Hitler's Home Front
A Family Surviving the War and the Peace

Don A. Gregory and Wilhelm R. Gehlen

Pen & Sword
MILITARY

First published in Great Britain in 2016 by
Pen & Sword History
an imprint of
Pen & Sword Books Ltd
47 Church Street
Barnsley
South Yorkshire
S70 2AS

ISBN 978 1 47385 820 6

A CIP catalogue record for this book is
available from the British Library

Typeset in Ehrhardt by
Replika Press Pvt Ltd, India
Printed and bound in England
By CPI Group (UK) Ltd, Croydon, CR0 4YY

Pen & Sword Books Ltd incorporates the Imprints of Pen & Sword Aviation,
Pen & Sword Family History, Pen & Sword Maritime, Pen & Sword Military,
Pen & Sword Discovery, Pen & Sword Politics, Pen & Sword Atlas, Pen &
Sword Archaeology, Wharncliffe Local History, Wharncliffe True Crime,
Wharncliffe Transport, Pen & Sword Select, Pen & Sword Military Classics,
Leo Cooper, The Praetorian Press, Claymore Press, Remember When,
Seaforth Publishing and Frontline Publishing.

For a complete list of Pen & Sword titles please contact
PEN & SWORD BOOKS LIMITED
47 Church Street, Barnsley, South Yorkshire, S70 2AS, England
E-mail: enquiries@pen-and-sword.co.uk
Website: www.pen-and-sword.co.uk

To the memory of our mothers

Contents

List of Plates

1. Will Gehlen, aged eight, in full Jungvolk uniform. (Wilhelm Gehlen)
2. A 1930s map of the Rhineland where Will grew up.
3. Will and other boys are allowed to inspect a quad 20mm flak gun. (Wilhelm Gehlen)
4. Will's troop with other Hitler Youth and Jungvolk in morale-building exercises in the Eifel. (Wilhelm Gehlen)
5. Group photo of Will's troop on an excursion to Bavaria. (Wilhelm Gehlen)
6. *Obergefreiter* Lorenz Gehlen, Will's father, in uniform. (Property of the Gehlen family)
7. Dad (right) on patrol near Cholm, Russia, in April 1942. (Wilhelm Gehlen)
8. Dad (far left) listening in while plans are being made; somewhere near Vilikye Luki, Russia, in 1942. (Wilhelm Gehlen)
9. Brother Len and his group of Hitler Youth on the march during training exercises in the Harz area, 1943. (Wilhelm Gehlen)
10. Len and five of his mates no doubt planning an attack on the invading Americans. (Wilhelm Gehlen)
11. A permit and receipt for having paid the tax for owning a dog. (Wilhelm Gehlen)
12. An official document granting a farmer permission to slaughter a pig. (Wilhelm Gehlen)
13. Ration card for children aged six to fourteen. (Wilhelm Gehlen)
14. Major General Reinhard Gehlen, Will's uncle. (US Army Signal Corps)

Overture

A twelve-year-old Hitler Youth single-handedly trying to save the Thousand-Year Reich from destruction in 1945 might seem a little far-fetched today, but it was not so far from the truth at the time. Millions of us had the same idea, but that is only a small part of what life was about during the last days of the war. As early as 1941, some food items were becoming scarce at home and in the final months of the war, most of Germany's soldiers and civilians were hungry. Trying to save themselves and their families became more important than continuing to fight for a lost cause. After the war, Germans began starving by the thousands. It was a struggle for many just to find enough food to survive from day to day. This book is my small contribution to history as seen through the eyes of a young boy growing up in a small rural community just outside München-Gladbach, or M–G as those who lived there called it. I was barely a teenager when the walls of the Reich Chancellery came crashing down but some events are as real today as they were then.

I never learned English in school and my first teachers for that foreign language were American GIs who spoke everything from New York Yankee to Mississippi Rebel. My native language is German or more correctly, a lower Rhine German slang. I don't have a high school education or a college degree in political science and I have never been politically active. I have never voted for any political party and do not support one now. I do listen to the politicians' promises, but when the voting is over and done with, those promises all go out the window, whether we are talking about Washington, the German Bundestag, the Kremlin or some capital in deepest Africa. As I have said many times since I became an adult, the only honest politician I ever remember was Adolf Hitler. In his campaigning he said, 'Give me five years and you won't recognise Germany' and he told the truth. The Germany of 1938 was nothing like the Germany of 1933 – but then the Germany of 1945 was nothing like the Germany of 1940 either.

Times were bad, much worse than just eating horsemeat or using discarded cement bags for toilet paper. Folks can get by without a broom or new clothes every year but one has to eat. Americans shouldn't say that could never happen here, because in fact it did. The Great Depression of the early 1930s didn't just happen in the United States; it was far worse in Germany and it had already been going on for a decade. Adolf Hitler promised us that things would get better if we would just elect him Chancellor. Contrary to what you may have been taught, we did have elections – and we elected Hitler, although maybe not quite fair and square by American standards of today, but by European standards of the time, it was not an unusual election. He got hold of the government in January 1933, the year I was born, and sure enough things got better almost overnight and kept getting better even after the war came. After the war was lost however, things were even worse than during the depression if you can believe it. Hitler's Thousand-Year Reich had only lasted twelve years, but for a young boy, twelve years is forever.

I want to describe in this book our daily life in the final years of the Second World War and shortly after. It was a time when the whole world went mad; when people in Germany lived on four ounces of rock-hard margarine and one egg per week and whatever else they could find that wouldn't kill them if they ate it. It was a time when a simple broom handle would cost you practically nothing but you had to have three or four permits with stamps and signatures to get one – if it was available. Seventy-plus years is a long time to remember some of these things but they're a part of my childhood and I do have some notes I made, and most importantly, I have my mother's cookbook where she wrote down recipes that she tried and then tested on us. Several of those recipes are included at the end of this book.

There is an old German dialect proverb that translates as, 'What a farmer can't grow himself, he won't eat'. Well, today, when food is plentiful, it is easy to pick and choose what you eat, but in the times described here, you ate what was available or you starved. Life was as simple as that and food was always on your mind. We ate without questioning what it was or where it came from. This however is not a gardening guide or a cookbook. It is the survival guide we created at the time to get us through another day. 'Skinny cooks can't be trusted' is one of my favourite sayings today, but when I was a boy, you would have had a difficult time finding a cook who wasn't skinny. There were new proverbs created toward the end of the war that reflected the times. '*Altes Brot ist nicht hart, kein Brot, das ist hart*' was often heard. This is not difficult to translate even if you don't know much German: 'Old bread is not hard; no bread at all is hard.'

Just recently I came across an article in the *Washington Post* online that said that 40 per cent of US domestic food production is wasted and goes into the dustbin. A quick calculation tells me that this is food for about 130 million people out of a population of 300 million. Germany had eighty million in the war years, not counting the occupied areas. If Germany had wasted 40 per cent of its food production then, no German would be alive today to tell the tale. A few days after that article was published, another guru predicted an acute food shortage in the not-so-distant future, not only in the US, but worldwide. My advice is to get your shovels and hoes out now and make a garden. The food will taste better and be better for you.

Thousands of good (and bad) recipe books have been published and they look good as exotic decorations on kitchen bookshelves, but most are never read by anyone preparing the meals. After all, a can of soup or a bowl of Corn Flakes is much simpler. Good cooking takes time and skill. Books have also been written about essential vitamins one must have to live a long and healthy life, but we had none of these books in our house. Nobody in our family knew what a vitamin looked like. I have never seen one; neither have I ever seen a calorie. We were given cod liver oil that is supposed to be full of Vitamin A, but believe me, the stuff was awful. It tasted like fish gone bad and looked like snot. To us kids who had to take a daily dose of the stuff, it was public enemy number one. Amazingly, there was a never-ending supply of it right up to 1947. Allied bombers had no problem hitting blacksmith shops and railway stations, but no enemy bomber was able to pinpoint the Hell's kitchen that made millions of gallons of cod liver oil. We kids, given the chance, would have told Winston Churchill right where it was and to bomb the place. In 1947, all of a sudden, supplies dried up. Why? We never figured that out, but nobody died of Vitamin A deficiency afterwards. Maybe all of us had enough cod liver oil stored up in our bodies to last a lifetime.

This is a true story and so I have changed some names and locations to protect the privacy of a few people still living among us. I should also like to point out that sometimes I might have the exact dates wrong but, remember, there was a war on, which was a common excuse for many things all over the world during those times. This book is not written as an exact historical reference, but as a bit of entertainment, black humour maybe; funny events – and at times, it's simply the story of horrible-tasting food.

Wilhelm Reinhard Gehlen
Telford, Tennessee

It's impossible to speak with Will Gehlen for very long without the conversation drifting toward something related to the war and food. I think this comes from his childhood in Nazi Germany when both were always on his mind. Today, most of us are familiar with disaster preparedness and food requirements in an emergency situation, but Will learned it first-hand. There were no books or movies or websites with vital information, and this was not a temporary emergency. It lasted for years. Things had to be learned by trial and error and they had to be learned quickly. Every able-bodied man, and by the end of the war, that meant young boys and old men, was at the front, even if the front was just down the street. It was left to the women to hold the home front together and that included feeding the children and keeping the house in one piece. Will's stories are not unique; similar stories could be written about millions of Germans in small towns and in rural areas throughout Germany trying to survive after the loss of a war they had been told they would win.

Will recently came across a letter that describes the frustration the ordinary German farmer had with trying to survive while at the same time trying to support the government. The letter is from February 1943. A woman whose husband was in the military was ordered to deliver approximately 300 pounds of hay to the local Nazi *Bauernschaft* (Farmer's Organisation). She wrote a simple letter of reply:

> I received a letter from you on Jan 7, 1943 with a request to deliver 150 Kilos of hay to your organisation. This order I cannot fulfil. My husband has served in the Wehrmacht since February 1940. I have one cow to supply milk for six children, an RAD maid, and myself. That is eight people. I also have to deliver some of the milk to another twelve people by order of your office. I have two other cows not yet giving milk.
>
> If I have to give the *Bauernschaft* 150 Kilos of hay, I cannot feed the cows and will be forced to sell them and have to buy my milk elsewhere, so I beg you to reconsider your demand.
>
> Heil Hitler,
> Amalie Pombergen

While times were hard for those in rural areas, they were much worse for those in the large cities that had been bombed constantly for more than two years. There wasn't much left that could be called habitable and certainly nothing to eat. In Will's community, there were people who had already endured one war and knew how to survive in desperate times. They became a source of knowledge for those trying to live through this one. These were the older parents and grandparents of children of Will's generation. They often lived in the same house or in the same community as their children and grandchildren and could be counted on for support and advice.

Germany could have become a third-world country after the end of the war – and according to some highly-placed Allied officials of the time, that would not have been such a bad idea. The US soon backed away from the hard-line punishment of the entire country and repealed JCS (Joint Chiefs of Staff) Directive 1067, issued in April 1945. The directive was essentially the 'Morgenthau Plan', named for President Roosevelt's Secretary of the Treasury Henry Morgenthau, and it called for Germany to forcibly be turned into a country of farmers with no capability of starting another war. There was as much hatred of the Germans at the time as there was fear of yet another war with them sometime in the near future. Germany surrendered unconditionally on 7 May 1945 and repeated the surrender on 8 May for the Russians. This gave the Allies complete control of the country and the Russians temporary control of Berlin, but to those who had survived the war, none of this was of any importance. Finding enough to eat to live another day was front and centre in everyone's mind. The bombing had stopped, but the dying continued.

Whatever long-term treatment the Allies had in mind for the Germans, it couldn't have been much worse than the conditions already in existence for them just before and just after the end of the war. The German economy and infrastructure was already a wreck and the inflation continued after the surrender with prices of essentials (if they could be bought at all) rising to double and triple that of 1943. Only the war industry continued to function reasonably well right up to the end. Parts of the intelligence-gathering section of the German military continued to function even after the war with the capture of Major General Reinhard Gehlen, Will's 'uncle', and a substantial portion of his command. In August 1945, they were transferred to 'Box 1142' at Fort Hunt, Virginia along with Gehlen's vast microfilmed records. Gehlen can arguably be called the father of our CIA.

A year after the surrender, the situation for starving German citizens, particularly those in large cities, was not much improved. The de-nazification of Germany took priority, with anyone wishing to maintain a position of responsibility, such as teachers and policemen, having to undergo the process immediately before being able to resume their jobs. This was no more popular with the American GIs who had to implement the order than with the ordinary Germans who had to endure it. The Russians in particular did not bother with such details. They had other ways of dealing with those suspected of being former Nazis. Many Germans resented the Americans' de-nazification treatment, as few of them were willing members of the Nazi party or had any political affiliation. A significant number of those who were members of the Party had joined under duress. The Allies, particularly the Americans and British, wanted the reconstruction of Germany to be a long drawn-out effort to allow ample opportunity to de-nazify the country in the process, and there was plenty of reconstruction to do. The almost unimpeded bombing had devastated the major cities, and the country was not able to produce enough to even feed its own citizens. More than 10 per cent of the total population had been killed during the war and agricultural output was barely a third of what it had been.

The German Red Cross was dissolved by the Allies immediately after the end of the war and relief agencies like the International Red Cross were prohibited from aiding the Germans with food and supplies. Even the Vatican was told not to interfere when an attempt was made by Catholic relief organisations to aid starving German children. Predictably, death rates rose among children to ten times that of pre-war Germany. The effects of the US-enforced starvation could not be kept quiet for long, however, and in early 1946 President Truman was forced by the public and their elected senators and congressmen to allow relief organisations into Germany. By this time, the entire population was on the edge of starvation, not receiving the bare minimum just to stay alive. The years immediately after the surrender were much worse than anything ordinary German citizens had experienced during the war.

With the realisation after the war that Stalin's idea of democracy was to allow everyone to vote communist, the repeal of JCS Directive 1067 began to be called for in speeches by Secretary of State James F. Byrnes and former President Herbert Hoover. They promoted the reestablishment of a government of some sort in Germany. JCS Directive 1779 in July 1947 was 1067's replacement and permitted German economic recovery in order to stabilise Europe. This led to the 'European Recovery Program', more widely known today as the 'Marshall Plan'. This was the first shot fired in what would become the Cold War. For young Will and his family and millions of other Germans, the 'cold' war meant something very literal. In the winters they *were* cold – and always hungry.

It was impossible to arrange this story in perfect chronological order because certain subjects would send my co-author into storytelling that would span the entire war and the years after. I have tried therefore to rearrange and group the stories around broad topics.

Special thanks go to Mary Chaires Damon, Samantha Jo Meiborg and Marjorie Miller for proofreading and commenting on the first drafts of the manuscript.

Don A. Gregory
Huntsville, Alabama

Chapter 1

Through a Boy's Eyes Clearly

I magine . . .

It's 1942 and you're a scrawny nine-year-old German boy who was born the year Adolf Hitler became Chancellor. He's the only German leader you've ever known. Germany has already been at war for almost three years. Your father and all your adult male relatives are in some branch of the Wehrmacht. Your country's being bombed from the west and the invasion of Russia is slowing down. You hear Stalingrad mentioned for the first time and there's talk of an enemy bent on destroying your homeland and enslaving its people if the war is lost.

And with a group of other boys your age, you repeat the following:

In the presence of this blood banner flag which represents our Führer, I swear to devote all my energy and all my strength to the saviour of our country, Adolf Hitler. I am willing and ready to give up my life for him, so help me God.

This was the Jungvolk Oath, administered to ten year olds in 1936 and afterward; although, after the war began, no one cared if you were not quite ten or maybe even not quite nine. Hitler's warning to others that, 'Your child belongs to us already . . . ' had come true.

* * *

Your world today might look like this: a nice house and flower garden, preferably a few miles outside the city limits, a happy family, a comfortable income; few debts, plenty to eat, and all the modern conveniences. Now, turn the clock back more than seventy years to Germany, or the Greater German Reich as it was called, where Adolf Hitler and his Nazi Party (the *Nationalsozialistische Deutsche Arbeiterpartei* – NSDAP) controlled everything from official government business down to how many rabbits you could raise. Your house has a hole in the roof from a bomb dropped by either a British or an American plane and your garden is not for flowers; it's your survival patch of ground for growing anything you can eat. Your family is one of the lucky ones – you have a garden; many do not. Your family is as happy as it can be, with your dad fighting a war somewhere near Stalingrad or in North Africa, and with the added worry that you might never see him again. All too many of your friends and relatives have had loved ones who had already laid down their lives for '*Führer, Volk, und Vaterland*'. No one has a car. They had practically disappeared by 1941 – requisitioned by the Party for government use, and besides, there was no petrol to run one anyway. Our local Leuna petrol station was selling carrot seeds and cabbage plants by 1941. We had a rusty bicycle that we used to get from here to there, but most of the town's electric tram system was still running and in fact kept running until near the end of the war. There were fourteen lines all total in our area which connected the cities of München-Gladbach, Krefeld, Rheydt, Wickrath, Viersen and a few smaller places. In March 1945, a few 2,000lb bombs destroyed the power station that ran the system, but it was soon back in operation. The #14 line was out after a bombing raid destroyed the whole 17km-long track and it didn't run again until mid-1946.

It is a fact that, when war comes to a country, no matter where the soldiers are fighting, the front line is always right at your doorstep. At times, *Obergefreiter* (Corporal) Lorenz Gehlen, my dad, was fighting 1,500 kilometres away in Russia, but back home, towns and cities were being laid to waste with bombs. The 'front swine', as our soldiers fighting in the east called themselves, dodged bullets and artillery, while at home the people dodged bombs and some of them were fifty times heavier than the 105mm artillery shells our *Heer* (land forces) had to contend with. The constant rain of fire from phosphorous bombs turned cities into infernos that burned for weeks.

From his earliest rise to prominence in the 1920s, many people regarded Hitler as the saviour of Germany after our defeat in the Great War. More thought that way when Germany recovered, under his leadership, from the world recession, which was much worse in Germany than in the United States. The Treaty of Versailles had restricted Germany's Army to 100,000 men, but that changed overnight when Hitler introduced compulsory military service for every able German. Then came the *Reichsarbeitsdienst* (RAD – Government Labour Service), the *Hitlerjugend* (HJ – the Hitler Youth), the *Bund Deutscher Mädel* (BDM – the Hitler Youth for girls), and many other paramilitary organisations, so that it was impossible for a foreign government to know exactly how many to count as being in the military. It was '*Sieg Heil*' all over Germany, even in our small nearby towns of München-Gladbach and Krefeld, in the Rhineland halfway between Düsseldorf and the Belgian border.

The ninety Great War deaths the community suffered were forgotten until Hitler came along. The few wilted flowers on the base of the memorial were replaced by fresh ones on 11 November every year, but that was all. The battles of Verdun, the Somme, Ypres and even Langenmarck sank into obscurity, but not forever. Hitler declared that those millions who fell in France, Flanders, and in the East had not died in vain. He said that Langenmarck, where 3,000 German students died in 1914 after only six weeks of basic training, would forever be foremost in the minds of those working for Germany's revival. Hitler's power grew year by year with the near-unanimous support of the people who yelled *'Heil, Heil, Heil'* at Party rallies, on Hitler's birthday, on Wehrmacht Day, and at every other opportunity. Reality hit the nation on 1 September 1939, however, when Germany invaded Poland from the west, and three days later, Great Britain and France declared war on us. What is often forgotten is that sixteen days after that, Russia invaded Poland from the east. Did those countries then declare war on Russia? I think not.

As Hitler's panzers rolled through Poland, then France and the rest of Europe, the nation celebrated victory after victory, but a few chips of the enamel of Hitler's holy aura were soon to be broken off. When the first casualty lists from the fronts came in and were published in newspapers, everyone knew the war was real. Great War veterans knew already, but the consequences of real war are forgotten quickly by those who were not in it. With the rationing of food and other goods, a few younger Germans also came to doubt the National Socialist leadership. The first air raids, life in shelters, lost sleep and sixty-hour working weeks made doubters of many more.

We lived on the edge of the industrial area of the Ruhr, so we naturally had a good number of anti-aircraft, or flak, batteries, in our vicinity. Most people don't know it but the word 'flak', which is used in many languages, comes from an abbreviation of the German word *Fliegerabwehrkanone*, meaning anti-aircraft gun. The huge Krupp Steel and Armaments Works was only thirty-two miles away and there were other vital industries near us: copper smelting facilities, stainless steel mills, Buna artificial rubber plants, synthetic petrol plants, the Mannesmann (steel tubing) works, and the DEMAG (heavy-lift cranes) operation, just to mention a few, that had to be protected from air attack. Near us were also factories that processed and packaged food, made paper products and one that made submarine parts. Other smaller enterprises were involved in manufacturing textiles and roof tiles, and there was a large creamery that bought the local farmers' milk for processing. Luckily, we had no ammunition plants near us, but there was a large railway shunting yard with a locomotive repair shop that was highly visible from the air. All of this had to somehow be protected just in case Churchill decided our area was important enough to bomb.

When men began being drafted into the services, several of the pubs and restaurants closed. A sign was usually placed in the window that said: '*Wegen Einberufung geschlossen!*' which means, 'Closed because of being drafted'. Some even added, 'See you back here after final victory'. By 1942, some of the pubs and restaurants had reopened and were being run by the woman of the house, but the quality of refreshments and meals had deteriorated. One never knew if the rabbit stew being served was made from the animal that hopped or the other kind. 'Roof rabbits' (cats) were eaten all over Europe late in the war. It was best not to ask the cook and no one did. The beer was watery and stale even if it was fresh. Wrought-iron tables and chairs were gone; probably melted down and reborn as Panzers or guns. The once-immaculate beer gardens were overgrown with weeds. Folks who were too old for military service and those who had returned badly wounded or were on home leave still frequented these establishments – mostly just to have somewhere to go and talk. The endless talk was always about the fronts. The old First World War veterans, pipes in their mouths, gave their advice to the young soldiers on how to send the Russians packing. Others drew maps on bare table tops with fingers dipped in beer and explained how they had beaten the 'Frogs' (the French) on the Somme river in 1916. At least all this talk could be had without a ration card and the beer was only twenty Pfennigs a glass. Getting drunk on the stuff after 1942 was impossible, however; one would burst before that happened. Some industrious men brewed fruit brandy from cherries, pears or apples but that was a hazardous occupation, mainly because of the improvised equipment they had to use and the ever-present *Polizei* (police) snooping around.

Most trades, small firms and workshops had closed by the middle of 1942 because anyone with a knowledge of cars, construction, carpentry and related things, ended up in the Wehrmacht. One tradesman that was hardly ever called up was the watchmaker. They were mostly old, retired people too feeble to fight in Russia, but their skill was always sought after. There were no battery-operated watches; all had wind-up mechanisms and in the intense cold of Russia, the metal gears contracted. Watches stopped by the thousands and those that ran didn't keep good time. Soldiers needed watches, especially those in forward areas. Attacks and retreats had to be coordinated so everyone would know precisely when to move or how long to hold out. In North Africa, on the other hand, fountain pens dried up in the heat. Pencils can be used for solving that problem, but telling time accurately requires something more complicated.

People began to stink, literally. No – baths were not rationed, but soap was and what we got didn't last long or get us very clean. In the early part of the war, baths were taken once a week, except for those who had really dirty jobs, like coal miners, manure spreaders and soldiers home on leave. The extra baths for them were encouraged to get rid of lice that have always followed any soldier around. Cars became cheap; we used to say you could have one for an apple and an egg. There was no petrol to buy for private use, so what were you going to do with a car? A sausage and a two-pound block of butter were far more important than a DKW or an Adler 4-cylinder. Anyway, most privately owned cars and motorcycles that would run eventually got requisitioned by the Wehrmacht. Doctor Kreutzer, our local doctor, was well known in Germany during the war, and she had an Adler sports car. Sadly, she was killed in the last air raid on our town in February 1945.

We got war news from a radio that Dad brought home from Poland in 1939. It had short, medium and long-wave reception. We were not allowed to listen to enemy radio broadcasts, but stations in Sweden, Switzerland or Portugal were allowed. Some people did break the law but if they had been caught, a heavy fine, a prison sentence or even a stay in a concentration camp could have been their punishment. Newspapers were all controlled, owned and printed by the NSDAP and censored by the office of Propaganda Minister, Dr. Goebbels. He had a couple of nicknames too: 'Herr Big Mouth' and 'Club Foot Jupp'. Occasionally, they would print world news but we never knew if the stories were genuine or not. For instance, in June 1940 an article in the official Party newspaper, the *Völkischer Beobachter* listed the UP (United Press) as the source of an interesting story. At that time Germany was not yet at war with the United States. The article described a test by a scientist at the University of Minnesota, a Dr. Alfred Nier, who had successfully produced Uranium 235 from the much more abundant Uranium 238, which was a major step toward making an atomic bomb. The article went on, saying that, 'Up to now, only a few grams of this new isotope have been produced and we doubt that this discovery will be of military value in the present war.' The article continued with a description of atom splitting and tests at Columbia University. So by no means was Germany completely shut off from the rest of the world in 1940; that would come later.

The Second World War didn't come to our part of Germany with a big bang. In fact it was only the radio and newspapers that kept us informed of things that were happening in Poland; that is, until the telegram came telling us that Uncle Fritz (Dad's sister's husband) had been killed in action there. My dad was soon drafted into an assault gun unit and left for training. In peacetime he had been the driver of an electric tram. I guess that made him qualified to be the driver of a tracked assault gun, although I thought there was a lot of difference between the two.

When the war started, the area we lived in immediately became part of the 64th Flak Air Defence Command, whose headquarters was in Münster. This area encompassed the whole of the Ruhr valley from the Dutch border in the west to just east of Dortmund and from Münster in the north to Cologne. By 1944 there were several flak divisions defending the area with almost 20,000 guns in all. Most batteries were positioned north and west of this vast industrial complex, but many positions were in close support of vital war industries. Ammunition factories were also present and it was not every citizen's cup of tea to live in a house knowing that just down the road from them, shells and bombs were being turned out by the millions and that these places were favourite targets of the Allies.

Since the beginning of the war, a total blackout had been ordered throughout the Reich and air-raid wardens were appointed to see to its enforcement. These wardens were usually men over sixty years of age, old wounded veterans from the First World War, or Party members without more important assignments. Their job was to patrol the streets after dusk to make sure that no light was visible from houses and factories. Violation of the order could result in a brick coming through your window. The wardens were also responsible for blocking access to bombed areas and keeping the roads open for firefighters and rescue teams. With us living in the Ruhr, blackout regulations seemed to be a farce at times. The Ruhr contained many steel works with huge smelting furnaces and the glow from them was visible for miles. Their chimneys billowed smoke and steam day and night. We had framed blackout paper covering our windows that could be removed during the day. Everyone had little crosses of tape on their windows to stop flying glass in case the window was shattered by the concussion of a nearby bomb explosion.

Mr Vink, our primary air-raid warden, was a veteran of the Great War and had served with Granddad Willem in the same infantry regiment, the 77th Lübbener Jäger. Lübben is a town in Brandenburg and a good 250 miles from the Rhineland, but Granddad and Mr Vink were in Lübben on a work detail when the war began. They enlisted there and then and joined the light infantry. They were both at the Battle of Verdun and both walked home from Belgium at the end of the war. In 1939 Mr Vink, who at the time was the furnace stoker at the nearby food-processing plant, was made our first air-raid warden. He was also the only person I knew during the war who had a flashlight. If the electricity went off during a raid, we had to make do with homemade candles or sit in the dark. We only had one 25-watt light bulb in each room, so we were almost in the dark anyway. Mr Vink even had a steel helmet given to him by the Party. To be honest, to us kids, he looked pretty ridiculous in it. He was about six feet four inches tall with a head like a large pumpkin and the helmet was about two sizes too small, but he wore it with dignity and in fact, to adults, he was a well-respected member of the community. He was the only person who could shout, 'Lights out, damn it' and be obeyed by young and old, regardless of who they were. Arguing with an official air-raid warden performing his duties was an invitation for trouble. He could have you arrested or even worse.

Actually, we should never have needed air-raid wardens, although a *Luftschutz* (air protection) law in 1936 required their appointment. Reich Marshal Göring had promised Hitler and the people in 1939 that, in the event of war, no enemy plane would ever be able to cross into the Reich. A few months later, a bunch of British Hampden twin-engined bombers dropped a few bombs on Wilhelmshaven, doing no damage, but nevertheless, the occasion gave Göring the nickname 'Herr Meier'. The use of this nickname is very old and has origins in a German expression of doubt about a prophesied event and it just seemed to fit the occasion I guess. After our Reich Marshal's promise proved to be as meaningless as most of the other propaganda, we were glad to have our wardens. Even though Göring knew all about his nickname, it was still not a good idea to use it around people who might report you to the Gestapo. We knew they got most of their information from ordinary citizens reporting on others they might want to see jailed, and everyone knew there was a large Gestapo office in Krefeld, not far from us.

*　*　*

Our healthcare before the war was probably the best in the world, but the invasion of Poland and the subsequent six-year war created problems that could not have been foreseen. Even before the 'Barbarossa' campaign against Russia in June 1941, there were almost a million wounded or sick soldiers in public hospitals, military hospitals (*Lazaretten*) or otherwise getting treatment for war-related injuries. Injured or sick civilians were generally better off than the soldier at the front. At home, there was always a doctor, a nurse, a first-aid station or a hospital nearby. As the war turned decidedly against Germany, it was a lack of medicines that created the real problem. This was especially the case with drugs like morphine, that were made from plants that we could no longer import. Dandelion flowers or Rose Hip tea won't do much for a broken arm or pneumonia.

Up until the First World War, the civilian population as a whole was not too bad off food-wise. It was not a densely-populated area, but the First World War and its aftermath brought famine to Germany on a scale that no one had foreseen. Hitler promised the Germans a better life, and for a few years after he became Chancellor, life was better. But twenty-one years after the guns of the First World War fell silent, a new war started and immediately another food crisis came over the country. Germany was again unable to provide the necessary food for its eighty million inhabitants. The country was first blockaded by the Royal Navy and later by the US Navy. There were battle fronts in all directions and the shortage of men and machines to till the fields made for a food shortage that would not be overcome. German citizens sensed by 1943, after the defeat at Stalingrad, that this war was lost, just like the earlier one. Unlike 1918, however, they knew that this time the war would be coming home to them before it would be over. By the end of 1944, the population of some towns in distant East Prussia had a taste of things to come when the Red Army crossed into Germany. News travels fast and bad news travels even faster and the news we got scared everyone. The distribution of rationed food that was available frequently broke down, due mainly to attacks by Allied planes on food-processing centres and transport facilities, but also due to the overall inability of the authorities to cope with a disaster of this magnitude.

The NSDAP's *Nationalsozialistische Volkswohlfahrt* (NSV – civilian welfare organisation) took care of people who were less fortunate than us and there were lots of them. In addition to recipes, they also provided clothing and essentials for those who had lost everything in air raids, took care of orphans and collected clothing. Given the circumstances at the time, when air raids had become a daily occurrence, they did a great job, providing one gave them a smart *'Heil Hitler'* salute as a thank-you. The NSV issued leaflets and books with new recipes for meals and medicines but most people asked their parents and grandparents what could be eaten and ignored the government publications. By the end of the war, there were lots of reasons for not trusting anything that came from a Party organisation, even the NSV.

The NSV women, who were cooking for thousands of people, also advised us on how to cook over open fires between the ruins of bombed-out homes. Some recipes were worth a try, but others were outright ridiculous or dangerous. One of their proclamations comes to mind and I give it here, but please don't try it. The leaflet we received went something like this:

Dear *Volksgenossen* (loyal Party members):

Our present economic situation requires us to make many sacrifices now so that we can look forward to certain victory against the Bolshevik menace and the Jewish-inspired gangster clique. We urge you do as much as possible to obtain your own cooking facilities if you have been bombed out. This will allow the NSV to attend to more urgent matters. Please do not waste any scrap of food. Search your cellars, your gardens, and report any dead farm animals (cows, horses, pigs, rabbits, chickens, dogs, cats, goats, and the like) to one of the NSV officers who will then make sure that nothing edible is wasted. Your cooperation in this matter is a duty to our Fatherland.

Heil Hitler

Chapter 2

Home, Family, School and Church

I suggested to my Brother Len that when he was old enough he should volunteer for an SS (*Schutzstaffel*) outfit, but despite his fanatical devotion to the Reich, he didn't like the idea. He was only fifteen near the end of the war, so he couldn't be drafted into the SS or Wehrmacht, but belonging to the Hitler Youth was a must. I still think it was two things that kept him at home: his stomach (he was always hungry) and his authority as a leader in the local Hitler Youth. He relished giving orders to lower-ranking members during duty hours, but I don't think many of them were obeyed. He was, however, a genius in finding something for the table in the winter or during really bad shortages. For all his faults and his fanaticism, I still think today that we might have starved to death without him.

Len was totally uninterested in anything other than the Hitler Youth. His duties came before everything else. Once he was asked to deliver draft notices to boys that had come of military age, which was eighteen at the beginning of the war but was sixteen by the end. Len, being the ever-devoted Hitler Youth, got on his bike and took off with a handful of orders waving in the wind. I got the full story of what happened when he returned. The first address was that of a Wehrmacht captain who was then serving in Italy. When Len knocked on the door, a dishevelled-looking woman answered with, 'What do you want?'

'Heil Hitler,' Len responded, 'I have here the call up orders for Heinz Bücker. He has to sign in my presence. Can I speak with him?'

'Piss off,' was the woman's answer to that. In German, it doesn't sound much different and means exactly the same thing.

'Pardon me madam,' Len insisted in an official sounding tone (according to him). 'This is by order of the NSDAP and the Wehrmacht.'

'Look, Hitler boy,' the woman shot back, 'I'm not your madam; my son isn't home, and I told you to piss off.'

'Frau Bücker, I have to report this to my superiors in the *Wehrkommando* [local military office] unless your son signs the order in my presence. They will send the police for him,' Len threatened.

She was not at all moved. 'I don't care if they send the Reichs Heini himself [a nickname for *Reichsführer SS* Heinrich Himmler and it means just what it sounds like]. My son isn't going anywhere, even if ordered by the Wehrmacht or the Pope. You got that?'

Well, Brother Len knew he was beaten and he never went back to Frau Bücker's house. Whether Heinz was eventually arrested, I don't know, but this woman had put a serious dent in Brother Len's crown.

At the next address he was invited in by the woman of the house. She was a widow; her husband had been killed in a freak sawmill accident in 1938.

'Yes, I do understand,' the woman said 'and my son will be pleased to serve our Führer, Volk, und Vaterland.'

Her son signed the orders. Len gave him a copy and told him to report on Tuesday to the local high school gymnasium at 5:00 p.m.. The woman shed a few tears and talked about garden work, meat rationing and the lack of eggs. Len, so he told me later, was disgusted with her story.

'Here I was,' Len said, 'taking an order of the highest importance to this house and all the woman could do was ramble on about food and her garden.'

'Well,' I asked 'did you volunteer to help with her garden while her son is away at the front?'

'I have better things to do with my time; more important things.'

'Yes, like digging tank traps that wouldn't stop even a horse and cart.'

'This is for a better future for all of us,' he bragged. 'Yesterday, I met an old man who complained no end about this war. He said he had seen it all, the Loretto and Vimy Ridge in 1915, and Passchendaele in 1917. We will show the older generation what we can do; no more Langemarcks or Ypres.'

'Hitler was at Langemarck and we still lost that war.'

'The Führer cannot win a war on his own.'

'I hope he wins this one,' I mumbled, 'these air raids are going to destroy our country, and in Russia our army's going backward.'

'We'll go forward again,' he said confidently.

At that point, I gave up arguing with Len. There was no point; he knew everything.

Len, who was three years older than me, was the sort of guy who thought he knew everything, and who had to be first in whatever the Nazis ordered. He was the only person I have ever known who would forcefully argue for or against any issue just to hear himself talk. He had advanced from Jungvolk to Hitler Youth well ahead of me and he never let me forget that he was my boss – and I never forgot to remind him that Mum was his boss. By 1941, he was already a sort of platoon leader (*Kameradschaftsführer*). Len liked the title 'Führer'; it smelled of Hitler, our real Führer. Anyone with even a molecule of authority was a Führer of some sort in those days, be it the postman or the tram driver. Brother Len of course thought he had many more molecules of authority than the average Führer. I was only a Jungvolk member, and not very keen on marching, drumming and taking orders from kids hardly older than myself, especially my brother. He was a full-fledged Hitler Youth and in his eyes that meant something very special. After all, anyone in uniform had official status, whether it was a soldier, a ticket seller at the tram station or even a porter operating a lift. Some of those with a uniform and a hat would use their new-found position to order people around who would ordinarily have ignored them. Ours was a small community where everyone knew everyone else and those things were not easily forgotten after the war either.

I remember clearly one day in the winter of 1943 when Brother Len came up with one of his great plans for catching a goose. There were many recipes in Mother's cookbook for how to prepare goose but we never had one during the war and when they did become available long after the war, we couldn't afford one. There was some swampy land with a small lake fed by a creek not far away from our house that even Brögger Flönz avoided. He was the *Forstmeister* (Forest Manager) who walked the woods and fields in our area. Brögger was his real name and Flönz derives from the word *Flinte*, which means shotgun in old English, so the name sort of fit. Sometimes in deepest winter, a few snow geese would congregate at the lake and Len had an idea how we could catch one. Somewhere he had found a book that described tricks that kids could play on chickens and he figured the same thing would work with a goose. So, late one evening we set off for this lake. Len brought with him about twelve feet of strong string and a piece of fatback. He tied the string to the fatback and placed it out in a clearing while I watched the operation. When he finished setting his 'trap', I asked him what the idea was and how this was going to catch a goose.

'Well, it's simple,' he said. 'Suppose four geese come and each one wants to swallow the greasy bacon and they swallow the string with it. They all start pulling and the bacon comes out again. They swallow again and again, until they get tired, then we just walk over and pick them up.'

Well, I didn't fully understand all this, but I stayed with him in the freezing cold until 9:00 a.m. the next day and finally asked, 'Why wouldn't the geese just fly away when we walked over to grab them?' He wanted to give it another try the next day when it was foggy and a light drizzle was falling. I flatly refused to go along with that plan, but he never stopped trying to find ways to catch geese and pheasants.

*   *   *

Early in the Third Reich, the NSV advised instituting what became called *Eintopfsonntag*, or literally translated, 'one pot Sundays' and it became the law of the land. On the first Sunday of the month from October through March, the Sunday main meal was to consist of a stew cooked in one pot. This was supposed to save the family money so there would be more to donate to the *Winterhilfswerk* (WHW – the Winter Help Work programme). Later in the war, this was extended to two Sundays per month and finally, out of necessity, almost every day's main meal was *Eintopf*. A leaflet distributed to all households by the NSV stated that the meal should cost no more than fifty Pfennigs, about twenty-five cents at the time. People with gardens had no problem reaching that target but adding meat to the stew and staying within the fifty-Pfennig limit meant that the housewife had to atomize an ounce of meat (if there was any) to add to the stew. The NSV leaflet did not mention meat and Hitler, being a vegetarian, decreed that only vegetables were to be used. Hitler himself was seen on many occasions in German cities on the first Sunday of the month having a meal of *Eintopf* at the local NSV meeting hall. When he invited the Party bosses to the Chancellery dining hall to have *Eintopf* dinner with him, they came in droves at first. The novelty soon wore off and by 1939, only a very few dignitaries attended these dinners. Average German citizens followed the *Eintopf* decree out of necessity, but you rarely saw a skinny Party *'Bonzen'* (big shot Party men), as we called them. There was another farce to this *Eintopf* day. *Sturmabteilung* (SA – the Brownshirts) snoopers could knock on your door on *Eintopf* Sunday and demand to see what was cooking on your stove and if you had a good-size piece of meat boiling away with the stew, you were branded a parasite on the rest of the community. This was serious business. In some larger cities – and it happened a few times in Magdeburg where an uncle lived – your name was published in the paper like a common criminal. One good thing came out of this stew Sunday however; never in history were so many creative recipes invented in such a short period of time.

I remember Granddad Willem Gehlen as a pipe-smoking, stomping and orders-shouting bundle of energy and only my mother was able to tame him to some degree. Of course, he was too old to be drafted into 'Hitler's war' as he called it, and it would have been below his dignity to support the Nazi ideology under any circumstance. 'Give me Kaiser Wilhelm anytime. I'll go with him through thick and thin' was Granddad's answer when discussions came around to anything to do with the Nazi government. Granddad Willem died in late 1942, but he continued to be our inspiration to survive the hard times that came at the end of the war and after. I never knew my Grandmother Gehlen; she died long before the war. Neither do I remember my Grandmother Zander from my mother's side, but Mum's dad I do remember. He came to visit a few times, but was killed in one of the Schweinfurt raids. He was a tool maker and worked for SKF (*Schweinfurt Kugellager Fabrik*), the ball-bearing company. This industry was a favourite target of Allied bombers throughout the war.

Granddad was in charge of our family's garden until he died, and after he passed away, the responsibility should have gone to Brother Len but he was our number-one shirker. He would do anything for Hitler including digging eight-foot-deep anti-tank ditches, but digging in the garden, planting vegetables or weeding was below his dignity, so the job became mine. What he did do well was order me about, making sure the freshly-planted onions stood in a row like a parade of stormtroopers. When he planted onions or potatoes, he did it with a measuring stick. 'Things have to be done exact,' he used to say. I didn't know what he meant by that until the onions sprouted their first shoots. They were all twenty centimetres apart, no more, no less. They looked like a company of RAD men on their way to work. Even in fruit picking he was mostly useless, despite the fact that he thought he knew everything there was to know about the subject, but he never failed at being first to the dinner table.

One day in the spring of 1942, Granddad Willem had an argument with Mum about his constant pipe-smoking in the kitchen and Mum got rather loud with him. He walked out into the garden to calm down and the two of us sat on the bench under the cherry tree discussing this and that and looking over the rows of newly-planted beans and onions. There was not too much to harvest as yet, but plenty of weeds were coming up. 'Okay,' Granddad said, 'Let's do a "*Quer durch den Garten*" (across the garden) dinner today.'

I was puzzled, with no idea what he meant.

'Come on, I'll show you.'

He slipped on his self-made wooden clogs and as I followed him, he explained to me what was edible and what was not. Granddad Willem made his and our shoes, which I guess would be called clogs today. It was something he had learned how to do from his father back in the late 1800s. They were made from freshly-cut willow blocks and Granddad had all the tools of the trade to make them. He made two sizes and they either fitted or they didn't. There was also no difference in left nor right; they (did or didn't) fit either foot. He had made a good supply by the time he died in the summer of 1942. If they were too small, you got the bigger size and if they were too large, you pushed a handful of straw into the end to make up the difference for a perfect fit. For the whole war I only got one new pair of shoes and that was in 1943. So, what did other kids less fortunate than us wear when feet outgrew shoes? *Klepperkes*, they were called; a wooden, inch-thick contraption with attached leather straps and if you wore them long enough, you ended up with flat feet.

He picked a few young onion shoots, some wilted leek leaves, dandelion leaves, some herbs, and a few stalks from leftover winter brussel sprouts. Then in the shed he picked up a few carrots, potatoes, and a preserved jar of rabbit meat and proceeded to the kitchen. These were *Eintopf* ingredients, he told me, and that evening Mum made a tasty meal from weeds, rabbit and wilted vegetables, so 'across the garden' became a favourite dish in our house. You might think that you can only eat the sprouts of the brussel sprout plant but you're wrong. Even today in most Balkan countries the local vegetable markets sell the stems too. You just peel off the hard outer part and cut the inner white part into small pieces and cook like any other sprouts.

Then there was Aunt Kaline; everyone called her Carol, my dad's sister, who also lived with us after her husband Mathias Hansen was killed in September 1942 and had been buried near Staraja-Russa. Died for '*Führer, Volk und Vaterland*' the telegram said. All of us felt sorry for her, but we also knew there were thousands of war widows who had no family at all. We were glad she came to live with us and she did more than her share helping with the housework. Her cooking, however, was something Brother Len and I feared. She hadn't had too much experience in that department, but probably Len and I were spoiled because of Mum's cooking skills.

The youngest Gehlen living at our house at the end of the war was Baby Fred. He was born during an air raid in late 1941. He was a happy baby in spite of what was going on around him. When he got old enough to walk, he was another one of my responsibilities whenever he was outside and he loved being outside. Maybe it was because he was born during an air raid, but he seemed to have no fear of anything and would walk right up to a 600lb horse and try to talk to it. I think Mum liked him best, probably because he never complained like the rest of us.

Mum was the boss of the house; well, most of the time anyway, even when Dad was home. When it came to things regarding keeping the family fed and clothed, no one argued with her. During the Second World War it took a lot of knowledge and imagination for a housewife to feed a family. She, or whoever did the cooking, had to make sure the food was healthy, somewhat palatable and free of known poisons. My mother was born in 1900 and as a young girl spent two years at a convent in Aachen during the First World War, learning how to maintain a household. Most important for us, she learned cooking and anyone who says there is nothing special to boiling potatoes or cabbage has never eaten either prepared correctly. There were ninety-five nuns in the convent and at one time, about sixty teenage girls. After two years' training, they had the opportunity to become a nun and some of the girls did. Even during the Third Reich, a few convents were still in operation that provided this training. Hitler had created a more promising future for young girls, however, and so most preferred to do a year of government service at a farm with the prospect of marrying a soldier and raising children. My mother's recipes were mostly her own inventions and dated from the inflation of the early 1920s. They were perfect for the bad times that were to come again. During the war, her skills developed into a fine art. We owed much of our survival and health to her foresight in writing down the recipes two decades earlier and creating new ones based on them.

*   *   *

We didn't have a refrigerator in our home so the only way of preserving food was to dry it or can it. Some things were a problem right away after rationing began, like keeping our small ration of butter in a reasonably solid state. This required expert attention. It was put into a small container and immersed in cold water in a shaded outdoor building. Most German rural houses had sheds built onto the side of the house you could get into from the kitchen without stepping outside. The darkest corner was selected for storing perishable food. There was also a wooden trapdoor in the shed that led to our air-raid shelter, but there was no room for us during raids. The shelter had rows of shelves with canned fruit, rabbit meat and vegetables, plus coal, wood shavings, and winter potatoes. During high alert we used the front-door lintel for shelter. It was the strongest part of the whole house. Granddad Willem never bothered with seeking shelter and he died before air raids became commonplace. Only once was he really upset about an air raid and that was when a bomb destroyed part of the food-processing factory he had helped build. He swore at the Party, the SS, and the SA for what they had brought upon the German people.

There were no washing machines or dryers in those days. Washing was done in a metal tub using a zinc washboard. You hoped for a sunny day so the clothes would dry. Bleaching your wash was done by laying the items flat on a grassy spot of ground in the sun. Most villages had a public *Bleiche*, a bit of grassy ground specially reserved for bleaching your washing, and letting kids play on the Bleiche was *verboten* (forbidden). Sometimes these white and coloured spots on the ground were an invitation for fighter-bombers to stitch a few holes in your clothes with their *Bord Waffen* (cannon).

One day in April 1940, a stray bomb was dropped by a British aircraft and partly destroyed a barn a few miles from us – not much really for a war being on, but Brother Len, who knew everything, commented, 'We will retaliate'. Yes, Brother Len knows, I thought. But Granddad Willem was not to be deceived by the tranquillity.

'War will come to us, probably sooner than later, you mark my words,' he said that evening while we were sitting around the table eating a meal of fried potatoes and sour herrings. This was a favourite meal for Granddad. He knew everything about herrings that there was to know, and there's a lot about herrings to be known; although he never saw an ocean and the only time in his life he was ever away from home was in the Great War.

Bismarck is well known to any reader of history; he was the Iron Chancellor of nineteeth-century Germany, but what isn't so well known is that one of his favourite foods was pickled herring. To this day, pickled herrings are called Bismarck Herrings in Germany. There is also of course the battleship *Bismarck* of the Second World War that came to grief in the Atlantic in May 1941, but only after it battled with the British battlecruiser *Hood* north of Iceland, and sank her with the assistance of the heavy cruiser *Prinz Eugen*. But here, we'll stay with the lesser-known Bismarck, the herring. There were no herrings swimming in ponds along the Chemin des Dames, or in shell holes on the Verdun Battlefield, but somehow Granddad had learned all there was to know about these fish. After the war, he had a thriving business selling pickled herrings and pulled a hand cart with a barrel full of the creatures around town. When he wasn't pulling herrings in a cart, he was busy with trowel and spirit-level building things. He built a workshop across the road from us for his friend Jupp, who later became a major food packing businessman and distributor in the area.

*   *   *

I went to school when Sütterlin script was still the handwriting one had to learn in Germany. This was replaced in 1940, but its use was not forbidden. Many wrote in this older style until well after the war. Today, it is difficult to find anyone who can read it, especially if it is written by someone with poor penmanship. For the first four years in school, children used slates to write on to save paper. Books were used until they fell apart. Teachers didn't have a higher standard of living than the parents who sent their children to the schools. No teacher had a car; some had a bicycle, but most of them walked to school like their students. School went from 8:00 a.m. to 1:00 p.m. but homework had to be done and that usually took an hour. Our school, like hundreds more, was called the 'Adolf Hitler School'. It was built in 1938 and Hitler himself came to the dedication. It was a major event in our town and it was planned down to the last detail.

We didn't get school meals, as there was no dining hall or kitchen. Outside in the schoolyard, there was a water fountain that, as far as I can remember, never worked. We took our own lunches to school, made from whatever Mum had. After the war, they were provided, brought by a horse-drawn cart from a communal kitchen in town. By the time the food reached us, it was inedible.

In the winter, it was stone cold and in the summer, it had gone sour if any milk had been used in its preparation. We ate it anyway if we were hungry enough and many of us were. Barley soup was a favourite of the kitchen, if not of ours, but at least it was nutritious and one could survive on it. There was also barley bread that was hard as paving bricks and no amount of dunking it in any liquid would soften it. A good friend of mine, who lives up north in Massachusetts, was captured by the German Army in Salerno (Italy) in 1943 and spent the rest of the war in a POW camp in Pomerania. He told me that they lived on potatoes and barley soup; fortunately it was cooked in real milk, as they worked on a dairy farm. We couldn't afford milk in our barley soup even when it was available, but at least we had ration cards to get other things if they were in the shops. The POWs weren't so fortunate; for them, they had to eat what was given to them or starve. To this day, I cannot bear to eat anything made from barley.

Large coloured posters were hung up in our school classrooms with pictures of plants, the parts of them that were needed for manufacturing medicines, and a description of the healing power of each one. In the beginning, at least to most of us school kids, the plants looked like a bunch of weeds, which in fact they were. During growing and flowering season, we were required to gather as many of these plants, their blooms and roots as we could. Of course, some kids weren't anxious to do this, but school hours usually ended at 1:00 p.m. and we were exempt from homework if we brought a bag of medicinal plants to school the next day. A lot of the plants we collected were totally useless and some were poisonous, like Deadly Nightshade and Fingerhut (Foxglove). Washing your hands after picking was mandatory, or you could wake up the next morning with a rash or worse. Over the weeks and months we collected the plants; we learned to recognise the ones we had seen on the charts. We knew it was important for the war and we all had relatives that were fighting on the front somewhere.

My father was one of the lucky ones. He was in the first wave of the attack on Russia (Operation Barbarossa) on 22 June 1941. He was the commander of a *Sturmgeschütz* (tracked assault gun) unit and his first battle was at Dünaburg (Dangavpils). In August 1941, his unit, Assault Gun Brigade 184, took Velikiye Luki on the Lovat River. His division was then taken out of the drive to Leningrad and assigned to break through to Toropez-Rzhev, move on to Selizharovo, and finally occupy Klin, just north of Moscow. Hitler came to visit the soldiers at Velikiye Luki on 30 August 1942. It's easy to find stories in modern history books about how Hitler never wanted to be with the men at the front, but I have a *Feldpost* letter written by a soldier who was there. He got Hitler's autograph on a scrap of paper and even took his picture, had it developed, and sent it to his family. In his letter he said that Hitler arrived at 11:00 a.m., had a pea soup lunch with the men, and shook hands with them. The letter continued with, 'He then walked right to the trenches to say hello to the men on guard duty. He told us he was glad to be with his soldiers at the front.' So-called historians who don't bother doing their homework would never write about such things.

Klin was briefly occupied by German forces during the Battle of Moscow but was presently retaken by the Russians. Parts of Dad's unit reached Cholm in December 1941 and ended up being surrounded while the rest of his unit escaped the pocket. Once inside the pocket, they soon lost their airstrip and were supplied by the Luftwaffe via air drops from Ju-52s and bombers, but ammunition, medical equipment and weapons had priority over food. The few motorised assault guns that were available had no fuel and couldn't be moved from one threatened point to another inside the pocket. The soldiers dug in on the south-eastern perimeter between houses and factories. There was one place that, in better times, had been a fur treatment facility that was stacked with untreated furs. These sure came handy in the bitter winter but they were so infested with lice that the German soldiers called the position 'the lice bunker'. German forward artillery observers directed fire to protect their position there. Our soldiers were supposed to live off the land, but they found out just how little there was to eat anywhere around. Supplies were dropped but there was never enough for the 7,000 soldiers inside the pocket. By February, rations had gone down to 50 grams (two ounces) of black bread and a slice of sausage or a spoonful of jam a day.

They held out until March when relief finally came. Dad was wounded earlier and flown out to recuperate, eventually being sent to the military hospital in Bottrop in Germany. He came out of Cholm with a stomach ulcer, a leg wound and a belated Cholm Shield medal, which was awarded to the survivors in May 1942. General Scherer, the commander, was awarded the Oak Leaves to his Knight's Cross. Whether he lived on two ounces of black bread and a spoonful of jam a day, I don't know. Dad recovered in time for the Belgorod Operation Citadel in August 1943, where they lost all their guns and trucks. He made his way back riding on a Russian Panje cart or walking. Due to his age, he was then assigned a job as a POW guard, then an instructor at Hillersleben and Ohrdruf Proving Grounds. The war ended for him in Denmark where he surrendered to a resistance unit that treated the Germans very well. He was back home in the summer of 1945 and a few months later, he was driving trams again.

*   *   *

Religion was a touchy subject for the Nazis and I can only write about our own experiences. The attempt to curtail the influence of religion on the German people as a whole did not affect us in our small town. New regulations from the government regarding churches were ignored by the pastors and their parishioners whenever possible. We couldn't see how the Nazis' meddling in religion was going to help win a war anyway. Living in a predominantly Catholic area, there were about a dozen Catholic churches, but I only remember three Protestant ones. Our own church, built in the 1890s, was designed by the *Kirchenbaumeister* (church architect) van Kann and we were very proud of it. At that time, our village had 970 inhabitants and 95 per cent of them were Catholic. Several of the well-off citizens donated the money to build the church and the land was donated by a local farmer. We even had a steeple built and it rose to a respectable height of about 160 feet, with a clock face that was visible for miles around.

German churches had always been a sanctuary for the hard-pressed of the population. Life wasn't easy in small villages; nobody owned a car, maybe a bicycle or a 125cc DKW motorbike, so a church within walking distance became a refuge you could get to. Catholic churches were usually packed at Sunday's High Mass at 10:00 a.m. Even the soldiers had the inscription '*Gott mit uns*' (God with us) on their belt buckles. Every battalion in the Wehrmacht had two chaplains assigned to it; one Catholic and one Protestant. You were one or the other in the Wehrmacht or you kept your mouth shut, especially if you were a Jehovah's Witness or a Jew who had somehow slipped through the net. The former *Gauleiter* (district leader) from Thuringia, Artur Dinter, tried unsuccessfully to create a German *Volkskirche* (People's Church) in 1934 and even held a few congresses, but the idea soon fizzled out. Hitler feared a rival to his NSDAP and had already dismissed Dinter as Gauleiter in 1927. He ran afoul of too many high-ranking Nazis when he started attacking Hitler in his newspaper and that soon got him kicked out of the Party for good.

Our pastor during the war was Father Andreas Gilles. He was born on 8 May 1879 in Nideggen in the Eifel and was pastor for our church until his retirement in December 1954. I still remember his often controversial sermons from the pulpit during the war, and to say he was an anti-National Socialist would be an understatement, but nobody ever denounced him. He would not allow any uniformed Party men to attend church services. Soldiers in uniform and even the Hitler Youth had to leave their military decorations and flags behind. Although the Party dictated school curricula and eventually forbade religious lessons in schools, the Nazis' authority, at least in our community, stopped at the church door. On weekdays, three services were held and on

Sunday mornings, there were six, starting at 6:00 a.m. On Sunday afternoons, there was a one-hour *Andacht* (prayer) service. Since the pastor was banned from giving religious classes in our school, parents were advised to send their children to church at certain times for religious education. For obvious reasons, care had to be taken by the church to ensure that the lessons did not clash with normal school hours or Hitler Youth activities, but as far as I remember, we never had a problem. After all, even the local Nazis were well-known members of the community and church. People quickly realised that a chicken or a dozen eggs given to them under the table did more good than arguing about religion.

The first restrictions on the church came soon after the war began and some seemed reasonable enough. Church bells were not supposed to ring and blackout restrictions were enforced. Our pastor and chaplain were required to open their basements as air-raid shelters, because there was no underground shelter in the church; they would have done that anyway. Later all electricity was cut off in the church; masses could only be held by candlelight. In early 1942, the church, with no way around it, was required to give up its two big bells to the war industry. Brass and bronze were needed in ammunition factories. Some of the largest bells then in existence, like the Cologne Cathedral bells, went into the melting pot. So in January 1942, the bells were rung for the last time until 1961, when two new bells were donated to the church.

By 1940, the first bombs had already fallen in our vicinity and the Church Warden was made an air-raid warden to assist Mr Vink. The WHW was forever begging for more clothing, the war industry wanted our aluminium saucepans to make planes, and iron railings were demanded to make tanks and guns. Earlier than that, in 1938, before the war, the Party confiscated the money that had been collected in the community for church renovations. Afterward, the WHW and other Nazi organisations didn't get much of anything from the people voluntarily. Even the stained-glass windows in our church were taken and normal windows, painted in different colours, were installed with blackout curtains. Our church was also forbidden to display Catholic flags on the occasion of the death of Pope Pius XI. The Party continued to introduce more and more restrictions; Corpus Christi Day, Ascension Day and All Saints Day, which were up to that time holy days, were officially abolished. We held our religious processions each year anyway. Ascension and Corpus Christi were both on Thursdays and observed as religious holidays throughout the war. I remember Ascension Day in June 1944 when a procession of about 300 people, men, women, and children, walked through the streets of the village at 11:00 a.m. with crosses in their hands singing psalms. Suddenly an alert was sounded. Everyone who could run disappeared under the huge chestnut trees, but no *Jabos* (our name for Allied fighter-bombers or *Jagdbombers*) came near us. The Lord was with us that day I reckon and nobody from our village ascended to Heaven on that Ascension Day.

Throughout the war, we celebrated Christmas the traditional way and there was never any interference from the Party. Hitler had no interest in changing that sort of thing, but Himmler did, and to get his hands around that holiday, he resurrected the *Sonnenwende* (Solstice) celebrations of 21 June and 21 December. The SS was required to participate and, as members of the Hitler Youth, so were we beginning in 1941. Granddad Willem, after some argument with Mum, finally gave in and let us go, but he himself refused to attend. Brother Len and I marched with the rest of the local HJ and BDM to a field outside town on a cold and windy 21 December. A big bonfire was lit and speeches were made by our Hitler Youth leader. We sang songs that had absolutely nothing to do with Christmas. Instead of 'Silent Night, Holy Night,' it was 'High in the Night' and 'Clear Stars Bridging Heaven'. Len, of course loved it. I didn't; simply because first, it was too cold and I had a runny nose and no handkerchief and second, instead of getting candy as we expected, we got a paper certificate saying that we had attended the festival. The homecoming afterward was much more to my liking. Granddad Willem was already busy setting up the Christmas tree and we decorated it with baubles that had been handed down in our family from almost a hundred years before. He had 'liberated' the tree, as he did every Christmas, in the middle of the night either from the cemetery or the nearby forest. Granddad Willem had the vision of an owl and he could smell Brögger Flönz miles away. He never got caught.

Younger children got toys at Christmas but most of them were war or Party related. There were wind-up tin tanks and guns and lead figures of SA and SS men and even Hitler, Goebbels and Göring. We could buy these for a few Pfennigs and today they sell among collectors for hundreds of dollars. Girls had jump ropes and hopscotch tiles and some collected *Glanzbilder*, which were small glossy lithographs. Whole scrapbooks were filled with them. The older children didn't have much time for playing with toys. They were busy with scrap collecting and searching for medicinal plants. Weekends were spent with the Hitler Youth – marching, singing and listening to Nazi-oriented speeches. Camping weekends were welcomed by all. It meant being away from school, living in tents, cooking over open fires and pretending to learn how to be a good soldier in the future. Most of the camping weekends ended after June 1944. Being out anywhere was downright dangerous by that time and a group of Hitler Youth was a certain target for the *Jabos*.

Mum was careful to save enough food coupons in the weeks before Christmas to make a good selection of candy, cookies and other goodies. No Christmas is completed in Germany without *Spekulatius*. Now the name might sound like the name of a saint of some sort (Holy Spekulatius?), or the name of an illness. Suffering from Spekulatius certainly sounds serious, but it is in fact a traditional German Christmas cookie. They can be bought today in most shops at Christmas but you can bake your own.

Chapter 3

Rationing, Gardening and Preserving

R ation cards came into use at exactly 11:00 a.m. on 3 September 1939. The *Reichsminister für Ernährung und Landwirtschaft* (German Food and Agriculture Minister – yes , there was one), Walther Darré, probably knew that the powerful British navy would somehow blockade our exits from the North Sea. This, of course, they did, but not only that; they also laid a mine belt covering all our exits to the Atlantic Ocean. Minefields were laid around Heligoland Island, the Faroe Islands, the Denmark Strait between Greenland and Iceland, and in the Channel. The only uninterrupted exit for the *Kriegsmarine* (German Navy) was the Baltic Sea, but even that route came under enemy bombing as the war progressed. At first, rationing didn't affect the German people a great deal, especially us out in the country. Most of the older people had lived through the great depression and inflation ten years earlier and had developed a sort of *Selbstversorger* (self-preservation) attitude. Those who 'had' traded with others who 'had–not'.

Hitler's aim in the early 1940s was to wage war with Russia and occupy the Ukraine, which was well known as the food-growing centre of Europe. *Kornkammer Europas* (Granary of Europe) as it was called. Yes, Germany was master of the Ukraine, but because of partisan activity and transport problems, the food situation didn't get any better. When war came on 22 June 1941, millions of soldiers had to be fed; soldiers can't fight on empty stomachs. So whatever was produced in the Ukraine in the summer of 1941 was mostly consumed by the troops. Some was sent home to feed the hungry population of Germany, and some was destroyed because of Stalin's scorched earth policy. What was left over went to the general Russian population and POWs – if they were lucky.

Rationing was put into effect along the same lines as in the Great War, or 'the war to end ALL wars', as it was called by some political optimists. The years up to 1941 were relatively peaceful with regard to running a day to day household. In those early days of the war there was only a small chance of a British aircraft dropping a bomb on your kitchen table or into the bean stew but nevertheless, restrictions and ration coupons were already in place. Up and down Germany, in every city's *Wirtschaftsamt* (economic office), pencils were sharpened and fountain pens were filled with ink for the anticipated flood of cards and applications to be signed. Many thousands of office workers were required to find a way through the maze of ration-card paperwork. They were mostly women, but some men too; who we thought should be at the fronts somewhere. We were sure NSDAP friends in high places got them their jobs. Corruption at any level, if proven, could mean the concentration camp, but it was rife in Germany nonetheless. We always suspected something fishy when a healthy-looking man stayed too long in a cushy job.

Yes or no was to be written on request forms authorising anyone to buy a tin of floor polish, fifty kilograms of lignite coal, or a bicycle inner tube. The Second World War turned rationing in Germany into a science. Long before 3 September 1939, ration cards had already been printed. There was a Wirtschaftsamt in our town, staffed by idiots whose job it was to write out permits for brooms, roof tiles, tap washers and sewing thread. It was in a big yellow building on Linden Street that got blown to bits during the February 1945 attack, and with it went all the permits and ration cards. The ration cards or coupons were in different colours for different things. As the war progressed, the items stated on the coloured cards became meaningless. A pound of pork loin on a dark pink card in 1941 could mean a pig's ear in 1944.

The first two years of rationing weren't so bad. Poland was overrun, next came Holland, Belgium, Luxembourg, France, Denmark and Norway, with booty aplenty to be taken. From France, we got household items and cotton materials. Holland and Belgium gave up vegetables and Denmark was a supermarket of all kinds of food. Norway had little enough for themselves, but Poland was flush with geese and chickens even after our troops were fed. Food parcels by the hundreds of thousands were sent by them home to Germany to feed their hungry families, and those families never had it so good. It was, as one German housewife put it, 'like sitting under a horn o' plenty'. Thousands of yards of coat, suit and dress material were sent home from France for busy housewives. Later on however, even sewing needles were rationed and hard to get. What we did get out of Norway was canned sardines and later in the war, Deuterium in the form of heavy water for nuclear research. This export ended when the so-called 'Heroes of Telemark' blew the heavy water plant to smithereens at the end of February 1943.

There were no real shortages early in the war, except of tropical fruit and spices that only grow in the Southern Hemisphere. Of course, oranges and lemons grow in Italy and Spain and Rommel's men in North Africa contributed a good deal of ship space to sending some of this citrus fruit home. Alas, we in our small village, far from Berlin, were the last in line and supplies regularly ran out before they got to us. Fortunately, vegetables, to my knowledge, were never rationed in our rural area, but there were shortages to come. If the greengrocer had no supplies from growers, the consumers had to grow their own or go without. Some, who had no garden or other honest means of obtaining vegetables, tried their luck at begging, stealing or maybe trading something for twenty pounds of potatoes. When harvest time arrived, there was food aplenty but many vegetables could not be grown in the winter, except for kale, leeks, turnips and rutabagas (*Steckrüben*) and we grew all of them. A leek for instance is one of the hardiest and most versatile vegetables you can find and it grows in Norway as well as it does in the Falkland Islands, providing of course you have good soil. They will still grow in poor soil but they are pretty skinny. The more manure, the more munch we used to say. You can even leave them in the ground during freezing weather, but you might need dynamite to get them out. Today you have to search long and hard to find a grocer who sells leeks and most gardeners won't grow them as the seeds are not easy to find. If we had leeks, Mum could make a meal out of them and not much else.

The supply chain of food and other goods eventually came to a near-standstill and many shops only opened at certain times. Everyone carried shopping nets in their pockets when they ventured out, just in case a shopping opportunity came up. A long queue always meant something was available and whatever it was, we wanted some. I still have my net and use it shopping at the supermarket because it's stronger and will hold more than those flimsy plastic bags that go into the rubbish. If word got around that something extra was available in a particular shop, and word did get around, a queue formed immediately. The added danger of getting shot at by a marauding fighter-bomber while standing in line for a half-pound of horsemeat, a pound of sauerkraut or a bar of soap was shrugged off most times because losing your place to seek a shelter of some sort usually meant doing without. The local bakery, before the war, could boast of having several bread delivery vans and managed to get the equivalent in horse-drawn wagons when petrol became scarce, delivering bread as far as fifteen miles away. Black bread, which is still sold to this day in Germany, came in foot-long loaves that were hard as bricks. We use to joke that if we had enough black bread loaves, we could build a bombproof shelter.

There were some things – mostly things you couldn't eat – that were sold without coupons or ration points, such as sand-based cleaning items. Sand soap was a mixture of sand, pumice powder and smelly salts. Real soap, or what we thought was real soap, was sold only on coupons and it was called 'swimming soap'. It wasn't called that because you were supposed to take it with you swimming, but because there was so much air whipped into it that it floated. We were told this was a great improvement over other soap because you wouldn't lose it in the bathwater. Even if Goebbels himself had told us that, I don't think anyone would have believed it. The stuff was yellow and looked more like a miniature Swiss cheese than soap. There was also a *Raucherkarte*, a grayish ration card for cigarettes, but most cigarettes went to the fronts. What tobacco was left, usually home-grown, was dried, cut up using a *Schwarzbrot* (black bread) slicing machine, and rolled into cigarettes. They sold for 10–15 Pfennings each on the black market. *Kippen sammeln* (cigarette-butt collecting) became a pastime for many smokers. The shortage of beer and spirits, including wine, was aggravating for most adults. Of course, grapes still grew along the Rhine and Moselle, the Ahr and in the Pfalz, but getting the labour to pick them and then transporting them to the presses was the problem. Beer was diluted with water to the point it was impossible to tell what it was.

Food rations were reduced every six months almost from the beginning of the war. There were coupons on the ration cards that were valid for 50 grams of sliced meat or 125 grams of bread, and you used them quickly because the next card's coupons might be for less. Salted lard was called *Schmalz* and it was shipped by the tons to the starving soldiers at the fronts, so at home we could only get a quarter-kilogram, about half a pound, a month. Buying sugar or anything similar, like flour, you had to bring your own paper bag, a triangular glued-together thing called a *Tüte* that held at most half a pound. These were made by *Tütenkleber*, ordinary common criminals that had been caught and put in the local jail. A sentence of six months or a year was a *Tütenkleben* and the prisoners were called the same thing. These criminals were different from hardened *Zuchthaus* (penitentiary) prisoners sentenced to hard labour. For anything you wanted to buy that had to be wrapped, you had to bring your own wrapping paper. One such wrapping paper, which was like our butcher paper today, was called *Pergament*, and it was used to hold jams and preserves – which were sold by the spoonful. If it got squashed by the sauerkraut and pumice stone, which were sold in paper too, you had a mess. Whatever items were not available on ration cards needed to be bought with a permit. These were issued by the local Wirtschaftamt.

Ration cards were printed in many fancy colours indicating what could be bought with them. A card for woollens and clothing, knitting yarns and so on was introduced in November 1939, usually with a total of 150 points on it; certainly not enough for a suit or a coat. There were normally seven different ration cards, but they weren't all issued every month. Food ration cards were issued once a month, clothing cards every six months (or once a year later). Leather shoes were only sold on coupons and you could get one pair every eight months – if they were available, and they rarely were. You were in serious trouble if you wore out or outgrew your shoes. Other goods could only be bought using special *Bezugscheine* (permits), which had to be applied for at the Wirtschaftamt. If you wanted a broom, first you had to go to that office and wait in line to fill out a form asking you how many persons were in the family, how many rooms the house had, if you had carpets or a wooden floor and even if you had a vegetable garden. Then, if the inspector thought you were eligible, you were issued a ration card and told where to get the item. A different form had to be filled out for every item you wanted to buy, and just because you got the permit; that didn't mean you got the item. Often it wasn't available when you finally got to the shop.

Blue cards were for meat and sausages, which meant *Wurst* or even pigs' knuckles, called *Eisbein* (ice leg is the literal translation) in German. There was nothing icy about it however; it had to be cooked, which usually meant boiling with sauerkraut. Generations have been brought up on it and even now it's a delicacy in Germany. Yellow cards were for anything not classified as meat. Butter, margarine, milk and cheese came under it. Butter was scarce and margarine came in hard one-pound blocks. White cards were for sugar, jam and marmalade. Later in the war when it wasn't refined properly, we didn't get white sugar anymore; it came as brownish crystals, but the colour of the card didn't change. During the heavy bombing raid on Julich, about thirty miles south of us, on 16 November 1944, an aerial mine exploded above a mountain of sugar beets, sending tons of them flying all over town. Not that it mattered much because Julich was almost completely destroyed by the attack. Fortunately most civilians had already been evacuated because the infamous battle of the Hürtgen Forest had already begun.

There were green cards for eggs, but people without chickens rarely got them except on the black market. Orange cards were for bread; they changed to red several times in the war, light pink was for Maizena starch, flour, tea or *ersatz* coffee, that, as the war went on, came to be called *Neger Schweiss* ('negro sweat') by a lot of people. Fish was seldom rationed and was sold while stocks lasted. There was always a fishmonger about with a barrel of salted herrings for sale. One thing that was particularly bad was a substitute for toothpaste which, according to people who knew, contained cigar ash, pumice dust, flour and a minty flavouring. It was made by Blendax and called Mint Max. The company still exists and they still make toothpaste, but I'm sure the ingredients have changed. Toilet paper was always in short supply during and after the war. Although not encouraged, the local newspapers, even those with Hitler's picture, were regularly used. Late in the war when newspapers were only two pages, such things as empty cement bags were used and haemorrhoids became more common than the common cold.

The milk we got, when it was available, already had the milkfat removed so it wasn't very nourishing. This non-fat milk was called *Magermilk* and even it got diluted later with water. This 'leftover' milk went sour in a few days without refrigeration and a sloppy white sediment called quark formed on the bottom of the container. We drained the whey from the curd and used this so-called cheese in many ways to supplement our meagre food rations. There was still protein in the stuff and that couldn't be wasted. It's an excellent diet food today, but nobody was on a diet during the war and right after. Fat people were rare and those who were fat usually wore a brown uniform and the only exercise they got was raising their right arm and shouting *'Heil Hitler'*.

There was never a real shortage of sugar for us during the war, but it was rationed. Germany had always had a flourishing sugar industry. The cool, wet late autumn climate of central and western Germany is an ideal place for growing sugar beet and refining factories worked full steam from October to early spring. Farmers lined up for miles with carts and trailers loaded with beets, waiting their turn to get to the washing ramp. After being washed, they were ready for processing and up until the winter of 1944/5, Germany still had refineries going full blast. These produced a lot of steam and during the war that was a beacon to enemy bombers. Germany had grown sugar beet as a major source of sugar since the late 1700s and by the middle of the next century; refineries were built for refining beet sugar on a large scale. By 1900, there were refineries all over Germany wherever sugar beet was grown. Nevertheless, sugar was rationed as part of Göring's Four Year Plan. Sugar beet molasses (*Rübenkraut*) is still made today but during the war, it was our main source of sweetener. It has a taste similar to sorghum. Pumpernickel was made, like the famous German 'black bread', but beet molasses was used to give it that distinctive flavour. We spread this molasses on our sandwiches instead of sausage and other meats which were strictly rationed. Our name for these sandwiches was *Kraut Lümmel* (which can have a rather vulgar translation) and a generation of German children went to school with them in their satchels. Today this molasses is added to cookie dough to make a special cookie called *Printen*. Until late in the war, we could get Printen spice that came from the spice warehouses in Rotterdam, but when we could no longer get it, we made our own from a teaspoon of ground cinnamon, a half-teaspoon each of nutmeg that we ground ourselves, clove and *Ingwer* (ginger).

Soldiers on leave brought their own ration coupons with them and at times were given something extra. The NSV often gave scarce things to soldiers on home leave. At Christmastime, the soldiers who were fathers got everything the NSV women could manage for the children. My dad went into town during one Christmas leave and came back with a big bag of nuts and sugar cookies. Even on leave, soldiers were required to salute any officer, but most lower-rank soldiers quickly changed into their civilian clothes to avoid, what they called '*Männchen Machen*' (standing on their hind legs, like a dog begging) many times a day. In civilian garb they had to conform like everyone else, seeking shelter in an air raid and obeying orders from air-raid wardens, firefighters and police. Many volunteered their services in emergency situations when out of uniform. Soldiers were called *Landsers* and most regiments were formed from local men, so the property and lives they were protecting were well known to them.

Almost everything had to be bought using ration coupons once the war with Poland began, but that was just a minor inconvenience at the time, as most everything was still available. That was not the case late in the war, but we at home were much better off than our soldiers on the Eastern Front. Our thermometer fell to –30°C (–22°F) in the winter of 1941/2 but in Russia, it fell to –40°C (–40°F as well) on a regular basis. A *Feldpost* letter from Dad reached us in January 1942.

Dear Wife, Dad and Children [Dad was Granddad Willem],

Thank you for your Christmas parcel. It got here on December 31, but I was unable to send you a letter earlier because the Fieldpost truck is frozen up. It is –43°C here. I'm now in a place called Selizharovo near a lake that is completely frozen. The ice is thick enough to hold up our tanks, if we can get them started. We have quarters in a Russian Kate [hut] and we are quite warm as it has an open hearth and we are surrounded by a forest that provides wood for the fire. Our field kitchen comes every day pulled by a Panje pony. We are only short of tobacco and cigarettes. The Wehrmacht Sondermischung cigarette brand is called 'hand grenade' here. You light one then throw it away quickly. If you can send some Halpaus or MB [Martin Brinkmann] cigarettes, please do so. There is no fighting going on here right now. Everyone is waiting for warmer weather. I hope you and the kids and Dad are okay. Please do not send me any more fruit. It was frozen solid when it arrived. Watch those boys and see that they stay out of trouble. I have applied for leave for White Sunday in April and I'm pretty sure our commanding officer will grant it.

Peter has written from Königsberg and says that he is getting married to a local girl named Gisela. This will probably not go well with Aunt Trina as Gisela is a Calvinist and you know what Aunt Trina's family is like. Well, it's Peter's life and I wish him good luck. I must end here. I'm on guard duty until 4:00 a.m..

Best wishes and kisses to all of you.
Lou

By the summer of 1944 there was also a general type of hoarding going on. Those people who still believed in a final victory were getting to be fewer and fewer. The prevailing mood was doom. Not many were convinced that the V-weapons were having much effect, even though every night after the Normandy invasion we heard on the radio, 'The bombardment of London and southern England with our V-weapons continues with devastating effect'. Well, a few V-1s never made it that far; one went down in a village next to ours that summer, missing a house by fifty yards but hitting a chicken coop. For many that meant no eggs for a while until they got more chickens from somewhere. We got a letter after Easter from an aunt in Fulda who, despite having an egg ration card, hadn't received even one egg in three months. She went on to say that she hoped there would be some by Easter next year. She didn't know that Easter 1945 would be even worse. None of us did.

We had no real coffee until after the war, but the older women often talked about *Bohnen Kaffee* or coffee from coffee beans and I wondered what it was. The tea we had was not very good and it was even worse when sweetened with beet molasses. I don't know it for a fact, but I bet acorn and barley coffee was invented in Germany during some war. There was even a specific name for acorn coffee. It was called *Muckefug* and it tasted much better than the name sounds to an English-speaker's ears. Whoever invented it should have been awarded a medal because both were pretty good substitutes. It required some imagination to figure out that barley or wheat could be roasted and ground into powder and brewed – but acorns? Now that really took some creative thinking. I wonder who first tried this and didn't suffer any health problems. Once it was manufactured, it was drunk all over Germany, except maybe at the Berghof. Late in the war, it was available without ration cards and it continued to be available after the war until about 1948. We had to bring our own paper bags to put it in after 1946.

Brother Len came up with the idea of making our own acorn coffee. There were plenty of oak trees in the area, but I had learned by this time to be wary of Len's hare-brained ideas, especially those that involved things to eat or drink. Arguing with him was pointless, so one weekend in the autumn of 1946; we collected about five pounds of acorns that were reasonably dry. He put about a pound of them into a cast-iron pot. We had no fat, only some strips of bacon and some beef tallow that looked like candle wax to me. Soon his 'roasting' process started to crack the shells and they were removed from the pot. After another thirty minutes, the acorns were turning dark brown and splitting. A few minutes later the acorns were black and producing an acrid smoke. He gave his roasting operation another thirty minutes and declared the acorns to be done. Alas, that was another idea of Brother Len's that did not work out. The roasted acorns were too large to go into the coffee grinder so he put them into a heavy cloth bag and hammered them into smaller pieces. We then ground them in our coffee grinder. Mum made one pot of Len's coffee and threw it out.

Another simple commodity that was unobtainable by people was cement. How could one mend a hole in an outside wall without cement? All houses in Germany were built of brick and there are still brickyards all over the country. Hundreds of years ago most houses were built of timber framing, then sided with either oak or willow slats. This was then plastered over with a mixture of straw, cow manure and lime. In 1938, we lived in a house built like this while ours was being re-roofed. That house was disassembled long after the war and re-erected as part of an open-air museum in Kommern in the Eifel Mountains. It's still there today and can be visited all year round. Repairing a damaged brick wall without concrete during the war used the same recipe developed two 200 earlier: straw, cow manure and lime. The patch would absorb bullets and shrapnel quite well. Roofs were made of clay tiles and to stop drafts and keep out the rain, each tile was bedded on straw matting.

Broken windows were a constant inconvenience because there was no replacement glass to be found anywhere. A piece of thin plywood served as a good substitute. Shop windows in the city were boarded up with planks. There were very few cases of looting after a destructive air raid. The penalties if caught were very harsh; even summary execution by a firing squad. The only thing that was permissible to take away was broken or partially-burned lumber for heating or cooking purposes.

Cotton was another item in short supply in Germany. Any old, torn, or worn-out cotton garments were collected and taken to a *Reisswolf* (now the name of an international company that provides document shredding), a machine that ripped the material to shreds. The fibres were then re-spun, dyed, and delivered to the weaving factories. Even paper was mixed in late in the war and shirts would be worn until they literally fell off your back. Washing them was a bad idea as they just disintegrated. This was called *ersatz* cotton but it wasn't much of a replacement for the real thing. After Granddad Willem died, we didn't have anyone who knew how to make the wooden clogs we wore, but Brother Len found his tools and decided he could make them as well as

Granddad. After all, he did know everything. His attempt went into the fire that cooked a pot of stew that night.

Spices were no problem during most of the war. We occupied Holland in 1940 and the Dutch owned a vast empire in South-East Asia now called Indonesia. There were huge warehouses in Rotterdam full to the roofs with all sorts of spices. Indonesia is still a main source of the world's spices. Nutmeg came in nuts and we had a very fine grater that worked well. Try a sprinkling of nutmeg in your mashed potatoes with a bit of dried parsley. You will be surprised at the delicious taste. The Germans love their spices. About forty years ago, on a visit to England, I observed that the average British kitchen spice rack consisted of salt, pepper, vinegar, a jar of Marmite and ginger. Times have changed since then, and even in the United States spice racks are overflowing with exotic spices, most of which are never used. I think the spice racks are mostly used as decorations for the kitchen.

Honey was unavailable and I never knew why. Surely we were not training artillery bees to fight on the fronts, although we would have if it could have helped win the war. We had our share of blooms on things and plenty of bees, so what happened to all the honey? Maybe it also went to the war effort. We did have a replacement, no doubt invented by some scientists in the food ministry. It was called *Kunst Honig*, which literally translated means 'art honey'. I have no idea how it got that name unless maybe there was an art to making it. '*Ersatz Honig*' would have been a better description of this stuff that came in two kilogram blocks that had to be cut with a sharp knife into thin slices. The texture was grainy, like pumice powder. It sort of tasted like pumice powder too. It was yellow and smelled like honey and was sweet, but there the resemblance ended. If there was pumice in it, we didn't suffer any effects from eating it. '*Dreck scheuert den Magen*' ('Dirt scrubs your stomach') we used to say.

If you wanted a good meal and had a little money, you might think eating in a restaurant was a good idea, but they were supposed to follow rationing regulations too. Some places were in operation throughout the war, but to get a meal, and these were not elaborate, one had to have a ration card with food points. The price of meals varied depending on the location and food availability, but in general they were cheap. What made it frustrating was that the point system was displayed right on the menu next to the price. A new term came into being in restaurants, *Flüster Menü*. Simply translated, it meant 'whisper menu'. If you did not have enough points for a certain meal, the waiter whispered into your ear that for certain favours, he could add an egg to your fried potatoes. A few Reichsmarks, a cheap bottle of wine or a bar of good soap would usually do the trick. The Gestapo soon put an end to this enterprise. They sent plainclothes agents into the restaurant and any waiter or restaurant owner selling *Flüster Menü* meals found himself behind bars and the place was closed down. The sign on the door might say '*Wegen Einberufung geschlossen*', but this time it was not a call to arms, but a call to court and maybe prison.

The meals in restaurants were not much different from those we had at home. During my visit with Mum to the Bottrop Military Hospital to see Dad, we went for lunch to a restaurant after an air raid was over. The fare was fried potatoes, sauerkraut, a slice of bread with *Schmalz*, and a cup of *ersatz* coffee to wash it all down. No 'whisper menu' was offered to us. We probably looked like we couldn't afford anything they had.

Rationing was hard during the war, especially for those with no spot of ground for a garden, but it was even harder after the war. The wartime proverb that went, 'enjoy the war because the peace will be terrible' certainly came true for most of Germany. For many, only the shooting and bombing stopped in May 1945; the dying went on.

*   *   *

At home, gardening was a must. If you had one, you worked in it and if you couldn't, you let someone else have it to grow food. We had a rather large garden, which wasn't to my liking because the constant digging, watering and weeding took all my free time, but then I realised if I didn't do it, I would go hungry and that's what happened to those who wouldn't work. One year a few kale, broccoli and leek plants managed to avoid being eaten long enough to go to seed, but we didn't have anywhere left to plant them. Brother Len had the grand idea of digging up the local football field. By 1943, all the young teenagers in the area had been called up to serve in the Hitler Youth flak battalions and the older ones were at the front helping the hard pressed old Landsers stem the Russian tide that was rolling relentlessly westward after the Stalingrad debacle. Permission was requested and given for us to work the field, but digging was easier said than done. It had been laid out in 1904 and years of trampling all over it, every weekend, by dozens of teenagers had made the ground as hard as concrete. In places, not even weeds would grow.

We used a pickaxe the first few days until a group of fighter-bombers (there was a railway track alongside the field) unintentionally gave us a hand. The pilots must have thought the soccer field was a convenient place to drop a few bombs. Of course, they missed the railway track, but four bombs hit the soccer field. Now, everyone thought, we had to fill in bomb craters as well as dig up the ground. Brother Len threw his shovel down in disgust, 'Look what the swine have done now,' he shouted.

'Never mind Len,;' I said, 'look at it this way, these four craters are loose soil now, all we have to do is fill them in and start planting, no digging. I hope those P-47s come back for a second helping and plough this field over and over again for us.' No one ever worked harder for a few vegetables.

We pickled everything that could be pickled and some things that probably had never been pickled before. There were successes and some downright failures that we couldn't eat and were pretty sure were poisonous. We pickled gherkins, onions and plums. Vinegar wasn't rationed but sugar was and you need a little sugar to take the sour edge off some things. Mum used to boil her vinegar mixture with a little sugar added, about half vinegar and half water and she used lots of dill from our garden; peppercorns too if we had any. Dill was something that every gardener grew and it was often added to anything being pickled for extra flavour. Ready-to-use bottled vinegar was not sold; it came as a strong vinegar extract in small bottles and had to be diluted with cold water. The stuff was highly toxic if not mixed with something. It's still sold in some shops in Europe as *Essig Essence*, or concentrated vinegar. Rich people diluted it with champagne to make things preserved in it tastier.

All food, cooked or raw, will go bad if not preserved properly; some will spoil in a day, some in a few days. That didn't happen very often during the war. If we had a surplus, like at autumn harvest time, we preserved it one way or another. Cabbage and beans went into a 100-litre (about 25 gallons) earthen jar. Enough salt preserves just about anything but it might smell so bad you can't eat it even after it has been soaked in fresh water for a day. We also dried vegetables and herbs on strings hung in the sun. After they were thoroughly dried, we packed them in pillowcases and hung them from wires attached to the rafters of our shed to keep the field mice from pilfering. Root vegetables like carrots, turnips and potatoes were stored in straw in our air-raid shelter. This shelter was only about ten feet by twelve feet and an adult couldn't really stand up in it, but it could hold a lot of food. Entrance was through a wooden trapdoor down some steps. An emergency exit to the road side of the shelter was added in 1939 by order of the local Reich Shelter Inspector (yes, there was one of those too). We never used the shelter for its intended purpose. We figured that if the house took a direct hit from a 500lb bomb, the shelter would not do us much good anyway. One side of the shelter had wooden shelves that Granddad Willem had built after the First World War. These shelves held glass jars filled with preserved vegetables, meat and fruit, and they were all lined up by size like Storm Troopers on parade. Brother Len loved to do things in a military manner, even if it was putting glass jars on shelves.

Preserving in glass jars was the best way to keep food but *Einkochen* (canning) was a tedious job. We didn't have pressure cookers or screw-top lids with seals on them. Our glass jars used a rubber sealing gasket and glass lids held down with a metal clamp. After the jars were filled, they were placed on a trivet that held six of them and lowered into a large pot. Cold water was added and the pot was placed on the cooking stove. Sometimes, depending on the contents, it would take several hours heating before the lids could be put on. The temperature throughout the food in the can had to be high enough to kill any bacteria. In the summer, the kitchen was turned into a sauna when canning had to be done. Most people didn't mind the work and heat because they knew that, come winter, there would at least be food in the house. Government food rations were reduced in late 1942 to just 1,600 calories a day and if that was all you had to live on, you went hungry most of the time. The promised food bounty that we were told would come from our occupation of the Ukraine had not materialised. The miles of Russian grain had been ploughed under by tanks from both armies or blown up by artillery shells. Our soldiers, who were supposed to live off the land in Russia, found only devastated countryside where even a live goat or chicken was a rare sight.

Food will keep practically forever as long as it is preserved correctly in airtight glass containers. In 1943 we ate strawberry preserves that had been canned by my mother in 1919 and they tasted as good as food we had preserved the year before. With commercially canned food in metal containers, the story was very different. The metal cans were lined inside with zinc which would oxidize after a year or so. The outside of the cans would rust through to the inside even if they were kept dry. After the war began, there weren't many metal cans because anything metal was needed for the war. Clay pots were used for preserving cabbage and beans, but that had its limitations too. We had fruit trees and bushes but not much sugar for making jams or jellies. A few pounds of preserving sugar were issued each fruit harvesting season, but the sugar didn't dissolve very well because the crystals were the size of grape seeds.

Granddad Willem pushed Brother Len and me to put every effort and ounce of our energy into our garden. That of course meant more digging and back-breaking labour, mostly for me. Len had a knack for avoiding hard work and, although I argued with him about it, if it came to a physical disagreement, I usually ended up on the losing side. When certain food became impossible to get, I got interested in gardening, cooking, and recipes that used what we had. Unlike Brother Len, who would only work in the garden if he had to, I was a nature person. We had a large garden with access from the house through a covered shed and from a gate on the road. There was a pigsty in the shed too, but we rarely had a pig. We also had several fruit trees and berry bushes: pears, cherries, plums, blackcurrants and raspberries. To have a good garden and grow plenty of vegetables, however, you needed a manure heap. A good manure heap was the pride of any real gardener. A farmer's wealth was judged by the size of his manure heap, which was usually situated next to the front door on the roadside, preferably under the kitchen window, or by the side of their slurry pits. We grew up with the smell and thought nothing of it. Plastic had been invented but it wasn't used for household items, so most of the household garbage could be composted.

We had no pesticides to control garden insects during the war and the German butterflies, caterpillars and other vegetable-eating critters probably didn't know there was a war on because they kept right on multiplying and eating their fill. It was a never-ending job keeping these pests away from our garden. After the war, the potato supply went from bad to worse because of this bug and schoolchildren were given candy bars for each glass jar of them or their larvae they collected and brought in. We were told that the Allies dropped the beetles during and after the war to destroy crops. All we knew was that we had never seen them before the ware. One summer we had an attack of Blackfly on our Fava beans. The bean flowers shrunk and the tops of the plant that normally were picked and cooked like spinach were useless. This wasn't just a bother; it could very well have meant we would starve, so Brother Len came to the rescue with another of his great inventions. He first tried hot water with soap and cod liver oil mixed in. I was hoping this would work because it would mean there would be less of that awful-tasting oil for Mum to give me. The flies loved the stuff and continued to multiply like crazy. Next he tried ashes from our oven but all that did was turn the flies grey. His last try was gunpowder which was stored in quantity in a few ammo bunkers near us. This was getting downright dangerous and I told him so, remembering what had happened when my mother threw my tobacco tin full of gunpowder into the fire one day and blew a pot full of bean stew all over the place. Len sprinkled the gunpowder between the rows of beans and then held a match to it. The result was a flash, singed eyebrows and hair, and burned plants. The black flies were gone, but so were our beans. We finally asked Aunt Maria for advice. She wasn't really our aunt but the wife of one of the local farmers we knew well. She was a sizeable woman with arms the size of tree-trunks and a first-class cook. When she was younger, she had a huge garden and grew Fava beans by the bushel. Her advice was sound and it worked; plant the beans in rows, but plant onions between each row. The onion smell (or something about them) keeps the flies away. Incidentally, this trick also works against carrot flies.

In 1943, rationing of seeds for most vegetables was introduced. I remember going into town to purchase white cabbage seeds, leek seeds and seed potatoes. First I had to show a permit from the local Wirtschaftamt, stamped and signed of course, confirming that we had a garden of about half an acre. Then I received seventy-five cabbage seeds, counted on the spot and not one more than seventy-five. Leek seeds were pre-packed, fifty in each pack, and I got one pack. Another separate permit was required for the seed potatoes. We got ten kilograms (about twenty-two pounds) and were told to cut them in half before planting. That was plenty for us as we always kept a few potatoes from the previous season for seed. Carrot seeds were sold in packs; probably the seeds were too small to be counted. We also got a half kilogram of onion sets (a little more than one pound) and no more. When you received your ration of seeds and plants, your name and address was recorded in a ledger indicating you had received your allowance and you got no more. Sometimes friends would not need their entire ration and would share with you, but no one had surplus seed potatoes. What you didn't plant went into the stew pot.

All that digging and sowing was no guarantee of food to eat later on. Insects, birds and bombs took their share but the most worrisome were the thieves who would come at night and dig up your vegetables and haul them away. If caught, the thief would get at least three months in jail; no fines, because money was worthless without ration cards or coupons. In extreme cases, the thief would find out what hard labour in Sachsenhausen was all about. We had no pity on these parasites that preyed on the hard-working members of our community. Few people got caught because word soon got around that this would not be tolerated and that those who did get caught would find no mercy from the authorities.

One of our favourite vegetables, apart from leeks – you can't eat leeks all the time – was called *Kappes* in proper German. It's called *Kohl* and *Kraut* in common German speaking, and cabbage in America. There is also of course, sauerkraut, a fermented white cabbage, which is easy to make at home. All you need is a stone jar, salt and the cabbage. Then there is another delicacy, which is boiled red cabbage; in Germany it is called *rot* (red) kraut. There is *grün* (green) kraut too. *Rüben* kraut (*Zuckerrüben-Sirup*) is a molasses made from sugar beets and *apfel* (apple) kraut is made from apples, and it has a rather sweet-and-sour taste. Then there was 'Kraut', 'Jerry' and 'Fritz' which were names given to us by the American, British, and Russian soldiers.

Sauerkraut is easy to make but I'm not fond of it anymore. I think I had too much sauerkraut soup in 1945. In our area, there were many acres planted with kraut and the 'have-nots', that is, those without a garden, would board the slow-moving local train that wound through the fields connecting the small villages. This train collected the farmers' cabbage and people would jump off the first car, cut as much cabbage as they could carry, then jump back on the last car. We gave the train the name, the 'Kraut Express' and it only went about fifteen miles per hour so it was pretty easy to steal enough to make a meal for a few days. Before the war, this was just an everyday occurrence and no one bothered trying to catch the thieves, but later in the war it became a serious offense.

I hung around the kitchen stove when I wasn't in the garden and watched how things were being cooked. True German cooking is a slow process even today. American-style fast-food restaurants have sprung up in major German cities but many people still cook at home and use the old recipes handed down over the decades. I suppose this has something to do with the lean times that have been experienced in most of Europe, particularly in Germany, since the Thirty Years War. Going back in history, at least two major wars were fought in that part of Europe each century. In the kitchen, I often I got in the way so much that Mum would chase me out. She was unable to do any garden work with Baby Fred on her knee and housework to do. Dad was in the Wehrmacht and Brother Len was an idle swine when it came to work at home, so I was responsible most of the time for the garden and the animals. Even though a good garden needs plenty of sunshine, after the spring of 1943 we prayed for overcast skies to keep the fighter-bombers away. I think the men who drove the ammunition trucks prayed hardest of all. I guess it was no fun driving a truck loaded with several tons of explosives through populated areas while being shot at from above.

Eating frozen potatoes is not everyone's idea of food, but in the First World War and also in the Second when potato storage was a problem in harsh winters, something had to be done with them and they were certainly not going to be thrown out. Potatoes were stored either in straw clamps (mounds) in the field they were harvested from, or bagged and stored in barns. Both were favourite targets for low-flying attackers, however. Clamps didn't burn and if one was hit by a bomb in the winter, there would be a free-for-all potato raid, but in -30°C weather, they would freeze in minutes. Waiting for them to thaw out was a bad idea. They rotted immediately and then you really could not eat them. Some old veterans from the First World War who had spent winters on the Galician Front had learned from Russian POWs what to do with frozen potatoes. First of all, they have to be prepared while still frozen and it's no use trying to peel them. They were boiled in salt water and mashed up. To me, they had a rather sickening sweet taste, and to overcome this, we added plenty of spices and whatever other vegetables we had. We also made a type of hash brown potatoes called *Schnibbels Kuchen*, which sounds rather exotic, but the only thing exotic about it was the spices. They are made with grated potatoes, grated onions, one egg (per three potatoes), parsley, fresh chopped leeks, salt, pepper, nutmeg, powdered clove and a tablespoon of cornflour, all mixed together. There is one additional spice that is found in every German kitchen that should be added. It is actually a mixture of spices called by the trade name 'Aromat' and a few shakes will do wonders for the taste of anything that hasn't much taste of its own. This potato mixture can be fried in a frying pan as a whole flat cake or as smaller cakes. Slow frying until brown and turning over a few times is recommended. The cakes are really good with apple butter and cinnamon.

Even the smallest potatoes were used during the war and after; none were wasted. The marble-sized ones were fried whole with onions and the peelings from the bigger ones were washed and turned into potato cakes. In mid-1947, Dutch potato farmers trucked untold tons of their yellow variety into western Germany to help feed the starving population. The Dutch called them something that translates to 'Earth Apples' and this yellow variety is still the main potato grown in Germany today.

A simple potato soup can be made with one medium-size beef or pork bone, or even a pig's tail. Boil this for half an hour in salted water and then add a grated potato and chopped leeks. Boil for another half hour and sprinkle fresh parsley in the soup just before serving. Pig ears were boiled overnight on a low heat in lightly salted water with a tablespoon of vinegar added. They were then either fried or added to a stew. Fried, they become very crispy like bacon or fatback and are very good for breakfast or in a sandwich for lunch. Potato roasting became a way of life in those days and it was the cheapest way of having a meal. Deep-fat frying had not come to Germany, and besides, nobody had enough cooking oil to do it. There were many other ways, however, to prepare potatoes even with limited resources. Most housewives had a clay crock in their kitchen for household fats. This fat was usually a mixture of whatever was available. Ours was rabbit, beef, pork, and sometimes chicken. Without a refrigerator, this fat would soon start to go rancid, especially in the summer but we used it anyway and would disguise the smell with leeks or spices. I doubt if there are many housewives or chefs today who are as inventive as the Germans were during those times. Today, if the result of a new recipe isn't very good, it goes into the dustbin. We couldn't afford to throw any food away and every trick was used to make it edible. Spices would cover up a cooking disaster and we knew that if we didn't eat it today, we would find it back on the table the next day or even the day after that.

One of our must-have kitchen utensils was a hand-operated grinder and you can find them today at almost any flea market or antique shop. I still have one and use it almost daily. I know there are modern kitchen gadgets by the score that will do the same thing without turning a handle, but on those modern machines I only know where the on and off button is, the rest is a mystery to me. We had five grinders in the kitchen for everything from meat to coffee. It was operated by holding it between your knees. We ground everything – except coffee beans. There were none for most of us late in the war, although probably the high society of Germany had some. Our coffee grinders were used to grind dried peas into powder, or hard *Kandis* sugar into manageable sugar granules. Our meat grinder came in especially handy making vegetable cakes from dried peas, beans, or lentils.

*   *   *

There was always a shortage of rubber and it only got worse during the war, so the Germans made their own based on a 1908 discovery by an IG Farben scientist named Hoffmann. The new rubber was called Buna. The Buna Works near us in Marl Hüls was built to make this valuable stuff for tracked or wheeled vehicles. Tracked vehicles used a great deal of rubber and it had to be tough. Synthetic petrol plants were soon built in Leuna-Merseburg, Marl, Ludwigshafen, Gelsenkirchen and other places, making petrol and diesel fuel from coal. Twelve refineries were in operation in the Reich by 1940. The whole Ruhr area has one of the largest coal deposits on earth, but no oil. There are no coal mines in operation there now. Germany buys coal from Poland, Russia and China. By the time the oil fields in Romania were targeted by the Americans, German synthetic petrol production was in full swing. Once they established their huge bomber fleet of B-17s and B-24s in England, bombing priority was given to eliminating the German synthetic petrol plants, but it took them until early 1945 to put the Leuna plant out of production for good.

Coal was strictly rationed because it was needed by all the war industries. In the winter we got about a hundred pounds a month and there were also briquettes made of compressed lignite coal which was abundant in our part of Germany without deep mining. It wasn't a good source of heat but the briquettes would burn for a lot longer than the same amount of wood. We carted coal dust home from the local coal yard throughout the summer and autumn whenever it was available. We mixed the coal dust with anything that would burn, like bits of paper, cloth and wood shavings from our neighbour who was the local cabinet maker. When we had a thick paste, we formed them into tennis ball-sized globs and dried them in the sun. My little brother Fred joined in the fun and one day fell into the black concoction and got covered from head to toe. Mum didn't see anything funny about it and got splattered herself when she came to rescue him. Fred thought it was all good fun but from then on, he was banned from briquette making. We couldn't spare the soap to clean him up. Then later, once the bombing really started and houses were reduced to ruins, we would go into town and search for broken beams and anything else made of wood. I had to pull the four-wheeled cart. Brother Len said he was carrying the responsibility in case we got caught, but it sure seemed like I was doing most of the work.

Coal could only be bought on a coal permit – if it was available at all. The local coal merchant and the food-processing plant were the only businesses in our area that had trucks. The coal merchant had an old two-ton Ford truck with a four-wheel trailer he took to the mine to pick up his allowance. Some clever people found a way of getting coal at the rail freight depot. At night the coal cars were shifted around and assembled into freight loads to be sent to other destinations, and because of the blackout, the yard was pitch dark. A few Railway Policemen patrolled the area and Hitler Youth boys were assigned to keep the points from freezing in cold weather by putting metal trays with glowing coals under them. These boys easily managed to get a load of briquettes into a bag, which they then took home. Furnace coal was also stolen by opening a slide on the freight car hauling it. Twenty-five tons of coal would pour out and dozens of kids with sacks crawled like dirty ants over the heap of coal scooping the stuff up. Before the Railway Police could get to the place, the culprits would vanish into the night. During night air raids, when even the police would seek shelter, the kids came out in force and took all they could carry. When the 'all clear' sounded, they were already gone and the Reich was missing a few tons of coal. It got so bad that the signalman was issued a special pair of night vision binoculars to spot the little thieves. In the daylight, everyone stayed away, not so much because they were afraid of getting caught, but because signal boxes were a favourite target for the *Jabos*. A plume of smoke from an engine anywhere on the tracks attracted them like ants to sugar. The freight yard was about four miles away and too far for us to participate in the coal theft and there was always the danger of running into a warden on our way home who would demand to know the contents of the sack. Four miles isn't that far in the daylight, but at night in pitch dark, it was a very long way.

Chapter 4

Duty to *Führer, Volk, und Vaterland*

M y youngest years were dictated not by my parents, but by the Nazi system and as far back as my memory goes, Nazi doctrine was the only way of life. We were brought up under the clearly-defined rules of the Nazi government; parents played a secondary role. We were not capable at the time of understanding these rules but we obeyed them. Hitler's aim was that from an early age children would be indoctrinated with National Socialist ideals and what better way was there than through the education system. Teachers were Party members; a few were old First World War veterans who didn't always agree with the Nazis, but they were soon relegated to minor posts. When we were able to read and become members of the Jungvolk, each new member was given a leaflet explaining how to live up to the standards of the movement. It went something like this:

How can the Hitler Youth help our war aims? Wars are not only won with weapons but can also be won politically and economically. We must try in our total war effort to defeat the enemy of our Reich with our Wehrmacht, but we also have to defeat him politically and economically, so that he is forced to sue for peace. Therefore, the home front is as important as the military front. Men who are still at home, as well as women and children, belong to our inner front and should be an example to those who might think otherwise. Hitler Youths, always remember that you are the future of a new era. Modern warfare requires mobilisation of all our strength. Our Führer, Adolf Hitler, is with us always.

We had to digest this propaganda from our earliest years, but that wasn't all. We didn't just learn about gardening and growing food and Nazi propaganda in the Jungvolk; we also learned to cook, how to sew buttons on our uniforms and how to darn our own socks. Of course the Party had a doctrine for all this: '*Sparsamkeitsparagraphen* [frugality instructions] *für die HJ*'. We were proud of our role and acted like it, but that was long before the Normandy invasion. Up to then, we were out of harm's way most of the time. Fighter-bomber attacks were not common until later and B-26s and A-20s were too high up for our quads. Even higher were the Fortresses and Liberators by day and the Lancasters and Stirlings by night. They flew in endless streams to the big targets further east, harassed by the 88s and our fighters. We had our share of bombing, but compared to targets in the Ruhr, we were safe. All this changed after D-Day. More and more kids were assigned duty on flak guns; the oldest I saw was sixteen, the youngest ten, but we all had the same goal, defending our homes from air attacks. We had said goodbye to school by then and our teachers had already been recruited into the *Volkssturm* (men too old or too young to be drafted) anyway. Schools were turned into hospitals or assembly points for the retreating Wehrmacht, or into recruiting stations for the Hitler Youth. Blackboards and desks were being burned for heating and cooking fuel.

The BDM girls had their own leaders and met on different days to learn about safety, first aid and homemaking. Girls were supposed to become mothers someday and bear children to make the Greater German Reich even greater, so they learned a lot about cooking, washing and running a household. They also had to do a *Landjahr*, or a year of service. That meant they had to work a year for the Reich and it was supposed to be in a job that was important for the war effort. Some worked at farms and lived with the farmer's family. Some were lucky, but some were placed with a Party man's family and were treated like unpaid maids or nannies. Most learned how to cook for a family, which was a useful skill during those times and I suppose it did sort of contribute to the war, but it was the RAD labour service for girls introduced later in the war that really contributed. They worked in ammunition factories and did a lot of the other work that men had been doing.

By the middle of 1944, time was running out for the Third Reich. New regulations came about that drastically changed the role of the youth organisations for boys and girls. Ten-year-old boys were now required to register for some sort of active duty and late in the war if you were nine and looked ten, that was good enough. I still have the leaflet that we received at home.

Ten year old boys, to your duty!

Death lurks above our flags, but God will judge our struggle as pure. Our fight and our life are hard, but the war does not rest. Fight for your nation. Do your duty; encourage the Storm Troops to hold fast! Do not despair; your will must be hard as iron. Remember, the enemy hates you, and there are many enemies against us.

If you despair, you must strike back. Even harder days are ahead of us, and much deprivation, but fighting means that you are one of us. Let the walls crumble around you; your fight is for a new day and a better future. Victory and death are never far apart. Yes, some fighters must die, but always remember that you, our youth, will live to see the dawn of a grand new day for Germany. Sieg Heil.

If that sounds rather silly today, remember that, seventy-odd years ago, these proclamations had to be taken seriously. Whether the brain of a ten-year-old boy could digest this propaganda is another matter, but the Party's indoctrination of the youth was a very serious concern for the Third Reich. All this talk of victory, a better future and the Greater German Reich probably did sound grandiose in the 1930s, and up to 1942, but then came the six-month long battle and defeat at Stalingrad, followed by Kursk less than a year later, and then D-Day. The Allies were knocking on the Reich's door. Goebbels had attracted millions of listeners in the early days, but now the people turned their backs on him. The novelty had worn off. The war was real. It wasn't happening someplace we had never heard of; it was coming home to the Reich. Citizens demanded bread, but guns were more important. Morale among the average German citizen was even lower than it had been before the Nazis came to power. Only the Hitler Youth stood fast. They still believed in final victory and young boys volunteered in droves for the newly-formed 12th SS Panzer Division Hitler Youth. At the age of sixteen, these German youths fought in the Ardennes and Hungary. They died by the thousands for a Reich that was crumbling right before their eyes.

To the people outside Germany it was unbelievable that children were holding down the home front and in some instances, the fighting front as well. US divisional reports tell the true story:

84th Infantry Division, Aachen, October 1944: Two ten-year-old German sharpshooters taken prisoner.

4th Infantry Division, Hürtgen Forest, November 1944: Three boys ten to twelve years old observed pulling a daisy chain of anti-tank mines across the road in Scherpenseel.

9th Armoured Division, February 1945: A twelve-year-old knocks out a Sherman tank with a *Panzerfaust* [a single-shot bazooka] near Bitburg.

In late 1944, GIs of the 84th US Infantry Division captured the city of Aachen and had to deal with many ten- and twelve-year-old Hitler Youth sharpshooters. At the end of March 1945, the 3rd US Armoured Division approached Paderborn to trap 300,000 Germans in the Ruhr pocket. Ten miles south of Paderborn, a combat company of the 3rd Armoured Division with mounted infantry entered a village and came under *Panzerfaust* and small arms fire from a row of houses. Several of the *Amis* (Americans) were killed or wounded. The Sherman tanks returned fire, wrecking the houses with HE (high explosive) rounds. When the dust settled and firing had ceased, the men entered the ruins and found seven teenage boys and a girl not more than fourteen years old – all dead. They had single-handedly taken on a combat company of a US infantry division.

Not only did the Hitler Youth substitute as flak helpers, they dug anti-tank trenches, cleared rubble from bombed cities, and marched in useless parades. We also dug in gardens and even turned vacant fields into farmland for cabbage, potatoes, and turnips. Then there was the never-ending search for scrap metal, old wool or clothes, medicinal plants, and of course, school had to be attended, like it or not. Aluminium foil, used to fool the German radar, was another item we collected. The first drops of the stuff were treated with suspicion. Nobody knew what it was. We were told to collect the six-foot long strips and turn them in with the usual scrap collection but the housewives used them as batting for quilts and they made nice decorations for our Christmas trees. We also collected Allied propaganda leaflets which were dropped on us by the millions. They were welcomed because of the shortage of toilet paper. We didn't hesitate to use Nazi publications for the same purpose.

At our annual Hitler Youth camps, we had a sort of cook from the NSV assigned to us. Cooking for 120 boys in a camp over an open wood fire is not every cook's dream, but we loved it, even when the food didn't taste like Mother's. Just being away from the back-breaking labour of our own gardens made us a happy bunch of kids. Even the barley soup was appreciated. All the meals at camp were *Eintopf* and the fire was kept going all the time, except at night. One of the foods I was fond of was Bratwurst and they are simply fried sausages, but the German soldiers out in the cold winter of Russia seldom had a frying pan handy, so they boiled the sausages. If water was not readily available or suspected of contamination, they boiled them in beer with onions, if they had any. We tried it, but the brats would split open, until we were told to pour warm water over them before immersing them in the boiling beer. We had them with mashed potatoes and gravy made from the beer the brats had boiled in.

In July 1941 a decree by Hitler, # 613 published in the '*Armee Verordnungsblatt*' (Army Regulations Paper) had something to say about the call-up of family sons. The gist of it was:

A decree by the Führer states that families with more than five sons, with four of them already serving in the Wehrmacht, will not have to give up their remaining sons. The fifth and any more will be exempt from service so that at least one male family member will be available to help with work at home. An investigation will be made to determine if a fifth or additional son is already a member of the Wehrmacht or hasn't yet been called up. The wishes of the fifth and additional sons who can be exempted will also be considered. Career service personnel are not included in this decree. All applications for exemption have to be submitted to the local Wehrmacht service office.

Sounds good, yes? But in reality, it never worked because there were very few households with four sons already in the Wehrmacht and labour service did not count. Everyone, male or female, had to volunteer with the RAD for six months and later it was a year. That sounds not too bad, but it was also paramilitary training for the men. Some RAD units went straight to the front without Wehrmacht battalion or regimental status.

* * *

The winter of 1942/43 had been uneventful in our community, but March and Easter were not far away and for our family, the tedium was about to change. On Saturday 6 March, after a Hitler Youth parade in town, we were asked if we would like to participate in another parade the next Saturday on 13 March in Bottrop, a medium-sized city in the Ruhr north-east of us. The area was known for its coal mines, gas and petrol-related products, making it a good place for us to get bombed. We asked our HJ leader about the danger of air raids. 'I don't think so,' was his answer. 'Oberhausen and Essen are much more promising targets.' What he forgot to say was that the three cities, Bottrop, Essen and Oberhausen, are next door to each other, without a real boundary between them. One blends into the other with just a yellow enamelled sign telling the traveller where he is. 'And besides,' he added, 'there are high-rise air-raid bunkers in Bottrop if the RAF decides to come for a visit.' The cost for the trip was one Reichsmark. Parents could come to the parade too, but they had to find their own way of getting there and they would have to bring their ration books if they wanted to eat out.

Thursday we set out at noon in a fleet of Borgward and Hanomag canvas-covered trucks with drivers from the *Nationalsozialistisches Kraftfahrkorps* (NSKK – the National Socialist Motor Corps). Our intention was to stay until Sunday morning and be back at home about noon. Bottrop was only some thirty miles away. We crossed the Rhine at Krefeld over the Adolf Hitler Bridge and rolled into Wanheim, a suburb of Duisburg. There was lots of bomb damage all around us. It was the same in every town we went through,

Duisburg, Mulheim, Oberhausen, Sterkrade, and even Bottrop showed a fair share of ruins from previous bombings.

Like any good youth group of the time, we brought our musical instruments with us; drums, fanfares (flugelhorns), fifes and the always present 'Dicke Doom' the huge banging drum, usually carried by the strongest boy. We were ready for the parade and could play along with any of the usual marching songs. Our favourites were *'Ein Junges Volk steht auf zum Sturm bereit'* ('The Youth Stands Ready in the Storm'), *'Der mächtigste König im Luft Revier'* ('The Mightiest King in the Sky') and *'Rot scheint die Sonne'* ('The Sun is Shining Red').

Several mothers and other relatives showed up at the school to collect their boys for meals and Mum came by tram from her hotel at 5:00 p.m. to pick up Len and me, but we wanted to eat and stay the night with our friends. We thought it would be more fun staying with boys our own age rather than being with grumpy parents in an even grumpier restaurant and hotel. The parade wasn't until Saturday so it was no problem. She said she would pick us up the next day at noon after she returned from visiting a friend in Karnap, a little farther north-east in Essen. Trams were running until midnight unless, of course, an alert was sounded.

That evening for dinner we had the obligatory stew-soup, the *Eintopf,* which one boy said must have been invented by a mean and not-so-hungry NSV woman. We ate whatever it was and complained to each other while she sat in a restaurant having truffles or caviar. That's what we imagined anyway. The vegetables in the stew had no taste at all – if they really were vegetables. To wash down the soup, what of it we could eat, there was 'no bean' coffee, and if you think that all coffee comes from coffee beans, you are mistaken. No other country in the world experimented more with coffee-making than Germany in the Second World War. There was the *ersatz* coffee, made by the Kathreiner firm in Munich, which tasted the most like real coffee. There was also roasted barley coffee, wheat coffee, and even coffee made from roasted acorns, but the worst was chicory coffee that could turn your guts inside out if you drank more than one cup. There was no point in complaining to the NSV; they did their best with the things available. Of course, those of us who were younger couldn't remember better days from before 1939, so we tried our best to eat the *Eintopf* and drink the coffee, all gorged down with a good slice of *Kommissbrot* (bread made from rye and barley flour).

The night passed without any alerts; not a sound was heard from above. Was it a holiday for the RAF bombers we wondered? The *'Drathfunk'* radio stayed on all night in the leader's room to warn us of any air attack. As long as it was quiet and the light on it blinked green, everything was all right above us. The *Drathfunk* was no ordinary radio; there was only one station. We got news, and music too if there wasn't anything important going on. Listening to foreign broadcasts on a regular radio could get you into a lot of trouble if the wrong person found out. Mostly that only happened in the big cities. No one ever asked us what we listened to. Breakfast was at 9 a.m. and it put us in a better mood because we had cocoa instead of coffee with our bread and butter, jam of some sort and a slice of *Jagdwurst*, which was sausage that, at the time, could have been made from about anything, but it was good.

After breakfast we did a bit of band practice. Len and I played no instruments so we waited for Mum to come. We knew how to march, so no sense in practicing that. She arrived later and found us standing clean and neat by the gate. She had a look at us and decided we hadn't suffered too much staying with the other boys. A few other mums and grandparents arrived too. Fathers and uncles were scattered all over Europe serving the Führer and Fatherland. We asked Mum what we were going to do all afternoon. 'Does Bottrop have a zoo we can visit or maybe there's a bicycle race?' The answer was no to both and the public outdoor swimming pool was still closed; after all, it was only the middle of March. Mum had much more important things on her mind. She found her ration cards and searched through them for the shoe allowance points. There were enough for a pair of church slippers each for Len and me, so we proceeded to find the nearest shoe shop. The saleswoman there refused to serve us and it sounded like she had practiced her excuse a lot. Our cards weren't issued in Bottrop, which meant we weren't residents of that town, so no shoes for us. 'Has it come to this? What a crummy world we live in,' Mum said, loud enough for the woman to hear her.

'Yes, I agree, the woman said, 'Germany today is like Pandora's Box; every time it's opened, something else evil pops out.' We were used to that kind of talk among older folks back home, but to hear someone younger in a town the size of Bottrop saying the same thing was a surprise.

'It's a pigsty.' Mother added, seeing that she had found a kindred spirit.

'That may be so, but I still can't sell you anything. You have to be a registered resident of the city of Bottrop. I'd lose my job and could be brought up on charges.' Len, who was always a bit too fast with his mouth and too slow with his head, almost told her what she could do with her merchandise, but Mum's warning glance kept him quiet.

The hotel we went to was near the rail station and a fair-sized concrete bunker was only few yards away. '*Räder rollen für den Sieg*' ('Wheels roll for Victory') said the black slogan painted on a large white panel above the station entrance. The room had two big beds with a table and a chair, but no radio. We washed up a little, combed our hair, and were soon ready for supper. I was looking forward to something better than what we had the night before. Our room was on the ground floor, so it was a short walk to the dining hall.

Before you could order what you wanted to eat in any restaurant, you had to show that you had the right ration cards, but unlike cards for slippers, food cards could be used anywhere in Europe where Hitler's word was law and it certainly was in Bottrop. We had a big bowl of fried potatoes and bangers – made from what, we didn't ask. In most restaurants, Bismarck herrings were the usual fare with fried potatoes and we wondered why we didn't get any. Finally Mum asked our waitress about it. Waitresses knew everything because they heard everything. I was pretty sure they could hear the grass grow. Friday was the traditional fish day in Germany and it was Friday. Nazis or no Nazis, some holy dignity had to be preserved even in hard times. Good Catholics ate fish on Fridays but they had run out, serving sausages instead. We didn't complain, but the waitress told us that a fishmonger across the street sold succulent Bismarck herrings out of a barrel and that no one would mind if we bought some to have with our potatoes. Len dashed across the street with a one Reichsmark note in his hand where the fishmonger had a barrel of herrings under a canopy. From where I was sitting, I could see the heavy lid secured with a padlock to deter thieves. I thought that nobody would try to take the whole barrel anyway. He returned with three herrings and some change; not a bad deal we all agreed. Our meal was complete and afterward we had some *brause* (fizzy) lemonade – so the herrings could swim, and listened to the radio in the hall.

It seemed all so peaceful with 'Juliska from Budapest' with her heart full of paprika, coming from the speaker, followed by music from *The White Horse Inn on Lake Wolfgang*. When they started with the news, we retired for the night because none of us believed the stories about how the Russians had done us a favour by chasing us out of Stalingrad six weeks earlier. In our room, Mum read a Free Corps novel by Erich Dwinger while Len and I played cards. He always carried a worn out deck with him and liked playing twenty-one. I lost almost every hand, finally gave up and went to bed. Mum had the little bedside lamp on while she read, and sometime in the night, it flickered and woke me up. I could hear a lone aircraft somewhere overhead, but no siren came on to alert us to anything important. That didn't matter; Mum got us up and told us to get dressed as fast as we could. We went into the dining hall to see if there was any news on the *Drathfunk* and we had hardly sat down when the announcement came. 'Enemy bombers are approaching Hook van Holland [in far south-west Holland], Terschelling, and the West Friesian Islands; course, south-east.' That certainly meant western Germany. We knew bombers headed for Hamburg or Berlin came in through different air space. True enough, the preliminary alarm came directly; a long wailing sound, lasting thirty seconds, and then repeating itself. There was no danger as yet, but we grabbed our bags and things we had left in the room and went out into the hall again. Folks were assembled around the radio. Juliska was quiet and the white horse had galloped away.

Out on the streets it was pitch dark as expected in an air raid. A few lone aircraft could be heard a ways off coming nearer, but nothing that sounded like a stream of heavy bombers. All of a sudden the sky lit up like a peacetime fireworks display or a celestial-size illuminated Christmas tree. We knew immediately what was afoot; those were target markers and the planes above us had been twin-engined Mosquito Pathfinders. Searchlights swept the sky and some distant 88 flak guns opened up. 'It's time for the shelter now, Mum announced. There was flak shrapnel raining down on roofs and into the street; some ripped through the green and brown canopy over the fishmonger's cart, only missing Bismarck's favourite food by an inch. Then we heard the still distant characteristic sound of enemy bombers, and anyone who has lived through nights like this – nights of fire and destruction – will never forget the sound of four-engined RAF Lancaster bombers. *Ami* bombers only came during the day until near the end of the war. Folks from all corners of the city streamed into the shelter, which was a huge block of concrete six stories tall that could house several hundred people. An air-raid warden was stationed at the entrance, sorting out the incoming human traffic. 'No pushing, no shoving; there's room for all,' he kept repeating. A few latecomers dashed in, among them a woman in a post office cap and uniform who sobbed the whole time. 'Will you shut up,' the warden blared at her, 'You're making everyone nervous.'

'I can't help it, I have two small children at home,' she replied.

'So what are you doing without them here in the middle of the night?'

'I was visiting my sister and I'm on the early 6 a.m. shift at the post office.' By now bombs were falling in the distance. Was it at Katernberg or even nearer? We couldn't tell. Then a whole series of explosions shook the shelter to its foundations.

'That was close,' someone screamed and the post-office woman started sobbing again.

'Where do you live?' an old man smoking a pipe asked the woman.

'Johannis Street, number 37, top floor.' More explosions, some near some far away, but obviously they were all meant for Bottrop.

'I hope we get home okay and I'd rather leave tomorrow than Sunday,' Mum whispered to us.

'And what about our parade?' Len whined.

'If the town's been hit hard, there won't be a parade and let's hope those friends of yours in that school aren't hurt.'

Finally, after two hours the all-clear sounded. People streamed from the shelter, behind the post office woman, who was the first one out. She ran down the street still sobbing. All around us houses were on fire and then a delayed-action bomb went off with a terrific bang a few hundred feet away. I think those were the worst, designed specifically to kill rescue workers. The hotel was still standing with some windows broken but otherwise no damage we could see. I noticed something silvery in the road and a strong vinegar smell was everywhere. 'Look at all those herrings,' Len shouted and began filling his Hitler Youth cap with the slippery fish.

'Bismarck is turning in his grave,' the warden remarked, watching people grab the free food.

'Is he buried here in Bottrop?' asked a dumb-looking fellow.

'Where did you learn history – in Russia?' The warden wasn't pleased to see such behaviour and this simpleton just made it worse. 'He's buried in Friedrichsruh, Holstein.'

Yes, our parade was cancelled; many people lost their lives that night, but none of the other HJ boys and girls were hurt and we had enough herrings to last the weekend. Everyone went home on the train because the trucks had been hit and were sent for repair. None of us complained about that. In 1940, the events we had just lived through would have been reported all over Germany, but by 1943, such things were barely noticed and quickly covered up by propaganda that no one believed anymore.

Chapter 5

Nine-Year-Old Flak Helper

In the debacle at Stalingrad in early 1943, Germany lost so many divisions that there was an acute manpower shortage on the Eastern Front. Hitler, with a stroke of the pen, decreed that the losses were to be made up somehow. Thousands of flak gunners were immediately transferred to front-line units. This incensed Herr Meier. He was commander-in-chief of the Luftwaffe after all, and the homeland flak was part of the Luftwaffe. The Hitler Youth was immediately mobilised to fill vacant spots on the light flak batteries. This was unheard of in Western armies, but young boys were required to do their bit for victory in Germany and that's exactly what they did. While most able-bodied men were fighting on the Eastern Front or in North Africa, or just idling away in Norway, France, the Low Countries or the Balkans, the boys of the Hitler Youth and the girls of the BDM kept the home fires burning and the home front defended.

I had been a member of the Jungvolk for a while before the end of the war, and as such I had to attend parades and meetings where speeches were made by the youth leaders who stressed our role in the Thousand Year Reich. All this was not much to my liking but there was no way out, and besides, on the weekends we had field instruction. That was a lot more fun and gave me the chance to take the weekend off from garden labour and school lessons. In the spring of 1942, forty-seven of us Jungvolk kids claimed an unused sandpit at the foot of a small hill as our command centre. We didn't have tents so we made our own shelter out of bushes we cut. Above the sandpit was an anti-aircraft position consisting of two quad 20mm guns. They were menacing weapons that looked like they meant business. After our weekend was over, I strolled up to the position to have a look for myself. In unmistakable terms a sergeant told me to leave immediately, but the commander of the guns, a staff sergeant, who happened to be my father's friend and drinking pal, invited me to stay. I persuaded him to assign me as a messenger for the position. They had telephone communications with the nearby 88mm flak position, but they were often disrupted. This would also get me out of a lot of the other details that Jungvolk kids had to do. Roland was the staff sergeant's name, and to me, he was a true giant, like Roland the Giant in the song '*Roland der Reis im Rathhaus zu Bremen*' which we all knew. He must have been about six feet six inches tall and he told me that he would ask his captain if I could be assigned to the flak battery. The other Jungvolk kids were more than a little jealous when I told them that I had been approved to be the new flak helper.

When the quad crew first arrived, they had only a wooden hut and their meals were prepared in town by the NSV and brought up by a truck. When two new bunkers were constructed by Organisation Todt (OT – a civil and military support contractor) engineers, a several-kilowatt generator was installed in another small concrete shed, but the main purpose of this generator was to supply power to the searchlight and the *Horchgerät* or '*großen Ohr*' (big ear), as we called it, sound detector. Cooking was done on a stove heated with wood or coal. Perishable foods were stored in another smaller underground bunker and once a week, a truck brought up six large blocks of ice from the city ice plant. Since I was a sort of flak helper, I was included in the rations but as I only lived a mile down the road, and their cook wasn't very good, I preferred Mum's cooking most of the time.

Germany is a country of many dialects and even languages. Western Rhinelanders speak a *Platt Deutsch* related to Dutch. A Bavarian can't, or more likely won't, understand what a North German from Holstein says and that goes the other way 'round as well; an *Oberlausitzer* (someone from Upper Lusatia) has a hard time understanding a *Saar Pfälzer* (someone from the Saar), so it made a lot of sense having men in a regiment who understood what was being said; some knew each other in private life and that made the men of the regiment even more responsible to each other. The ever-inventive *Landsers* soon developed a litany of words that everyone in the regiment could understand, whether they were from the Lithuanian border, Aachen, Slesvig or the Brenner Pass. Here a few examples:

Wanzenhammer (bedbug hammer) . . . a tobacco pipe, or to kill bugs or lice.
  Stalin Torte (Stalin pie or tart) . . . dry bread.
  Taschenflak (pocket flak) . . . a pistol.
  Rollbahn Krähe (runaway crow) . . . light aircraft.
  Küchenbulle (kitchen bull) . . . military cook.
  Krüppelgarde (crippled guard) . . . *Volkssturm*, older men drafted into military service.
  Hühner Alarm (chicken alert) . . . late alert, as in bombs fell and then the alert was sounded; first the egg, then the chicken.
  Flieger Bier (pilot's beer) . . . lemonade.
  Eiserne Kuh (iron cow) . . . canned milk.

Donner Balken (thunder plank) . . . simple toilet.
Blech Cravat (tin cravat) . . . the Knight's Cross medal.

These are only a few, but there were hundreds of them, understood by any German soldier and late in the war, we had men from all over at the quad and 88 emplacements.

We were part of the Ruhr defence and came under the 64th *Abteilung* [Battalion] Düsseldorf. There were sub-commands of the 64th in Münster, Cologne, and Remscheid near us, all known as '*Luftgaukommando* [regional air command] VI Münster', plus an assortment of fighter bases. One was only about four miles away from us and from our elevated quad position we had a good view of the base and could watch the planes take off and land. At one time, early in the war, Adolf Galland, the well-known fighter ace, was in command there. There was also the 88mm battery not far from us; in fact one gun was only a few fields away. One man in our flak crew, Willi Strauss was his name, had been in the outfit since 1941 and he was a real artist. He made several drawings of our position, including the 88s and these were later published in a picture book in late 1942 under the title *Flak an Rhein und Ruhr* ('Flak on the Rhine and Ruhr'). I still have the book; my uncle, Major General Reinhard Gehlen, gave it to me on my birthday in 1943 and he had got General von Axthelm to sign it. Von Axthelm was the top flak general in the Reich.

By the end of 1943, about 4,000 enemy planes had been shot down over the Reich or been so severely damaged that they were unfit to fly. Almost thirty-five million AA (anti-aircraft) shells of all calibres had been fired to accomplish this. That was a lot of metal going up and there were many flak guns that never shot down even one plane. Flak men, especially those on the 88s, were well trained in the beginning, but later in the war, it was a different story; some were good, but some were downright useless. Allied bombers came over at a high altitude, from 20,000–22,000 feet and it took twenty seconds for an 88mm round to reach that altitude and explode. By that time the target had moved on about a mile, depending on air speed. At the quads, we fired over open sights. We could see the target because we only dealt with intruders that came in below 6,000 feet. We had a rangefinder, but for the quad crew it was mainly ears and eyes that counted.

My messenger duties allowed me to eat with the men if I happened to be there at mealtimes. The flak battery eventually also had running hot water and a shower cubicle installed in their bunker and I was allowed to make use of it as well. In late 1942 and early 1943, things weren't too bad and the cook, who was also a magazine loader, had some choices in what to make for the men to eat. Later, however, the cook had to make something of whatever was available and kraut was always available. The sauerkraut soup was called *Gorilla Rotze* ('gorilla snot'). It not only smelled terrible, it didn't look like anything edible either. It had the taste of something between rotten spinach and bad onions. The worst part came a few hours after eating it when your guts would explode. The cook did the best he could with what he had and often that's all he had. In civilian life before the war, the man had been an assistant to an undertaker and he should probably have kept that information to himself. The men never let him forget it. I suppose there were bad undertakers who were good cooks and good cooks who would have been bad undertakers; this guy was probably a good undertaker because he sure wasn't much of a cook. The war made soldiers out of all men and you could never guess what some of them had been in the real world. There is an old saying that's true in any army: 'Never piss off the cook; you will regret it', so we didn't make too much fun of our cook's former job, at least not when he was around.

*   *   *

In February 1942, when Mum went to the military hospital in Bottrop for a few days to visit my father, we had to fend for ourselves and we almost starved; Aunt Carol was not a very good cook. We avoided her meals whenever we could and I stayed with the quads as much as possible. As some sort of payment, I volunteered to help the cook prepare dinners for the thirty-one men. He was glad to get the help and I was glad to avoid Aunt Carol's cooking. I brought a big bag of carrots and a freshly-killed rabbit up to the position as my contribution to one of the meals. The cook, two men from the flak crew, and I washed and scraped about twenty pounds of carrots while the rest of the crew was sleeping, playing cards, or writing home. It was a misty foggy day, so we knew we wouldn't be disturbed by *Jabos*. When I told the cook that I wanted to make a carrot soup, he told me it had better be good.

'Trying is not good enough boy,' he said, 'If these guys don't like it, I'm in trouble and will have to start all over again.'

'You ought to be thankful for the free twenty pounds of carrots and the rabbit – and for a rainy day with no alerts,' I told him.

'Those guys are spoiled; they'll come down on me hard if the food isn't good.'

'They might yell at me too, but if they do, it'll be the last time I bring any food up to them.'

Giant came in from an inspection tour. Because of the wet day, he had to make sure all the guns were covered with tarpaulins to keep out as much of the moisture as possible.

'What's going on here?' he demanded.

'I'm making lunch for all of you, Sir,' I said, 'cabbit soup.'

'What is cabbit soup? I've never heard of it.'

'Well, it's like rabbit and carrot stew Sir.'

'It has to be better than sauerkraut soup, so go ahead boy. The cook is your servant for today, so get going.'

At 1:00 p.m. the lunch gong, which was an empty 88mm shell, was hit with a hammer to call the men to eat. Each man received a good ladle full of the cabbit stew and a piece of black bread. There were no complaints and in fact, Gunny, our senior non-commissioned officer under Giant, remarked that they should make their cook the messenger and have me prepare their meals every day. Gunny, who originated from Finland and had an unpronounceable surname, had been a butcher, a bricklayer and a cobblestone layer in civilian life.

The most common meal for everyone, and that included soldiers at the front, was pea or bean soup. Every company had their own 'Gulasch Cannon', a mobile field kitchen with a huge cooking pot. When not in use, it was towed behind a *Kübelwagen* (the German equivalent of the Jeep). With the stove pipe laid flat, it looked like a cannon from afar and even became a target of the fighter-bombers late in the war. Today, modern versions of this stove are in use at fairs and large outdoor gatherings. A stray cow or even a pig, if available, was duly slaughtered, skinned and cut up into small portions, depending on the size of the company, which was usually 120 men. Water (or snow in the winter) was added to the pot along with dried peas, leeks or other vegetables. Salt, pepper and any available spices were also thrown into the pot. This whole concoction was then boiled for hours. Dried peas need time to cook. Later in the war, the dried peas were ground to a fine flour-like substance and that shortened the cooking time considerably. Ground pea powder is still sold to this day in Germany and I have it sent from Germany once every two months. It is sold as *Erbswurst* and if you know any German at all you know *Bratwurst* – and *wurst* means sausage; *erb* is pea, so the literal translation is 'pea sausage'. It's called this because it comes in a cylindrical roll like sausage. It cooks in just a few minutes which was a good thing for soldiers at the front. At our flak position we didn't have a Gulasch Cannon because our guns were not mobile. The cook used a cast-iron stove fired by wood or coal and, unlike most of the cooks at the front, ours never learned how to cook for thirty-odd men. There was always too much or not enough. If there was too much, we had to eat it the next day but most of the time there wasn't enough.

Things were exciting at times, but serving in an anti-aircraft battery, even in your own back yard, wasn't always fun. You were as much in danger as a soldier hundreds of miles away at the front, whether in Russia, Italy, North

Africa, or France. The duty of an AA gun crew was to try and stop attacking enemy aircraft shooting at you, and to not jump into the nearest trench or ditch. If a P-47 made a beeline toward your position, you had to brace yourself for the worst while keeping your gun sights on the plane. The only consolation the home flak had was that they were at least on home ground. That could still mean you were 400 miles from where you lived. If a crew member was from East Prussia and served along the western border, he was a good 400 miles from home. My Uncle Peter served in the flak in Königsberg, and that was 400 miles from his home in Aachen. Even a few Russian auxiliaries were later added to the batteries. They were ex-POWs who thought serving Hitler was a better choice than living under Stalin. The eastern POWs had a hard life, but a daily crust of bread and a mess tin of hot stew promised by recruiters from the Vlasov Army was enough to lure them into the Wehrmacht. Andrey Andreyevich Vlasov was a Russian general who decided he'd rather fight on the German side after being captured by General George Lindemann in July 1942.

Since I was exempt from Jungvolk and Hitler Youth parades most of the time because of my duties at the quads as a messenger, I had more time to help with work at home. I was sort of the mascot at the quads as well as the runner for messages when the phones went out, which was often. Whatever duties needed doing, I did them if I could. Mum at first said that I had to come home in the event of an air raid but she was soon convinced that her boy was safer under a foot of concrete at the quad position than at home under a wooden table. Besides, the fighter-bombers did not announce when they would arrive and I sure didn't want to be out in the open after the shooting began. There were two concrete bunkers at the quad battery, one for the crew and the other for the loaded ammunition magazines, and both would withstand anything short of a direct hit. The crew's bunker had a sleeping room with eighteen field beds. Later, when a searchlight crew was stationed nearby, things got rather crowded. The searchlight crew of course slept during the day and was at their positions by sunset. We had a generator in an old shed about twenty-five yards away, and later the generator was put in its own bunker and trenches were dug for the cables that ran to the searchlight. The quads really didn't need electricity but it was sure dark in the bunkers without light. I still have a drawing our artist did that shows the shed before it was turned into firewood.

*   *   *

When Len became a group leader in the Hitler Youth, he got a dark green braid to wear on his uniform with all the efficiency badges he had won. I was still in the Jungvolk, but I had a more important job at the flak battery than anything he ever did. I was in good stead with the light flak crew and I wanted to keep it that way, so whenever I had free time I was at the battery helping out with loading magazines and emptying the collection bins that held empty shell cases. Since this was a sort of official duty assigned by the captain and Giant, I was exempt from town parades to the envy of Brother Len. He thought my job was just for show.

'Look Len,' I told him, 'you dig holes and ditches and you march twice a week, strutting around town like a peacock, don't you think that's useless?'

'It's for the defence of the Reich and it's very important.'

'So in other words Len, what you're saying is that the flak is not that important and that a ditch is a better air defence than a brace of quads, not to mention the 88s. Well, I can tell you that you'd better keep that opinion to yourself around the men from the flak position.'

'We're all important in this war.'

'Yes,' I shot back, 'I know we are, and you think you are the most important of them all.' And with that I left him standing.

My Jungvolk duty required me to be on the flak battery, but on quiet days, I loved the garden and farm work. Quiet days were also rainy and foggy, if not snowy, and the planes we were often bothered by couldn't fly. Only the big boys high up, 20,000 feet or more, kept going in that weather, but even they had days off when their home bases in England were shrouded in fog. On these gloomy days, half the flak crew had time off. I usually went to help on a neighbour's farm or worked in our garden. After Granddad Willem died, I was responsible for most of the garden work. Len always had excuses but he never shirked from digging slit trenches or anti-tank ditches for the Führer. He was so indoctrinated by the system that, even at the end of April 1945 when our area was under Allied occupation, he still believed in the Führer and final victory. In 1943 an offer was made to Brother Len by the Party-organised *Kinderlandverschickung* (KLV – Children's Evacuation Office) for his evacuation to the Tyrol Hitler Youth camp for his safety, but he flatly refused to go. I myself could have gone to deepest Mecklenburg but Mum wouldn't hear of it, and besides, I felt quite happy and safe under a foot of concrete at the flak battery.

Our quad battery was in a fixed position near M-G and Krefeld, but when bombing of the Buna plant at Marl threatened to decrease production, our crew got a two-week transfer to the area. We were to bring the guns that had been hastily brought up to us on halftracks driven by Luftwaffe soldiers. Our guns back home stood idle with only a skeleton crew, but fortunately, during our absence there were no major attacks. That Buna plant never ceased production during the war. There were too many flak batteries in the Ruhr area. I still have a picture that shows the skyline with all the barrels of the AA guns in the vicinity pointed upward. That must have been a frightening sight to the pilot of a fighter-bomber.

We set off in a truck on a warm July morning in 1944, reaching Marl in the afternoon where we were directed by a captain to a position just northeast of Buer (Gelsenkirchen) and about four miles west of the Buna plant. The position was on an old coal mining spoil heap and, although the spoil was mostly overgrown with grass and bushes, the hot summer wind blew clouds of black dust everywhere and soon we looked like a bunch of Zulus. The emplaced guns already there included a 20mm quad and a 37mm RB (Rheinmetall-Borsig) 18 that fired explosive shells from six-round magazines. The RB was something we didn't have at our position back home. We stayed an unsuccessful nine days. The Allies had decided to give Marl and the Buna works a miss for the time being. A truck came to pick us up for the three hour journey home. We had just arrived in Karnap near Essen when out of the blue sky three fighter-bombers roared down at us with guns blazing. They were circling the huge smoke-belching chimneys of the town.

'Damn it, we've got nothing to shoot back with,' Gunny cried. A quad hitched to the back of a truck could be made ready to fire in less than two minutes by a well-trained crew, but we didn't have one, and besides, we knew the bombers would be gone by then. We all dived into a roadside ditch hoping the enemy pilots would not spot us. Somewhere over Bottrop they turned around and came back for a second helping. By then, several light AA guns in the vicinity had opened up and tracers were crisscrossing the sky. We made ourselves inconspicuous, but the truck was too tempting a target and took a couple of cannon rounds through the canvas into the wooden flooring of the bed. Then, just as quickly as they had appeared, they were gone, followed by a few angry streams of AA fire, but we didn't see any damage to the planes. There were none of our planes to be seen, but we didn't expect any that late in the war.

'Those flak guys were sure lousy shots. They need their butts kicked for wasting ammunition,' commented Gunny.

'It was probably Hitler Youth kids on those guns,' someone added.

'Now hold on there, they have to learn too and learn fast,' Gunny replied, and looking me over, he asked, 'You okay? No peeing in your pants?'

'No Sir. I'm fine, but I agree, those guys were lousy shots.'

We inspected the few holes in the tarpaulin and in the bed of the truck and decided it was minor damage. We were saddling up to continue our journey toward Meiderich when a Wehrmacht staff car stopped by. A major and an NCO driver stepped out of the car.

'You both okay,' he asked, 'no damage? I see you're Luftwaffe flak; are you going far?'

'Sir, we have come from the Buna works in Marl and we're supposed to get back to our unit near Krefeld. We got a few scratches but no real damage was done,' Gunny said. 'We have our *Marschbefehl* [transport permit] here.'

'No, that's okay, but if you need anything, stop at the OT canteen in Duisburg-Wanheim. You can get something to eat and a rest there.'

'We'll be almost home then, Sir; that's not far from the Krefeld-Uerdingen Rhine Bridge, but thank you all the same.'

'Okay. Well have a safe journey then. *Heil Hitler.*'

'*Heil Hitler,*' we all shouted back.

'We could do with a bite to eat,' Gunny said. 'It's almost noon and for breakfast we had bread, beet molasses, and barley coffee. Who's up for a stop in Wanheim so we can see how the OT engineers live?'

We were all for it, so we turned on a road west of Mühlheim and picked up the Duisburg-Düsseldorf Highway. Soon we passed the huge Mannesmann Armament Works, probably where our quads and 37mm guns were manufactured. The OT yard was just outside Duisburg-Wanheim. We pulled in, told the guard our predicament and showed him our travel permit.

'Yes, okay, no problem,' he said. 'The mess hall is on your far left'

'What's for dinner here?' Gunny asked the guard.

'It's all good. Go and see for yourself Sergeant. I had two helpings just minutes ago,' he said as we drove away.

We got into the chow line with our mess gear that we always carried with us.

'Ahh, the Luftwaffe is here,' a guy from the OT remarked.

I saw the grin on Gunny's face. He knew I would not let that go past without saying something. 'We are flak gunners,' I corrected the OT guy, 'light flak, as you can see from the red piping and collar tabs on our uniforms.'

'Flak, flak; that's all I hear around here,' another OT man chimed in. 'Are you shooting much out of the sky? I don't think so. We had two near misses this morning and the flak crew put enough explosives into the sky to kill every sparrow in Wanheim, but I didn't see any planes go down.'

'We're not one of your outfits around here,' I replied, and Gunny just let me go on. 'We're from near Krefeld and we look after our area.'

'What unit?' the OT man asked.

'*Pssst, Feind hört mit,*' [the enemy listens too], our gunner's mate Kremer whispered to me.

A bit sheepishly, the OT guy looked around, but he asked no further questions.

The chow was excellent. Their cooks were mostly professionals, drafted from long-since closed restaurants. A good cook needs good ingredients to make a good meal and they surely had what they needed. We had potatoes, green peas, a slice of pork covered in juicy gravy and apple sauce, and second helpings were available. We ate more than our share and thanked them before going on our way.

'We ought to send our cook here for some lessons' I said to the sergeant.

'That won't help much if our supply truck only delivers sauerkraut, but they sure must have an excellent supply depot here. Too bad it's too far for us to come for lunch every day.'

Around 3:00 p.m., we crossed the Rhine River, and on the west bank we met a group of RAD men and POWs who were busy filling in a few shallow bomb craters. An hour later we rolled up the hill to our home base.

'Welcome home Kameraden. Did you have a good time?' Giant shouted.

'Naaa, nothing doing,' Gunny answered, 'we got black as Zulus from coal dust and there were no attackers within our range, but we did have some good food prepared by real cooks.'

'Be happy to be home Sergeant. Our cook made something special for today's evening meal.'

'Did he now? I'm open to surprises.'

'Yes; he has made a first-class chicken ragout.'

'Where in Hell did he find a chicken?'

'A woman brought it up this morning to thank us for being on guard here and protecting her home and life.'

'What woman?'

'It was that Mrs. Brögger, the Forstmeister's wife.'

'I didn't know Brögger Flönz shot chickens. He normally shoots rabbits for the Party *Bonzen*. For that matter, I didn't know he had a wife either.'

'We got a rabbit too. It's all in the ragout; the cook has been busy.'

'A chicken and a rabbit isn't much for sixteen hungry mouths.'

'Well, the searchlight crew's not in on this. They had pork in town and conveniently forgot to bring a share up for us.'

The evening meal was palatable, but not exactly excellent. A few ingredients that needed to be added were missing, and besides, rabbit and chicken is not a good mix cooked together. The left-out searchlight crew slept through it all. In the summer, with long daylight hours, they had the best job in any flak battery.

Our family occasionally invited some of the crew for dinner, but either Giant or Gunny had to be at the quad position, even at night. Most nights the 20mm guns were silent because the enemy raiders flew at an altitude that they couldn't reach. To the crew, these dinners Mum made were a welcomed change from those made by the flak undertaker cook. Not that I had anything against undertakers : after all, my Uncle Hermann was a gravedigger at the local cemetery and supplied us with a Christmas tree every year after Granddad Willem died, but that flak cook just could not get his meals right no matter how hard he tried. To stretch our meagre rations we often made an *Eintopf* stew when the men came to dinner. After the Finnish-Russian war of 1939, Gunny had somehow made his way to Germany. His mother was German, and when he joined the Wehrmacht, they found out that, apart from knowing the ins and outs of cobblestones, he was also an expert in small-calibre gun mechanics. He quickly rose from private to corporal and then went for more schooling to the Rheinmetall-Borsig Plant, the makers of light flak cannons. After a successful examination, he found his way to the 64th as a gunnery sergeant.

The stew was made in our big three-gallon kettle if we were having visitors and it was usually started very early in the day to give the meat (usually rabbit) time to cook into small pieces, otherwise, someone – the first to be served – got the lion's share of the good stuff. Halfway through the process of cooking, chopped leeks were added, along with potatoes, cabbage, carrots and ground peas or beans, if available. All this had to be cooked with an exact dose of herbs and spices. We even tried cauliflower stew, but that didn't turn out to be very good because the cauliflower cooked to a creamy white soup with no texture. Of course we still ate it. If we had pork, we used that instead of rabbit. Beef was very seldom seen and you probably had to know someone high up in the Party to get some from the butcher. My mother's recipe book also shows stew made with a whole chicken, and we had it occasionally before the war, but plenty of bones had to be picked out during the meal. Chicken meat was unobtainable during the war. Chickens were much more valuable as egg-layers than as ingredients in a stew but if ever a chicken refused to do its job, we had to put it in the pot. We couldn't feed things that were of no use to us. I guess that's why I always wanted to be useful.

Late in the war, when the meals at the battery were becoming unpalatable, some of the men asked if they could get a *Blitzmädel* ('Lightning Girl') to do the cooking. I was not very keen on that idea because these *Blitzmädel* were also used as messengers, meaning I could lose my cushy job at the guns and have to parade around town or dig trenches like Brother Len. They were called 'lightning girls' because their uniforms had a patch with a lightning bolt on the sleeve. It was a Signal Corps patch, but when young girl volunteers were authorised to wear the uniform, they were given the somewhat unflattering nickname of *Blitzmädel*. Giant ignored the men's request and assured me that my job was secure. He was the chief and besides, the few girls in our area that might have been suitable were needed on the farms. I had the captain on my side too and he was the final decision-maker.

It was in the spring and summer of 1943 when the US Air Force began throwing its weight about over our area with bombing raids. When bombs were first dropped on M-G, I was asleep in the upstairs bedroom and almost fell out of bed. At that time there was only a single battery of 88mm anti-aircraft guns near us capable of firing on them at night and the racket was enough to wake the dead. The ground shook like an earthquake. That air raid was nothing compared to what would be in store for us two years later. In school, we had identification charts of all known enemy aircraft and classes were taught in how to identify them. We could eventually tell the difference between a B-26 Marauder, an A-20 Havoc, a B-17 Flying Fortress and a B-24 Liberator. Later there were other aircraft that were a worse problem for us, especially during the daylight when I was sent out as a messenger for the quads. Our quads were capable of firing about 2,000 rounds per minute. However, we didn't have ammunition belts, only fifteen- or twenty-round magazines that emptied in a few seconds, and then they had to be replaced to resume firing. Another disadvantage was that quads in fixed positions had no shields like those at the front. Our quads were set up in open pits with no protection whatsoever against low-level attacks until we built a sort of earth and log embankment around them. Our 20mm flak was only used for lower-flying attackers and later, in 1944, we had plenty of them to deal with.

Chapter 6

Bombings and Fighter-Bombers

G ermans seldom mourned the loss of property to bombs; that could always be replaced after the war. It was the starvation rations late in the war and the failure of their government to rectify the situation that brought on a feeling of helplessness we'd never experienced. Going hungry day in and day out was more depressing than a home destroyed by bombs or even a loved one killed. Any other country might have found a leader who would lead a revolt against such a system, but Germany had no other leaders. They had long since been thrown into concentration camps or murdered. There was no opposition political party the people could turn to and even expressing an opinion that was critical of the Party could be dangerous.

Why then did the German people not give up when all around them, cities were being laid wante? The German bombing of England had no effect on the morale of the British people, and it was the same for us. The Allied bombing was on a far more massive scale than the Luftwaffe's puny attacks on Great Britain, even including the so-called 'Baedeker Raids' or the V-Weapon attacks. However, after the war, many Allied bombing analysts agreed that bombing German population centres was not a major contribution to ending the war. Destroying oil refineries, communication centres and industrial plants made much more of an impact. Allied commanders like Carl (Tooey) Spaatz, Ira Eaker, Arthur (Bomber) Harris, Charles Portal and a few more, however, were convinced that bombing civilians was just as important. By the beginning of 1944, America alone had built some 150,000 aircraft and those in charge were determined to do something with the ones still flying. Millions had been spent on their construction and they would be worthless as soon as the war was over, and by this time everyone knew it would be over very soon. Certainly if Germany had the planes, fuel and pilots at the time, there would have been a great deal more bombing of English cities late in the war as retaliation for the devastation we were enduring.

* * *

By the middle of the war most people had some sort of air-raid shelter. For centuries, houses in Germany were built with underground basements, and during the Third Reich, building regulations required any newly-built house to have a basement. The exterior of all houses was brick and mortar so everyone had at least some sort of protection in an air raid against anything but a direct hit. A direct hit by even a small 250lb bomb would wreck the house and basement and probably kill someone. Big cities were also big targets and there was a problem providing any sort of shelter for the inhabitants of apartment buildings. The shelters, if they existed, were rarely large enough to hold everyone and some preferred to take their chances in the lower floor apartments rather than be buried alive. Huge above-ground public shelters were constructed in the largest cities and they could hold thousands of people. They often had ceilings that were eight feet thick and made of reinforced concrete. Some even had 88mm anti-aircraft guns and quad 20mm positions on top of them. These *Hochbunkers* (high, above-ground bunkers), as they were called – like the one in Bottrop – had no windows and only a few small openings with inch-thick steel shutters over them. They were safe even from multiple direct hits and saved the lives of many city-dwellers during the last year of the war. A number of these shelters can still be seen in large German cities if you know what to look for. The Allies decided it was not worth all the explosives it would have taken to blow them up. They're mostly used as storage facilities today. These remains of the Third Reich will probably be around for a dozen more generations.

Not until after 10 May 1940 did the real bombing begin, when civilians were killed en masse. That first raid, which was on Freiburg in May 1940, was a bombing by Germany's own Luftwaffe. Some sixty tons of bombs were mistakenly dropped on the city's train station because of a navigational error, killing dozens of civilians. Of course Goebbels blamed the British and Göring retaliated by attacking London, missing military targets altogether and hitting civilians. The British retaliated in kind and so it went on, both sides blaming the other. Luckily, the air-raid wardens, jokingly called 'Meier's Drovers' were out in force. The air-raid sirens came to be called 'Meier's Hunting Horns'. Every city or town had an engineering detachment, usually a platoon or company of the OT or the *Technische Nothilfe* (TNH – Technical Emergency Corps), supplemented with labour from nearby POW camps. The constant bombing of bigger cities put an enormous strain on the resources of these organisations. They were always short of transport, fuel and equipment for removing rubble after the bombings. These people worked wonders to get jobs done that were essential to maintaining communications, water and power supplies.

Any fighter or bomber pilot from the Second World War can tell you that of all man-made structures they bombed, high bunkers and chimneys were the hardest to demolish. Just look at post-war photographs of the cities in the Ruhr and you will see miles and miles of destroyed factories but hundreds of chimneys defiantly standing.

Around December 1941, the first British plane was shot down over our area and crashed in the centre of town, burning a few houses and injuring several people. Brother Len was not entirely satisfied with the results and blamed the civilian casualties on our flak defence. I told him he should blame Herr Meier. After the first bombings, a verse circulated among the civilians that I think the Reich Marshal would not have appreciated. It went something like this in a loose English translation:

A Walk in the Blackout – Father and Son

'Father, who's that walking through our streets in the night;
all blacked out, no lights shining bright?'

'My son, that's a stupid question I hear,
that's our blackout Kommandeur.

He's the man who safeguards our beds,
when enemy bombs come down on our heads.'

'My father, my father I can see very dim,
in the blackout, someone is following him.'

'My dear son, yes, I can see him as well.
Is it Herr Meier? Yes, sure as Hell.'

'Who is this Herr Meier? He looks like a thief.'
'Well, yes son, he is one and our own Luftwaffen Chief.

So please don't approach him, just walk by and be quiet,
like tits on a bull, he is useless tonight.'

'We're protected by our wardens from dusk until morning,
and your mum's in the fire service to give us all warning.'

We then heard a shout from our warden, 'Hear, hear.
The air raid is over; I'm sounding 'all clear'.'

A five-ton bomb was dropped near our church, in the pastor's garden, in early 1942, but luckily it didn't explode and was made safe by the local bomb disposal unit. In our little community, we didn't experience any real destruction until September 1942 when a few bombs fell on a farm not far away and the house and barn were burned down. Incendiary bombs set the home of the chaplain ablaze and the home of the holy sisters was hit too. Our pastor gave all of them temporary shelter until things could be sorted out. A phosphorus bomb hit the chaplain's house in a later bombing and burned the roof. It was five months before the house was completely repaired. This bombing was reported in the official Wehrmacht War Diary I read years later. On 3 October 1942, an aerial mine was dropped near the church, killing a parishioner and breaking a few windows. One of the enemy bombers our 88s shot down crashed into a factory near us and the engine ended up next to the church but there was no damage that day. Several schoolchildren died in the early summer of 1944 when they gathered around a hole in the road that a time-delayed bomb had made. The children were curious and the bomb exploded as it was supposed to. There was some precision bombing by low-flying P-38s or P-47s, but the damage was minimal; a few dwellings were destroyed. During the heavy bombing raid in September 1944, the rest of the church windows were blown out.

There was a raid during one of our visits (February–March 1942) to see Dad in the military hospital in Bottrop. Sometime around midday, the sirens started up. We were ushered out into the street and an air-raid warden took us to a nearby Hochbunker. People were streaming in from all directions in the inner city for shelter. There were mothers with baby strollers, old men and women clutching a few belongings, and of course, the ever-present Party officials in their brown uniforms, demanding respect and the best seats in the place. Many of our soldiers came home on a short leave only to find their homes in ruins and the family missing. If they were lucky, they would find a crude sign stuck in the rubble telling them where their family was. The soldiers who had lost everything had no desire to stay in Germany. The front became their home and their only friends were their comrades in arms, so they boarded the next train back to their lice-ridden bunkers or their lonely bases out in the steppes. Millions never came back.

I sat next to an old man and his wife. He was holding a small wooden suitcase and his wife was clutching a few pillows. He told me that he lived in Oberhausen, which was only a few miles away, and that he had worked in the coal mines for fifty years. He had lost a son during the fighting in Yugoslavia. We talked for a while and I found out that he was also a gardener, so we had something in common. His garden was much smaller than ours but we grew some of the same things. After talking to him for a while, I realised just how much better off we were.

'So, how are you set for manure for your garden then?' he asked.

'Animal droppings, kitchen waste, straw, weeds, the list is endless, Sir,' I answered.

'Well, he said, 'I haven't seen horse manure for years and have forgotten what it looks like.'

'We have plenty,' I told him, 'but sorry, it's too far from here to share it with you.' I could just imagine this old man running through the streets with a shovel and bucket looking for horse droppings. 'In the country we don't live like rich folks but we manage to get by.'

'We just get by too,' he said with a chuckle, 'but every day I have a slice of bread with four sausages on it.'

'Four sausages!' That's a lot more than we have. How do you manage to get four sausages every day?'

'Imagination son, just imagination,' the old man replied.

'Well, if imagination can fill my stomach, I would sure like to know how?'

'Okay boy,' the man whispered, 'I'll let you in on a secret. Just get a slice of black bread, put your four fingers on the top and your thumb below the slice, then hold it in front of your mouth and look at the four fingers. Then imagine those fingers being sausages and before you bite into your imaginary sausages, pull your fingers away. It works every time. You can even put mustard on your fingers for a little extra flavour. Mustard isn't rationed; not yet anyway.'

Well, what could I say? I thanked him for the tip, and heard far away a few rumblings of exploding bombs. The 88s on the roof let loose with a few rounds and everything went quiet again. In the last year of the war, city people went through this exercise almost every day, sometimes more than once. I couldn't imagine having to be cooped up like that very often.

'Alert over, alert over,' an air-raid warden shouted. I was glad to see the sun again. Bottrop was spared that day and we took the next train home.

In mid-June, it never gets really dark in north-western Germany. The sun sets well after 10:00 p.m. but the western horizon never gets dark and by 2:00 a.m., daylight starts creeping up again in the east. These were days when I did most of the garden work, at times well into the night. Brother Len didn't do much garden work but he did like picking blackcurrants. I think it was because he could fill his belly with them while picking. In mid-June 1943, on a clear night, about midnight, a huge stream of aircraft approached from the west. We didn't bother seeking shelter because bomber streams high up were not interested in a little village like ours, so we kept picking blackcurrants. Then a few minutes later, the sky to the east of us lit up as if by brilliant fireworks.

These were the bombing markers that the Pathfinders dropped to show the following bomber stream where to drop their loads. The searchlights in our area had already been alerted and their silvery white fingers were swinging back and forth across the clear sky. The dozen or so 88 batteries in our area then commenced firing. Instantly we knew the city of Krefeld was on the receiving-end of this attack. The city had a huge steel works, the DEW (Deutsche Edelstahlwerke), a chemical plant, many cloth manufacturing and food-processing plants and an inland harbour on the Rhine.

Krefeld had been bombed several times since 1941 by the RAF but not much damage had been done. In mid-1943, the USAAF joined in with better and more advanced bombing sights, better incendiaries and much bigger bombs, but that night's attack was courtesy of the RAF. Over 600 Avro Lancasters and Halifaxes dropped several thousand tons of bombs in multiple waves of attack. Our vantage-point on top of the only hill in the area gave us a panoramic view of the attack. We were about thirteen miles from the city and the huge fires started by phosphorus incendiary bombs lit up the sky; at times we could clearly see the attacking planes. A few German night fighters tried their very best to interfere, but they could never have stopped the attack. The AA flak had to stop firing when the night fighters released green and red flares to indicate their presence. A few of the bombers were shot down but not enough to make a difference. Brother Len reported to his Hitler Youth unit the next morning and was detailed to a rescue squad that went to Krefeld. The city, he told us, was flattened. I have no idea how many people died, but it must have been thousands. The city was attacked a few more times after that. In November 1944, Krefeld had another heavy raid but I wasn't home at the time.

This particular raid on Krefeld seriously affected our food supply. Krefeld-Uerdingen was at that time the largest producer of Maizena or cornflour; another plant was in Bielefeld which also got its share of bombing in an earlier raid. Cornflour was used extensively in every kitchen, not for its nutrition value, but more for thickening watery soups and stews, gravies and pancakes. Some of the bombs hit the cornflour storage facility and the subsequent fire set off a huge corn-dust explosion. In a nearby high-rise concrete bunker with 1,500 people seeking protection, the air was sucked out of the ventilation shafts and many suffocated. Brother Len nevertheless brought some ten pounds of cornflour home two days later, mixed with ashes and dirt of course, but we put the stuff through a sifter and used it. This raid stopped production for a considerable time and we had to use plain flour until the factory was halfway back in operation. We didn't grow corn because we had no facility for grinding and refining it. Our primitive coffee grinders just barely managed to grind rye, wheat or barley. There were plenty of oat fields too but processing oats requires a complicated bit of machinery to separate the oat grain from the chaff. We nevertheless cooked the whole thing anyway when we could get it, then strained the stuff and used the water in soups. The chickens and rabbits got the rest and they loved it.

Destroying a sugar refinery was an easy way to disrupt the local economy. By the winter of 1944/45, there was not a single one in operation. The refinery in Euskirchen had been bombed the day before Mum and I arrived during a trip through the Ardennes. Thousands of tons of sugar beets, waiting their turn to be made into sugar, were blown all over the town. The city of Jülich, only twelve miles north of the Hürtgen Forest, also had a large sugar factory. During the Battle of the Hürtgen Forest, still the longest battle the US Army has ever fought (19 September to 16 December 1944), that city and another, Düren, which was just east of the forest, were attacked by 650 American bombers on 16 November and totally destroyed.

Not only did the raids kill Germans; there were also thousands of foreign slave labourers in every major city working in the war industries, and they suffered the same fate. The bombs killed them as easily as they killed Germans. On 9 February 1945, we had our first heavy bombing raid. Up to that time, our city had only experienced the occasional scrap with fighter-bombers or the odd night bomb dropped by returning RAF bombers. On that early February day, things changed; the town was situated in the very centre of the path being taken by the advancing US XIII Army Corps commanded by Lieutenant General Alvan C. Gillem, Jr. during Operation Grenade. In mid-February, the IX US Bomber Division with a hundred B-26 Marauders and about forty B-26 Invaders attacked M-G just after 1:00 p.m.. There were 175 people killed in that raid, including many schoolchildren and several Russian POWs. The centre of the city was hit hard but the railway tracks, the main target, were quickly repaired and trains were moving again a few days later. The *Amis* decided that another attack was necessary, so on 24 February a second raid began. This time the IX US Bomber Division attacked with 110 A-26 Invaders, seventy-five B-26 Marauders, and for good measure, fifty fast twin-engined A-20 Havocs, protected by a swarm of P-51 Mustangs. They came in at 10,000–12,000 feet, just out of range of the quads, but we were busy nevertheless, targeting the escorts and flak suppressors. The 88s got two Marauders; one crashed about three miles from us with a full bomb load, the other hit a factory chimney as the pilot tried to get the damaged plane home on one engine.

There were fewer casualties during this attack. Most people who had survived the first bombing had already left the centre of town. The phosphorus bombs burned most of the inner city this time. The town's old market area with the large Catholic cathedral was especially hard hit. After that raid, I went in search of Brother Len. I knew he had gone to a Hitler Youth meeting in M–G about mid–day, but I wasn't very concerned about him getting hurt. He always managed to get out of any bad situation. I found him and several other Hitler Youths at a burning house on a side street by the cathedral. There was not a fire engine to be seen; the town only had four, and they were busy extinguishing fires in more important buildings. Brother Len and two more boys had just pulled an old couple out of the cellar. They were shaken but unhurt. The house, however, was in ruins. Len went back into the cellar and through the small basement window; he started handing canned peaches to his two mates. Under normal circumstances this would be looting, but these were not normal circumstances. They pulled the rubber rings and drank the peach juice like it was cold water and a few of them were taken home. By late afternoon, the whole block of houses had collapsed. Nobody felt guilty about taking the peaches, least of all Brother Len.

'Spoils of war,' he said.

I had heard that before somewhere. If I'm not mistaken, Dad said the same thing about the radio he brought home from Poland in 1939.

We walked the old couple to an NSV first-aid shelter and later, Brother Len got a commendation for helping rescue them. He didn't get to show it off for long though. The war was over for us eight days later. We got home that afternoon by 6:00 p.m., avoiding a few delayed-action bombs that went off around us. No doubt the pilots had dropped them to delay the rescue operations. If that was their intention, it worked. Five more people were killed the next day when some of those hellish devices exploded. In that last week of February, the *Jabos* were constantly patrolling the sky from dawn to dusk and venturing outside in broad daylight with no cover was just dangerous. The 88s were absolutely useless in holding them off, so the job fell to the quads, the few 37mm guns in the area and an assortment of single and twin heavy machine guns. The days were long gone when we were able to defend the area with ease. The P-47 Thunderbolts we called *Heckenspringer* ('Hedgehoppers') now had armour plating underneath, self-sealing tanks and, for good measure, four rockets under each wing. Only a lucky hit in a vital part of the engine could bring them down, and with the front line only a few miles away, a damaged plane could easily glide to safety. The pilot would be back the next day to shoot at us again. On 26 February, we made a sieve out of the port wing of a P-47, but the guy got clean away and dropped two 250lb bombs on the old motorcycle track before veering off. If that had been one of our planes with damage like that, the pilot would have pulled up and bailed out.

The bombing of Viersen on 24 February 1945 by six American bomb groups did not affect the outlying areas much. They were going after a communications centre there and didn't scatter their bombs. Three days later our house took a 105mm artillery hit that we didn't get repaired until well after the war. One of the bombs, a 500-pounder dropped on Viersen, didn't explode until 18 September 2012. It was a controlled detonation by a German bomb-disposal team, but there was still considerable damage. The disarming or detonation of such bombs is an almost weekly occurrence in areas that were especially targeted.

By late February 1945, things were getting bad for our church too. When the Allies advanced toward us, the Wehrmacht retreated and left many German cars, trucks and other vehicles parked near the church. On 28 February 1945, an attack by P-38s targeted this assembly of vehicles and a bomb fell on the home of the chief Church Warden, next door to our church. He and his daughter and some relatives who had taken shelter in the house were killed. The fighter-bomber pilots didn't know what was below; all they could see was a Wehrmacht field kitchen and halftracks parked nearby. In addition to being an air-raid warden, our Church Warden was also the person responsible for church business and he played the organ during mass. The kindergarten next door to his house was also hit but thankfully no children were present at the time.

An artillery forward observer sat in the church steeple directing our return fire. All this attracted fighter-bombers and a squad of P-38s raked the area with cannon fire and bombs. The next morning I went up to the quads as usual and watched as an American halftrack opened up from more than a mile out with a .50 calibre machine gun, using our clock face for target practice. The whole mechanism came crashing down into the church. Our artillery observer in the steeple was chased out with a few well-aimed rounds from a 105mm gun. The next day, the Americans arrived. The vicinity of the church looked like a battlefield with burned-out cars, trucks, dead men and animals. That was the end of the war for us and our church. It took years to repair the damage after the war, but by 1950, it was back in good shape. The church was once again the centre of religious activity and it still stands today, 120 years after it was built, more than seventy years after the end of the war and the end of the Thousand Year Reich.

*   *   *

The bombings were bad, but the fighter-bombers were our biggest worry. They could fly in low, sometimes lower than the hedges that divided the fields. Coming in at 400 miles per hour, flying over and around the hedges, they were a tough target for our quads. We discovered the best way to get a shot at one was to put up a curtain of fire across the path we thought they would be taking. We called this a *Harmonika*. The P-47s soon figured out what we were doing and began flying in from crossing directions at a separation in elevation of a few hundred feet. They had two bombs, or wing-mounted rockets and up to eight machine guns or cannons. A single fighter-bomber could do an incredible amount of damage to a small town and there was rarely just one of them in an attack. In July–August 1944 they came in from captured airfields in France, about 20 miles away, and they were equipped with 75-gallon drop tanks to give them either a longer range or more time over a specific target. These drop tanks came in handy after the war as small boats or bathtubs. They made better bathtubs than boats. Even a small ripple on a lake or stream could turn them over.

Air defence positions were built around many towns by 1942, mostly in prominent places with a good view in all directions. The biggest concern was the north-western direction since that's the direction the *Tommy* (British) and later the *Ami* fighter-bombers were coming from. To say our quads were in an excellent position would be a bad description of reality however. Firing from our position was like a doctor trying to remove an appendix with a kitchen knife and a corkscrew. Trees, chimney stacks, church steeples and other obstructions hindered the view in any direction. On top of that, a railway track ran only a hundred yards off, and to the east, about two hundred yards away, there was a large motorcycle race track, nicely oval shaped like a football stadium. Both made excellent references for a pilot looking for us. The motorcycle track had seen better days even when I was a kid. Nobody organised a race anymore, but as a reference point for bombers, there it was, and since we had no means to demolish it, we just ignored it. The demolition was finally taken out of our hands, first by P-47s with a few 250lb bombs and later, in February 1945, a misplaced salvo of 500lb bombs dropped from an A-20 Havoc finished the job. They were not aiming to destroy the racetrack of course; they were after the railway track. Gunny remarked that the bombing raid had been a terrible waste of explosives. In 2006, I visited the area for the first time since the war. The racetrack had turned into a wilderness but a few bare spots and parts of the concrete ticket booth were identifiable. A local resident who was walking his dog nearby said that he never knew there had been a racetrack there. He told me he was born in 1962 and had lived there all his life. A few shallow bomb craters can also be seen in the area and our old gun position is now part of a bird sanctuary. There were three huge factory buildings within a mile or so of the track, a food-processing plant, a cotton mill and a machine manufacturer, plus a few minor enterprises, and all of them had huge chimneys that were visible for miles. The cotton mill chimney was 240 feet tall and was the highest structure in town. Trees were not a big problem, they could be cut down, and they were in 1944. Church steeples and chimneys were a different matter. Brick chimneys were immune to machine-gun fire and even 20mm cannons hardly scratched them.

München-Gladbach, the city we were supposed to protect from air raids, was about three miles away from the quads, but there was also a fighter base a few miles to the south-east. From our elevated position, we had a grandstand view of both. Only to the north and west was our view largely restricted by chimney stacks, high buildings, and tall poplar trees. The *Heckenspringers* always used these trees as approach cover. Of course they knew where all the flak positions were, and even their best pilots hesitated to tangle with the eight barrels of our two quads. The chimney stacks were something we couldn't do much about, but in all our time up there, I can't recall ever hitting one. Gunny always knew the most direct solution to any problem so he suggested that we sneak up to the stacks at night and blow them up ourselves and blame the destruction on enemy raiders. He didn't get much support for that idea.

Many factories, and especially the food-processing plants, had ceased operation by early 1945 because of the daily bombing raids. Those that were still in operation had *Volkssturm* men and air-raid wardens guarding them. They were known to occasionally help themselves to whatever was being produced, but they also knew that, by this late date, they would likely be shot if they were caught. The Hitler Youth had been required to guard these facilities, but Goebbels' proclamation of early 1945, *'Der Führer erwartet Dein Opfer'*, which means, 'The Führer expects your sacrifice,' changed everything; even younger boys were being called up. Ten- to sixteen-year-olds died by the thousands defending Germany at the end of the war. 'The Hitler Youth fights for our lives, our freedom and greater Germany – and we will win' was another slogan we heard everywhere. I'm not really sure if we believed this propaganda anymore, or if we were just afraid of what would happen to us if Germany lost the war. By this time war had become very personal for all Germans.

At times, when enemy fighter-bombers had nothing better to target, they would attack livestock in the fields. I guess they figured a dead cow couldn't give milk and less milk meant less food for the enemy. A dead German was a dead German, whether he died from a bullet or hunger. That surely sounds cruel today but war is cruel, especially for civilians. I remember a quote I once heard but I can't remember who said it. I think it was a general. 'The will to resist can only be broken by killing the willing.' That is what total war is all about. Any cow that unfortunately got targeted by a P-47's machine gun was not wasted by any means, but if you wanted your share of fresh beef, you had to have a sharp knife and nerves of steel. You had to get your cut while the fighter-bombers were still roaming about and the farmer was still in his shelter. If the pilots got a glimpse of you, they would turn around in an instant and you became the next target. You also had to have a good excuse if someone happened to see you walking around with a slab of beef under your arm after any attack. It was still stealing, whether the cow was alive or dead.

*   *   *

Except in the winter, our garden was the place to be during the day, but because of the constant threat of air raids and particularly fighter-bombers, it was also a dangerous place to be caught unaware. The *Jabos* came unannounced; alerts were sounded usually after the culprit was gone and had left behind a trail of destruction. Many gardens, including ours, had a sort of shelter dug in one corner, about six feet deep and eight feet square with a corrugated iron roof, topped with two feet of soil. This was not exactly a safe haven against a direct hit, but a near miss from a 250lb bomb could be survived if you were in the thing. We also built a *Laube*, a sort of crudely-camouflaged gazebo as a place to hide from spying observation planes. We had no front garden and so we were exempt from the law requiring us to have a ditch about ten feet long and four feet deep to be used by the public walking along the street in the event of an air raid.

One minute, you were on your hands and knees, peacefully thinning out rows of carrots, and the next minute all Hell would break loose. It was not the peaceful gardening one has today. We were not so much afraid of the bombs however. We had figured out that a bomb exploding in the soft ground was much less dangerous than the machine guns on a *Jabo*. If the bomb happened to hit a house, that was a different matter – bad luck we would say. *Jabos* were fast, but they couldn't disguise the sounds they made. Even children could distinguish between turbocharged Allison, Pratt & Whitney, and Messerschmitt BMW engines. Our planes weren't often seen but when they were, they were greeted with much fanfare by the schoolchildren. For people living in large cities, the fears were reversed. *Jabos* rarely ventured low over them because of the church spires, chimneys and high-rise buildings. City dwellers feared the bombs that rained down from the high-altitude bombers. They didn't drop the small 250-pounders either. Their loads were 2,000lb to 10,000lb destroyers. The Allies didn't waste that kind of munition on farms and gardens. Even in daylight, when only high-flying bombers were up, life was by no means peaceful. Our 88mm flak that harassed the Allied planes had to throw up a tremendous number of shells to hit their targets and what goes up must come down. Our 88mm shells took about twenty seconds to reach an altitude of 20,000 feet before exploding and raining down shrapnel. From that height, even a small piece could kill.

One day in September 1944, we had a soccer game that I will always remember. Our opponents were from a school in Neuss, which was about fifteen miles away. The team and a few of their supporters came by tram to our soccer field for the match. Kick-off was at 2:00 p.m. on a sunny afternoon. The crowd roared when a Nazi official presented each team member with a nice triangular banner. '*Sieg Heils*' could be heard miles away. I think maybe the *Amis* heard the noise as well. The front line was in the Hürtgen Forest and that wasn't very far away. A couple of P-47s came over to investigate and there was not a single German plane in the sky to defend us. The local quads began firing and the crowd scattered like the inhabitants of a disturbed ant hill when the planes came back around. Luckily, there was a brick wall surrounding the soccer field and it provided a bit of shelter. Two small 250lb bombs hit the field, but the twenty-two players had already run into the dressing room. The other bombs went wide of the mark into a nearby wheat field. A few spectators were killed and several more were wounded. The game was called off that day and the only winners were the P-47s, which went home without a scratch. All open air games were cancelled from that day forward and the Hitler Youth was ordered to dig a five-foot deep trench outside the stadium gate. I have no idea what for.

*   *   *

Night raids by the RAF were a spectacular fireworks display for us, but daytime raids by the Americans were shrouded in dust, and the easterly winds brought the dust clouds right up to our door. By 1944, these raids were commonplace and were hardly even discussed anymore unless our area was on the receiving end. Even the radio didn't talk much about the 'terror attacks by gangsters' as they were called by our Propaganda Minister. Goebbels promised revenge for every bomb dropped on Germany, but by then we knew that would never happen. Soldiers home on leave were often glad to get back to the front where they could at least fire back at the enemy. At home, they were in the same predicament as the rest of us. Some still believed, even as late as the first months of 1945, that Germany's V-weapons would somehow change the course of the war in our favour.

During quiet nights, we could hear the faint roar of the V-2s heading westward. They travelled faster than sound, and at 70,000 feet, we couldn't see them. Several mobile launching sites were in our area but they were heavily guarded and we never got a close look at any of them. At times the gyro compasses in these rockets went haywire and they ended up far from where they were supposed to. One crashed into a hotel not far from us and killed several people. Another did a soft belly landing near Cleve in February 1945 without exploding. It landed in the front line of the 1st Canadian Division and was delivered intact into the hands of Montgomery's 21st Army Group. It became a showpiece in London after the war. By the end of the war, many V–1s and V–2s had been captured and some of them can still be seen in museums in the United States and Great Britain. The team that developed these rockets was captured by the Americans and eventually taken to Huntsville, Alabama. *SS-Sturmbannführer* Dr Wernher Magnus Maximilian Freiherr von Braun, the father of German rocket development was made an honorary citizen of Huntsville and under his guidance, the *Saturn V* moon rocket was developed at what is now called the Marshall Space Flight Center (named for General George C. Marshall of the 'Marshall Plan' by the way). Whether the Americans fed the captured German POW scientists in Huntsville on sauerkraut soup and black bread, I don't know, but I very much doubt it.

Chapter 7

Regulations and Propaganda

After 1939, we would occasionally have a Party official call on us to conduct a *Viehzählung*, or animal counting, but it didn't include cats and dogs and no one kept fish or birds as pets. He was interested in animals that were normally slaughtered for food like pigs, rabbits, chickens, geese and goats. Farmers had to register every one of these. We figured, since there was a war on, somehow this must be important. The problem was, if you had too many, and we never knew from one visit to the next how many would be too many, the animals were liable to be confiscated without payment. Often the goose you had been fattening up for Christmas dinner would end up on some Party member's table if you had a couple more running around in the yard. Now we didn't know that for certain, but we always thought it. To have more animals than you were allowed for your family's survival was not a crime as such, but you could very well have them taken away after you had fed them for a year or longer and that was a waste of feed for us. You also had to have a permit (of course) to slaughter anything bigger than a rabbit and if you got caught, that was a crime and the punishment could be severe. This kind of slaughter was called *Schwarzschlachtung* or 'black slaughter' because people who did this were usually selling the meat on the black market. In times of rationing, when you have to have a ration card for a pint of watery milk, the black market flourishes.

Meat or other food was traded for everything from accordions to porcelain figurines, award medals to wooden clogs. In our household, after Baby Fred was born and before Granddad died, there were six people including Aunt Carol, so we were allowed twenty-six rabbits and six laying hens. We had stopped raising pigs in 1939. They ate too much and had to grow for too long before they could be slaughtered. Neither was true of our rabbits. They would eat most anything vegetable and they grew quickly and multiplied. In 1941, we had fifty-six of the little crunchers and that many rabbits eat as much as a pig, so it was a daily job finding enough food for them. One August day in 1941, the official Nazi animal-counter came to our village to check on every non-farming household. He looked like a true National Socialist with his brown peaked cap and a grayish uniform. He saluted Granddad when he answered the door with a smart '*Heil Hitler*' and proceeded to ask questions about our rabbit population. We were told that we could only have twenty-six and that he would be back for the rest. Well, he did come back but he only found twenty-six live rabbits. The rest had gone into our stomach or into the canning jars. It was not a crime to slaughter rabbits and we were not about to give them away after caring for them and feeding them since they were born. We had no reason to believe that our rabbits would go to hungry people and no idea what the Party man would really do with them. Granddad didn't trust them to do anything they said they would do and the rest of us were beginning to think the same way.

We kept about five egg-laying hens and they produced one egg each per day in the summer when they were doing their jobs. They didn't do as well when daylight was really short in the winter months. We had ration cards for eggs too, but that would only get you one or sometimes two eggs per week per person, and most of the time, they were not available at all except on the black market. Often we traded a rabbit for ten eggs or whatever else we needed. Eggs need to be consumed if you can't keep them cool, but we found out that if you don't wash fresh eggs they keep much longer. We would sometimes boil them for ten minutes, then crack the shells and put them in a basin and cover them with a strong salt-water solution. After twenty-four hours in this brine, the eggs would float to the surface. We then took them out and put them in an egg box and kept it in a cool place. They would be edible for up to four weeks. We used these eggs for making breakfast by warming them up in tomato sauce, mushroom sauce, mustard or bacon gravy and have them with rye bread. Then there is waterglass (sodium silicate) which can be used to preserve eggs but not many people know how to do it. It's simple: a solution of 10 per cent waterglass with 90 per cent water is poured over the unwashed eggs and they are stored in the coolest place you have. The eggs will keep a few weeks in this solution. In times when we needed more eggs than were available on ration cards, or if our hens went on strike, this was one good way to preserve them for things like traditional Christmas baking. Mum could also make four sandwiches with one egg. She would beat the egg in a bowl and add three tablespoons of unsweetened condensed milk and a teaspoon of cornflour before frying it in a hot skillet with oil. American GIs supplied us with powdered egg right after the war and we traded Nazi trinkets for them. They were all looking for some sort of souvenir to take home with them.

Other regulations in addition to rationing that affected our community were introduced soon after the war began. I remember one day a leaflet was distributed throughout the town and a copy was put in the letter box of each household. In big letters the title read: '*Entfernung eiserner Einfriedungen*', which means: 'Removal of all Ornamental Iron Fences'. It went on to say,

'We need your ornamental fences for the war effort. The Reich must have a reserve of important metals; therefore a new law has been signed that calls for the removal and confiscation of all iron fences. Violators who do not comply or hide their fences will be prosecuted beginning 1 June 1940. All demolition and transport costs will be met by the NSDAP.' Well, we had no iron fences so that left us out, but our school fencing went into the smelter, and so did the school's iron bicycle shed. Iron manhole covers were replaced with concrete ones, and the huge automatic gates at the food-processing plant were replaced by a 65-year-old First World War veteran sprouting a Hindenburg moustache, a dark blue uniform, and a cap with an eagle on it. He was armed too – with a walking stick.

When milk was rationed, it was only little babies that were entitled to full cream milk and even they didn't get it very often. The rest of the people and older babies had to be satisfied with watered-down skimmed milk. The NSV realised in September 1939, when milk rationing was first introduced, that they would have to do something to make sure that newborn babies would receive proper nourishment. Of course, newborns can be breast-fed, but if the mother is undernourished, she won't produce enough milk, and by the middle of the war, with all the rationing, that was usually the case. A breast-milk collection point was established in Magdeburg in 1939 and it was managed by the *Reichsarbeitsgemeinschaft für Mutter und Kind* (Reich Work Organisation for Mothers and Children). The NSV became the appointed overseers of breast-milk collection points and by mid-1940; there were more than a hundred of these well-run facilities. Soon, of course, the Nazi Party *Bonzen* started meddling in the organisation and split this institution up into several segments, all under the supervision of the NSDAP. They quickly realised that there was more to it than milking a mother and storing the milk in a refrigerator. Each mother who had breast milk to give away had to be tested by a doctor who made sure that the donor was healthy and not of Jewish ancestry. The Party was responsible for keeping morale up at home and they somehow thought this would make a difference to mothers of starving babies. Most of the *Bonzen* were shirkers and never fired a shot in the line of duty. It was not that we disliked the NSDAP at the time or even what they stood for; what irked the people at home was that many of these able-bodied men and women were useless in the positions they occupied within the Party, while the Wehrmacht was bleeding to death on the battlefields of Kursk, El Alamein and Leningrad.

When the programme was first established, the women with milk lined up at the collection points like cows in a milking parlour and that was just not acceptable. Later, to give some respectability and dignity to the process, breast pumps were given to mothers so they could do the job themselves at home. The milk was then collected every other day by the NSV 'milk man'. This was also an extra source of income for mothers. They were paid three to four Reichsmarks per litre and then the milk was sold by the NSV to mothers who needed it for five Reichsmarks per litre. Mothers who could not afford the cost got it free through the National Health Service. The NSDAP even advertised the milk-collection programme in their Party publications. This sort of thing might seem abstract today, but these milk-collection services saved the lives of many newborn babies. We had a baby at home and a father on the Russian Front, so anything to do with the welfare of our family and other families like ours was of major importance to me, even though I was just a boy myself. All this was naturally of no concern to Brother Len and the older Hitler Youths. They had other duties to fulfil, as Goebbels reminded all of us in one of his many proclamations. 'The destiny of Germany's youth is to carry the final victory in their hands.' We all wanted to do that because, since our first day at school, we had been told that we were the building blocks of the future Reich.

Everyone who was not in the military had a job, but only coal miners or steel workers were entitled to *Schwerarbeiter Zulage* (extra rations). It was a serious crime to quit your job and try to find a better paying one. The National Socialist Labour Office kept close track of that sort of thing. Every worker had an *Arbeitsbuch* (work book) and the employer kept those books up to date along with the worker's insurance payments. Everyone had an identification card but the phrase, 'Papers please' was rarely heard. Your ID was mainly used for visits to municipal offices. The local police in our area knew most of the residents anyway. Even many POWs, especially Russians or Polish, were issued ID cards. They worked on farms, sometimes in groups, guarded by a wounded soldier or elderly *Landsturm* (reserve military) man, but often with no guard at all. The farmer who had hired them was responsible for the prisoners' welfare. As long as these prisoners did their job, the farmer was happy and some POWs on farms lived better toward the end of the war than German citizens in large cities. Sabotage in our area was unheard of, but the prisoners would attempt escape occasionally. After all, France and Holland with their large resistance movements were only a few miles away. Some made it and joined the Polish Resistance Brigade in France; most didn't make it. Getting recaptured was a sure ticket to a concentration camp or an SS firing squad. Some never went back to Russia or 'liberated Poland' after the war and settled in the western occupied zones of Germany, preferring to live in a foreign country to living under Stalin.

Poor city-dwellers with no gardens travelled by the thousands to the surrounding countryside, usually many miles out, to beg or trade for food.

Will Gehlen, aged eight, in full Jungvolk uniform. This photograph was taken as part of his official Reich identification papers. (*Wilhelm Gehlen*)

A 1930s map of the Rhineland where Will grew up. München-Gladbach was too small at the time to be included, but it is about ten miles southwest of Willich. Krefeld is about five miles north-east of Willich.

Will and other boys are allowed to inspect a quad 20mm flak gun that would soon be set up in their area. (*Wilhelm Gehlen*)

Will's troop with other Hitler Youth and Jungvolk in morale-building exercises in the Eifel. This looks like some version of a tug-of-war. That's Will in the centre about to take a fall. (*Wilhelm Gehlen*)

Group photo of Will's troop on an excursion to Bavaria. Will is near the back row, left of centre with only part of his head showing. Being short was a problem sometimes. (Wilhelm Gehlen)

Obergefreiter (Corporal) Lorenz Gehlen, Will's father, in uniform. This was taken soon after his enlistment as part of his military identification. (Property of the Gehlen family)

Dad (right) on patrol near Cholm, Russia, in April 1942. (*Wilhelm Gehlen*)

Dad (far left) listening in while plans are being made; somewhere near Vilikye Luki, Russia, in 1942. (*Wilhelm Gehlen*)

Brother Len and his group of Hitler Youth on the march during training exercises in the Harz area, 1943. Len is front and centre; in command as always. (*Wilhelm Gehlen*)

Len and five of his mates no doubt planning an attack on the invading Americans. Photo probably taken right after the end of the war. (*Wilhelm Gehlen*)

A permit and receipt for having paid the tax for owning a dog. Not many people had pets and if you did, you paid the Reich for the privilege; in this case six Reichsmarks. (*Wilhelm Gehlen*)

An official document granting a farmer permission to slaughter a pig. To do so without a permit could get you arrested, but farmers had ways of getting around such regulations if the need arose. (*Wilhelm Gehlen*)

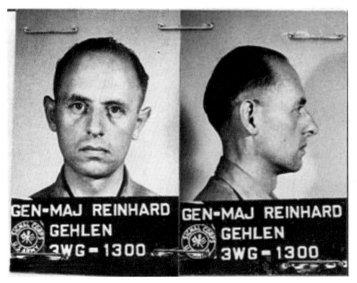

Ration card for children aged six to fourteen. Valid only for part of July and August 1944, it states that the coupons are only valid in occupied Luxembourg. Potatoes are listed, but looking closely, the coupons are for potato flour and only 25 grams; considerably less than an ounce. (*Wilhelm Gehlen*)

Major General Reinhard Gehlen, Will's uncle; often called 'Hitler's spymaster'. This is a photo of his identification card after he surrendered to the US Army Counterintelligence Corps in Bavaria. (*US Army Signal Corps*)

This was of course forbidden and in 1944, Himmler sent out a directive to all Gestapo and police officers to check any large bags being carried by people. If the person could not give a good explanation for how and where he obtained the cabbages or potatoes, the food was confiscated and he could find himself in court. You could get three months in prison for this or even be put in a concentration camp if someone in the Party wanted it. Himmler, in his memo, called it *hamstern* (hoarding, like a hamster) and that word stuck with the German people until June 1948 when the new Deutschemark currency was introduced and the economy began to recover.

* * *

In any country with a one-party system, propaganda is a must to keep the voters, and those who don't have an opinion, happy at all times. Germany was no exception to this rule. In a free and democratic society, you don't need a special Minister of Propaganda. Imagine one sitting in Washington today with a staff of several hundred and a billion-dollar budget. Americans would get the same thing we got from 1933 to 1945. Propaganda, in simple terms, is a method used to keep the population happy with the present government, whatever it is. German propaganda was specially geared to National Socialism and later the war. The words 'National Socialism' might sound nice today to some people's ears, even Germans – if it hadn't already been used by the Nazis.

Radio and newspapers were the essence of propaganda. The other source of news was the Wehrmacht reports, but not many people back home believed them and even fewer soldiers at the fronts. A radio was always in demand for the entertainment, the musical concerts and the evening news reports. Telefunken, Loewe Opta and others made radios before the war and they were dearly sought after, but they had not been mass produced. Hence, the *Volksempfänger* was invented, which was a small black-cased radio that was cheap, about seventy Reichsmarks at the time, and it soon got the nickname 'Goebbel's mouth'. It worked only on the Decimetre frequency and one could only receive German transmitting stations. The *verboten* transmissions of the enemy came over short wave and the older radios were able to receive these transmissions, but listening to a BBC transmission could bring you a world of trouble. After the defeat at Stalingrad, the mood of the population at home was so low that the government decided enough is enough. On 18 February 1943, as 100,000 German prisoners were being transported from Stalingrad to the far reaches of Russia, Goebbels, in front of a crowd of Party members in the Berlin Sports Palace, declared his 'Total War' programme. At first, not much was done to enforce this new policy and the Allies answered his declaration with an intensification of bombing raids on German cities. Only after the Normandy invasion was his plan better implemented.

What Goebbels lacked in physical stature, his mouth surely made up for it, with the masses following his speeches in the beginning as if he was the messiah. All slogans, in papers, on the radio, or even just painted on house walls, had to be approved by the propaganda office of the relevant local Party Headquarters and they all had propaganda offices. The slogan 'Wheels roll for Victory' on the wall of a railway station made sense, but that slogan painted along the wall of the local motorcycle track didn't. Late in the war nobody had a motorcycle anymore and this just reminded us of it, and almost nobody owned a car; roller skates were all we had left. I didn't see how they could roll for victory. The only wheels still rolling were train wheels and factory machine wheels.

Nazi propaganda wasn't only confined to Germany either. Goebbels' tentacles reached out to the occupied countries too and even to the front. Soldiers were inundated with leaflets, news reports of imaginary victories, and maybe excuses for the bad food over their radios that could only pick up Radio Belgrade. 'The Homefront goes hungry too' was a slogan often heard on the radio we had. Yes, we knew about going hungry, but until the very end of the war, we also knew our soldiers ate better with their rations than the coal miners in Dortmund. Many sent their butter or chocolate rations home; even packages of bacon, sausage, soap and *Papyrossi* (Russian cigarettes) were sent through the Reichspost. In the other direction went cigarette lighters, flints, gloves, scarves and the well-known honey cake, made of course with *ersatz* honey.

Then there was the propaganda beast named '*Kohlenklau*', a villainous-looking character who stole coal or used more of it than he needed. A lot of homes were heated with wood and food was cooked on a wood-burning stove, but I never heard of a '*Holzklau*'. Probably by the middle of the war there were so many bombed-out houses, there was plenty of wood around in the cities. This conservation propaganda was directed at children as well as adults. There were even board games and storybooks with this *Kohlenklau* character to indoctrinate the very young about the need to save energy. Sounds like something you would hear of today, doesn't it?

Of course, even the best propaganda can turn sour if fed day after day to a population that has no illusions about the outcome of the war, but no soldier wrote home to his wife that, in his opinion, the war was lost and that Hitler had made a mess of it all. Feldpost letters were censored frequently, so if he had something to say regarding the state of the war, it was mainly, 'We will win this war; let's wait for the V-weapons; let's believe in the Führer who has mastered other bad situations'. Even death notices in the newspapers eventually got censored to something like: 'Heroic death for the Fatherland and Führer'. There were no exceptions; death came to generals with the Knight's Cross the same as to the private. The bullet found the eighteen-year-old Hitler Youth as easily as a sixty-year-old *Volkssturm* grandfather.

When the assassination attempt on Hitler occurred on 20 July 1944, propaganda was quick to declare it had been the act of a few treasonous officers. That was half right, but there were more than a few officers involved. The Party promised to eradicate the treacherous vermin wherever they were found and put them in concentration camps. From that day on, the Party took over what they hadn't already gotten their hands on. That's when we began to hear propaganda that the Wehrmacht, and especially the generals, had failed the country, but that the Party would nevertheless lead Germany to victory. Of course, those few who listened to enemy radio stations knew better. We all knew, or we thought we did, why the war was in such a bad state. With old men, young kids, women, and even the sick and feeble the only ones left defending the Fatherland, what could be expected? We kids were even told by Party propaganda to denounce the eternal churchgoers, the lazy and the workshy. Party members who had never fired a shot in anger were promoted to Wehrmacht company commanders. Propaganda at the end of the war said that anyone not living up to the situation we were in would be arrested and dealt with accordingly. We knew very well what that meant. Most of those arrested were marched out into the fields at gunpoint to construct mile after mile of anti-tank ditches.

One good example of propaganda at the end of the war was a directive issued by Adolf Hitler to defend the old city of Trier on the Moselle River.

By Order of the Führer!

We will defend Trier with all our might. This order is to be perfectly clear; our resolve will be seen in the *Panzerfaust*. Now only our weapons will speak. Our eyes are directed toward the enemy day and night and our hearts are full of hate. We will block the gate to the Moselle. With the cry of revenge on our lips, we will fight the enemy; every street will have a barricade; every house will be a fortress. Trier will not surrender. Soldiers of the western front, you understand the Führer's orders the same as our comrades understood in Courland, East Prussia and in Silesia. Not one foreign soldier will enter the city even if we have to kill him with our bare fists; even if we have to strangle him. Trier will stay German.

The capture of the city by Patton was much less dramatic and went almost like a comedy. General Eisenhower in late February 1945 had told Patton to wait outside Trier until he could spare four divisions to take the city. Nevertheless, Patton went ahead with two divisions and took Trier without any heavy fighting. An old saying in Trier was, 'When the ravens leave the Porta Nigra [a Roman gatehouse in Trier], the city will fall to the enemy'. The ravens left that day and Trier fell.

Chapter 8

Food (and Everything Else) Was Where You Found It

W ell-meaning government officials of the Third Reich food ministry (there were a few) intended to cart all the food in Russia back home for the Germans while the conquest of that vast storehouse continued. This did not happen – simply because there was not much left when the Russians retreated from the Ukraine. Some greedy officials were much more interested in filling returning trains with loot anyway. You can't fry a painting or make a stew from a statue, so that sort of booty did us no good. Party officials were the last to suffer from a food shortage, if they ever did. When Dr. Robert Ley, the head of the *Deutsche Arbeitsfront* (DAF – German Labour Front), was captured by the 101st Airborne near Zell am See in Bavaria, he had a whole railway car of hams standing in a siding, not to mention all the other things he had accumulated to enjoy a life of luxury after the war. He was a loyal National Socialist to the end and never accepted the charge of 'War Criminal'. Maybe he wasn't much of a war criminal compared to others, but he was a criminal nonetheless. He committed suicide while awaiting trial in Nürnberg and I doubt if many Germans shed a tear.

What then did the people live on you might ask? An old German proverb goes something like: *'In der Not, frisst der Teufel Fliegen'* ('When the Devil is really hungry, he will eat flies'). Germans didn't eat flies, but when food was in critical short supply during the winter of 1944/45, and especially during the two winters after the war, substitutes were invented that would make a well-fed 21st-century person sick. There were many wild plants we were told were edible that we had never tried before, but we learned them well. One was known in Germany as *Huflattich*. Tussilago and Coltsfoot are other names for it. The rather large leaves were cut up and prepared like spinach. This herb was well known as a medicine too. It was dried then burned in a basin and the smoke inhaled for treating a cold or any breathing problems. It was also used for bandaging open cuts. We collected many bags of the leaves for the WHW. Because of the leaf's whitish soft underside, the leaves were sometimes called *'Wanderers Klopapier'* ('hiker's toilet paper'). There were also groundhogs

(*Murmeltier*) in our part of Germany and I'm not really sure if we ever ate one, but we probably did. What I do remember was that groundhog fat was used as a treatment for rheumatism and today in Germany it is an accepted scientific fact that it works. I use it now but I have to get it from Germany. I have not found a source for it in the United States even though we certainly have plenty of groundhogs.

In the spring of 1944 Brother Len attended a *Gemeinschafts Klassen*, which was a class for boys and girls and the topic was mushrooms. They grew by the millions in forests and fields and Len said they were told the things were an excellent source of protein and that they needed to be harvested. But the point was – one had to know which ones were edible and which ones were poisonous. Coloured posters were unrolled in the classroom and the fungi were marked with green for edible, red for poisonous, and brown if the instructor didn't know. There were a lot of them marked in brown. The next day Brother Len took off into the woods, a basket in hand, searching for mushrooms. About 6:00 p.m. he came back with a basket full of them. We stood in awe, gaping at his collection, but Mum had an eye for these things and went to work sorting them out. She learned all about mushrooms in the convent in Aachen where she lived when she was a girl. Len, it turns out, didn't know quite everything about mushrooms. Mum threw out almost all of them. They were toadstools and could have killed us all. After this lesson, we mostly left that source of cheap food alone, but we did collect dandelion leaves for salads. Although they tend to have a bitter taste, if one uses the fresh green ones and adds plenty of onions and a bit of mayonnaise, they make a very good salad. One can make a salad from almost anything whether it grows in the garden or not.

What Brother Len was good at, however, was slaughtering rabbits; Dad taught him before he was drafted into the Wehrmacht. Rabbits were bred for eating, not as pets. Len could slaughter seven of the crunchers in a day and dress them ready for the canning jars.

'I'll be a general one day,' Len announced at dinner after a day of slaughtering.

'Generals don't kill rabbits,' I answered.

'No, I mean at the front,' he tried to explain.

'Look Len, you might not have noticed but generals are seldom at the front line, and neither do they do the fighting and killing. They leave that to the soldiers in the trenches.'

'Okay, maybe when I am a general, I'll suggest that all generals fight on the front line alongside their men. General Paulus and the other generals who were taken prisoner at Stalingrad were on the front line.'

'Yes Len; in a bunker with six feet of earth and steel beams over their heads.'

Every year in the autumn, after the grain was taken in by the farmer, people would be allowed to walk over the stubble and pick up anything that was left. This was put in a pillowcase and when full, it was beaten with a stick – a sort of home-made threshing machine. Winnowing was done by the wind in the yard. The kernels were then collected and ground into flour using a hand-held coffee mill. We had three of them and no coffee beans to grind. In the evenings, we sat around the radio grinding away, with most of the chaff going into the resulting flour. It was a tedious job but it was better to have bad bread than no bread at all. When baked, the bread was hard as a rock when it cooled and had the texture of a sanding block. By the end of the war, our stomachs could digest about anything, but worse was to come.

It was a lot of work to make a three-pound loaf of bread twice a week. This was true wholegrain flour and I would not recommend it for sensitive stomachs, but we ate it regularly and never had to worry about getting enough fibre in our diet. Fresh yeast was usually available from the local baker, but we discovered that even with fresh yeast, some flour was totally unsuitable for baking bread. You can make bread from barley and late in the war, canned turnips and barley bread was about all the Wehrmacht had to live and fight on, but the stuff would never rise, no matter how much yeast was used. As long as it was warm, it was easy to cut and eat, even if digesting it was a challenge. After it got cold, it was hard as concrete and had to be chopped with a bayonet or an axe. Some people even used old barley loaves to patch holes in walls. Earlier, when times were better for the Wehrmacht, the bread was made from rye and it was called *Kommissbrot* and despite the name, it had nothing to do with Communists. It was very good bread and it would keep well without turning to stone.

From early times, the German Armed Forces were called *Der Kommiss* by the soldiers themselves because of how important this bread was. It was different from the well-known *Schwarzbrot* (black bread, not pumpernickel) made from rye and molasses, which is still made in Germany. *Kommissbrot* was sort of greyish-brown and soft in texture with a hard crust. It was baked in shallow pans and the finished loaves looked like eight-inch wide by two-inch thick bricks that could be a couple of feet long, usually stacked two together. It certainly was of better quality than the stuff civilians had to eat. We had a *Kommissbrot* bakery in our village and at times, the soldiers who operated the military part of the bakery would give us a loaf. The Wehrmacht had their own bakeries, usually far behind the front, and they often shared facilities with a privately-owned bakery. There were also mobile bakeries, but to supply a battalion or regiment of a thousand men with bread required enormous supplies to be brought along and that space was needed for arms and ammunition. By the time the US 102nd Infantry Division occupied our area, the Wehrmacht bakers had fled to the east, but they left a hoard of several thousand loaves and we made good use of them.

One of the favourite uses of *Kommissbrot* came from the Turnip Winter of 1917, during the Great War. The bread was hollowed out and stuffed with mashed turnips and the inner part of the bread was used to make bread soup. In the Second World War, we stuffed the inside of the bread with mashed potatoes, chives and onions. Then the bread was put into a baking pan in a hot oven for about twenty minutes. When done, it was stored in a cool place and later sliced and fried in whatever fat was handy. This can only be done with bread that has a hard crust and is soft inside, and rye bread was the most suitable. The inner part of the bread was used, just like in 1917, to make bread soup. We added a handful of raisins if we had them. Turnips were also used to make a vegetable stew and made into a sort of jam too. My mother made a simple turnip preserve to put on black bread. Three turnips were cut into small pieces and cooked until soft and then mashed. A half-pound of sugar and a spoonful of pectin were then stirred into it. I remember that it had to be eaten within a week or so. Sugar was rationed, but in the autumn every household was allotted four pounds for making fruit preserves. When Spam arrived after the war, it was diced and added to the mashed potatoes we baked inside the *Kommissbrot*. After the loaf cooled and was sliced, we dipped the slices in a beaten egg, and then in breadcrumbs and fried them in a pan. This was like manna from Heaven for us.

Graupen (barley) grows in abundance in Europe, but it was not often eaten before the war. It was mainly used with malt to brew beer. Beer was a washout during the war because barley flour was used to make bread or sold as whole grain to use in soups and stews. Beer was last on the list for barley use. Graupen soup was on the menu at least twice a week. Some genius in the food supply chain had the idea of changing the name of Graupen soup to 'Rum Fordsche Soup'. This was purely psychological; it was still barley and had nothing to do with rum at all. I have not seen whole barley grain offered in any shop since 1947. Maybe it can be found in health food shops; I don't know. Barley grain needed a very long cooking time and we noticed a lot of chaff in the soup it made, but nobody cared. If it was sold in shops, we thought it must be okay to eat, so we ate it.

*   *   *

The high-altitude bomber streams going toward the east didn't bother any of us. Then, in August 1944, everything changed. The Allies finally got the better of the stubborn German Army in northern France and broke out into the central plains. Advanced airfields were captured and that brought fighter-bombers within easy reach of our area in western Germany, only a stone's-throw from the border with Holland and Belgium. Then they could hunt anywhere between Paris and the Rhine River for something worthwhile to shoot up. Trains, trucks, farmers in their fields and even single persons out walking weren't spared. Worse than that were the twin-engined Havocs and A-20s that dropped fire cards over the ripening fields. The cards were about six inches square with a greenish-yellow spot in the centre that was covered in some kind of wax. The spot was phosphorous and when the wax melted in the sunshine, it burst into flames. Whole grain fields went up in smoke in 1944 and so did our hopes for something to eat in the coming year. Picking them up was dangerous too. After a few burned Hitler Youth fingers, the order came out saying we were not to take the cards to a collection point but deposit them by the side of the road where they could burn safely. There was also the added danger of getting hunted by the *Jabos* after the cards were dropped. The pilots knew that we would be out to collect the cards before they could ignite and made sure that our task would not be easy. Haystacks were not recommended as shelters because one tracer bullet could set the stack on fire. We played hide and seek with the *Jabos*, sometimes with dire consequences.

People have eaten horsemeat for centuries and in some countries they still kill horses and dogs for human consumption, but eating a horse, cat or dog that might have been lying dead out in the summer sun for several days is a different matter. From mid-1944, however, it was done by many bombed-out people because there was no other way to survive. You might say today you would rather die than eat your pet, but, those who did eat them back then survived, those who didn't, died. We didn't have many vegetarians during the war. You ate whatever was available whether it came from critters or cauliflowers. We all knew Hitler was a vegetarian but he could afford to be, with all the vegetables he could get that we couldn't. Hitler didn't raise rabbits and his greenhouse on the Obersalzberg was only for flowers, not vegetables. The NSV would tell you that you could eat almost anything, short of grass and cobblestones. Whether they tried some of their own recipes, I don't know, but I personally never saw a skinny NSV official. The NSV also acted at times like the Red Cross, giving out cigarettes, beer and meals to soldiers at railway stations.

When milk was available, barley was boiled in half milk and half water. If the soup was too watery, cornflour was added. POWs had to exist on a diet like this, but by mid-1944 we didn't live on much better, but unlike those poor souls in the Stalags, we at least had ration cards. Whether the items listed on the cards were available was another matter; most of the time they were not. Complaining got you nowhere; besides, public complaining was *verboten*. My dad did a short spell as a guard in a small POW camp that housed seventy-five Russian and

Polish inmates who worked on local farms in our area. The farmer employing these prisoners at harvest time was also responsible for feeding them. They worked in the fields supervised only by the unarmed farmer or his deputy. Any POW had the chance to escape, but not one tried. Rumour had it that Stalin had ordered any ex-POW to be shot if he managed to get back to the Russian lines. This was maybe the reason that no POW ever attempted an escape, or maybe it was because the nearest Russian front in mid-1944 was still 700 miles to the east of us. With US and British POWs this was another matter. Belgium and France were only a few miles to the west but the Germans, with foresight, put the Western Allied POWs in Stalags far to the east, in Pomerania, Silesia and Mecklenburg. Some of the camps were as far east as Danzig. Several POWs tried to escape and were caught, some made it to the borders, and the resistance groups were only too pleased to help these guys back to the Allied lines.

One former POW named Bob that I met years after the end of the war was taken prisoner at the Salerno landings in 1943. He and a group of forty-four others were put into a Stalag near the concentration camp at Stutthof (now in Poland). They had no contact with those held in the concentration camp and worked mostly on farms, digging potatoes, beets, and turnips. When the Russian front advanced westward, the prisoners were marched on foot to Pomerania and Schwerin by Wehrmacht soldiers who were in a hurry. Thirty-eight of them made the trip and lived to be liberated. Bob said that sauerkraut, potatoes and hard black bread were their staple foods. By 1945 we didn't live any better. Long after the war, I met a few people who had survived life in concentration camps. Those people knew what hunger really was, along with a constant fear of death – and not from bombs falling on their heads either.

Millions of ordinary people died of hunger during the Third Reich, but concentration-camp inmates were even worse off than we were. I doubt that even a sparrow could be found alive in those camps. The Wehrmacht also went hungry at times, especially in Russia, and they had to fight an enemy that was hell-bent on winning a war. The front-line soldiers learned to live and cook like Ivan. Soon they were making Russian *Borscht*, *Kapustra* and even fish soup. *Borscht* was something of a staple diet for both sides at the front. My father survived the first terrible winter in Russia on the northern front. That's where he learned to cook the stuff. During lulls in the fighting, they all searched gardens, which were under two feet of snow, for stalks of rotted frozen cabbage, shrivelled beets and whatever had been grown by the former owners. Once, they found a dead horse, frozen solid by temperatures that reached -40°C, and using axes and hand grenades, they managed to break lose a few pounds of frozen meat. All this was then boiled in an old rusty dye cauldron they found inside the fur-processing plant they had occupied. Salt used in the dying process was used to add a little flavour to the stew. The smoke from the cooking fire gave Ivan an aim point for 7.62cm short-range guns they called *Ratsch-Bums*, but who cared. They would rather have died with a full stomach than live hungry and become a prisoner anyway. Luckily, it never came to that; Cholm was finally relieved in the spring of 1942 and Dad's unit was relieved and shipped back to Germany for recuperation. Thanks to Ivan, *Borscht* became standard fare in Germany in the two winters after the war.

Unlike modern cooking that is expected to be finished in thirty minutes, stews and *Borscht* need several hours to cook. No one today has the time or the patience to wait hours for a meal. Fat from pork or beef is especially frowned-upon in today's kitchen, but we made *Schmalz* out of it. This was invented during the First World War by desperate German housewives and it still sold today in butchers' shops, but it is made with better ingredients. Many former Allied POWs who were held in German Stalags for long periods of time have asked me what *Schmalz* really was. It was served to them almost daily. It was simply raw animal fat from skin and bones, and it could be from any animal, including horses. The skin and bones were slowly boiled in water to remove every bit of fat until almost all the water was boiled away. This was then put through a meat grinder, bones and all. It was then boiled again with milk or water for about thirty minutes until most of the water or milk had evaporated. Salt, pepper and parsley (or whatever else was available) was then added. It was allowed to cool and spread over bread or used later for frying something else for a little flavour. It can be kept for a day or two without refrigeration and for much longer if kept cool. We sometimes made pancakes with it but mostly it was used for frying potatoes. Cooking oil was unheard of, so we used what we had.

One clear day in late winter 1944, two fighter-bombers came in low from the west and targeted a turnip bunker in a farmer's field not far from our house. Two 500lb bombs opened up that bunker and scattered turnips everywhere. For good measure, they also fired two rockets into a haystack and set it on fire. Melting snow soon put out the fire so no real harm was done. Not to be caught by the farmer stealing his turnips, we waited until dark and then Len and I set off, each with a small hemp sack. Apparently others had witnessed the brutal attack on the defenceless turnip bunker and had the same idea. We all filled our sacks and went home with the pilfered vegetables. We didn't bother telling Mum where our harvest had come from and she didn't ask. I took a few of the turnips up to the quads' cook the next day and everyone there thanked me for the change in rations. Even turnips are a welcomed improvement over sauerkraut soup. The following day however the men were not so appreciative.

'What's the matter with you guys, didn't you enjoy the present I brought to you yesterday'? I asked.

'Well, half the turnips were good and we made soup from them, but the other half had worms in them, so you can have them back for rabbit feed,' Gunny replied.

'Well, I'll be more careful the next time I steal turnips for you while being shot at. You're an ungrateful bunch and by the way, I don't remember hearing any firing from the quads while those planes were bombing the turnip bunker.'

'We never heard a thing,' Gunny shot back. 'There was no alert and no planes came our way.'

They were never short of excuses. Later we would all eat turnips, raw or cooked, worms or no worms.

Fish soup might not be to the taste of the ordinary 21st-century person but it was at least a change for us during and after the war. There were many lakes around us, and of course the Rhine wasn't far away. We fished in the lakes and rivers before the war, but for some reason this was forbidden after the war came. Of course that didn't keep us from poaching when we could. It was hard for the game wardens to watch for fishing lines tied to a tree and put out in streams or ponds. What we used for fish soup were the heads and the fish bones, usually the stuff that's thrown away these days. The fish flesh would have already been eaten with potatoes the day before. The fish heads and bones were put into boiling water with chopped onions and leeks and cooked for an hour. The fish pieces were then removed and fed to whatever would eat them; chickens will eat most anything. The soup was then brought back to the boil and two ounces of flour or cornflour dissolved in a cup of milk was added. We added some grated cheese, chives and parsley if it was available and let the soup come back to a boil. If we had to use salted fish, we didn't add salt but with fresh fish, it was a good idea. Our fish soup wasn't really good but it was a hundred times better than sauerkraut soup. I guess if we had made it from better parts of the fish, it would have tasted better.

We also made beer soup. Making soup from the beer that was available near the end of the war was a lot better than drinking it. During the war, beer was a weak watery concoction due to a lack of ingredients. The schnapps distilleries were doing good business however, because our soldiers in Russia especially couldn't get along without it. They said it warmed them up if no hot food was available and that at least it wouldn't freeze even at those temperatures. Pubs and public drinking establishments were well visited during the war; mostly by older First World War veterans. As beer was sold without ration coupons, some wise know-it-all published a recipe through the NSV on how to make a nourishing soup with it and my family received one of the leaflets. At times, the NSV gave out bulletins with new recipes and we tried some of the more sensible suggestions. We didn't have beer soup very often though, because it required an egg and late in the war, one egg was a week's ration for one person.

An interesting food invention from the First World War was called *Pannas*, similar to American Scrapple, and it's still made and sold today, but with better and healthier ingredients. My mother learned to make it when she was younger and she began making it again beginning in 1942. The ingredients soon became hard to get for individuals, so butchers started making and selling it. Friday and Saturday mornings were usually reserved for meat rations and Thursday became *Pannas* day. Butchers had huge cooking vats and in it went all the bones that couldn't be sold for making soup. Small cuts of fat, liver, sausage and leftover meat scraps of all kinds were added to the pot. No one ever asked what was in it. This was boiled for several hours to extract the last atom of flavour from the bones. They were then removed and coarse-ground rye, barley, flour or whatever was available, along with salt and pepper, was added. All this was boiled again for several hours until it was thick and then poured into bread loaf tins. It took twenty-four hours for the stuff to set, and then it was sold to customers without requiring ration cards. Each person got a half-kilogram slice. Everyone was registered with a particular butcher so you couldn't just go from one to the next and get a slice from each; we tried that. By 1944 many butchers had developed this recipe into an art and eventually buckwheat, mouldy flour and other leftovers from meat processing went into it. Although this stuff had been cooked at the butcher's shop, Mum had to fry it in order to make it halfway edible. One day, in the spring of 1944, on a *Pannas* Thursday, a bunch of Marauder planes and a half-dozen P-38s decided to drop a few bombs into the centre of town. One 250lb bomb hit the butcher's shop on Long Street and wrecked the front of the building. Amazingly, no one was hurt and the *Pannas* pot continued to bubble away, now with a generous dose of ceiling plaster added. This didn't stop the butcher from selling his batch to eager takers, but he did sell it a little cheaper than usual.

Getting a pound of pork or beef bones was a special bonus for us. If the butcher was a good friend, a few cigarettes or a pound of sugar could do wonders when it came to things like that. Soup bones were usually bones from beef, already stripped of the last milligram of meat by the butcher. These were sold by the kilogram as *Suppen Knochen* and were boiled by the housewife for an hour, and then a few herbs and noodles were added. When times were really bad, the bones were cooked the next day and even the day after that. By then the soup was just warm water with a few noodles and herbs. Today bones are for the dog but a properly-made soup using them is still one of my favourites. First, it is important to use the right amount of water for boiling the bones;

adding cold water while the soup is cooking is not recommended. The boiling time varies, but about two hours at medium heat per pound of bones is a good starting point. Cut-up leeks and fresh parsley can be added about thirty minutes before the soup is done. Fresh parsley has a tendency to turn from green to grey if cooked too long. If you use dried parsley, it has turned grey already during the drying process and will not turn green again. The taste is about the same, but a bit of green in the soup adds to the appearance, and we eat with our eyes as well as our mouths. If you prefer a somewhat darker soup, a cut-up roasted onion can be added. This will give the soup a light brown colour and a nice flavour. Add a whole stick of cut-up celery about halfway through the boiling and salt to taste. Liquid Maggie seasoning does wonders for any soup and you can add that anytime. Meat in Germany has always been sold as *Braten* (roasting) or *Suppe* (soup) meat. Soup meat might be pork or beef that has been shaved from bones or it might be kidneys or other less appealing cuts. Kidneys are always from calves but there might be pork in the package as well, but late in the war and just after, we didn't ask what it was.

*   *   *

Farmers had it better in the bad times, despite being controlled by the Reich Agriculture Commission, who had their men in every village to tell people what they could and could not grow. Farmers usually ignored the inspections because those doing the inspecting had no idea what they were doing and could usually be paid off with a slab of bacon or some fresh sausage. We were allowed to keep six chickens and twenty-six rabbits. Farmers kept geese, chickens, ducks and other meat-producing animals on their property in any quantity they could feed, providing the Party got their share occasionally. Farmers had the reputation of hoarding food during and after the war, but nobody dared search a farm for hidden items. After all, these were the people who supplied the nation with food. The 'don't piss off the cook' rule applied to farmers just like it did to military cooks. In the spring we all helped the farmers in the area plant and thin rows of sugar beets, and as pay we got a good meal. One spring Aunt Maria was preparing a goose and I watched her make goose sausage. I wrote down the recipe for my mum but she was not very interested because goose was out of the question for us.

The goose was already plucked and gutted but the long neck and head was still in place. She chopped the head off using a cleaver and with the skill of a guillotine operator she chopped off the long neck just above the torso. With an expertise that astonished the rest of us, she pulled out all the inner parts of the neck, leaving just the fat neck tube. She then sewed one end of tube together and filled this neck tube with ground goose liver and kidneys, fresh parsley, onions, salt and other spices. Then she sewed the other end together making a sausage shaped tube about eighteen inches long by three inches in diameter. This she put into a large cauldron of boiling water for about thirty minutes. While this was boiling away, a huge round loaf of rye bread the size of a small cartwheel was fetched by the maid – yes, maid. Farmers really did have it better than the rest of us. Aunt Maria got a bread knife the size of a Brazilian machete, made a cross under the loaf, like all good Catholics did in those days, and began slicing off inch-thick pieces. I was afraid she would cut her arm off but she was an expert. A few divisions of women like Aunt Maria would have made a big difference at Stalingrad. A crock of real butter was produced and slices of bread were covered with the stuff. When the goose neck sausage was done, we gathered around the spotlessly scrubbed table and said our prayers. Each of us who had worked in the beet field was given a generous piece of that sausage, and believe me, it was good. Aunt Maria's goose neck sausage recipe would be perfect at modern-day Christmas.

We had our own fruit trees and bushes that grew everything except peaches, which didn't do well in that cool climate. However, one distant neighbour did have a peach tree that usually bore fruit in September, but they never ripened enough to eat. One night in mid-September 1944, Brother Len had the great idea that we should raid that garden and liberate some of the unripe fruit. The garden was about a half-mile outside our village. We took a sack with us and made sure nobody was watching from their blacked out windows. Far out to the west, the horizon was full of flickering lights. The battle of Nijmegen (Operation Market-Garden) was raging there. RAF bombers high up in the sky were heading eastward on their nightly bombing run and a few searchlights were trying their best to get one of the Lancasters into their beams. We climbed the peach tree and searched in the darkness for the peaches. Suddenly the entire sky lit up. A bomber had been hit by the 88s. In the light, we could see the owner of the garden coming toward us with a rake in his hand. It was time for a quick departure, but that Lancaster saved us from a certain thrashing. The burning plane jettisoned its bombs and they came whistling down; one exploded in a clover field 200 yards away and the rest hit the ground farther to the north. The plane crashed about four miles west of us. The owner of the garden ran for his air-raid shelter and we made our getaway with twenty-five hard green unripe peaches. If Mum was pleased to have us back with the fruit, I can't remember, but I do recall the stomach pains we got from eating our stolen peaches.

Rationing bred black-market trading and those people who had stocked up on items before the war could trade what they saved for anything they needed. This was highly illegal and a Gestapo memo I found recently from 1942 forbade these transactions and threatened fines, prison or concentration camp for those caught. Many were caught by the police and the Gestapo, but the black market was never totally wiped out. A clever way to avoid getting caught was to place an ad in a newspaper advertising something like an accordion for sale. Then, when the two parties would meet, the accordion would be traded for a pound of coffee or whatever the person had. It was not *verboten* to sell an accordion of course, but it was illegal to trade it for something that had to be bought on ration coupons. Even broomsticks could only be obtained with a permit, and if you think you could just go out into the woods and cut your own, you would be risking your life. Brögger Flönz was surely somewhere around, and with his binoculars, he could be watching your every move.

Poaching was too dangerous and cutting down a tree, even if it was small enough to be a broomstick, could land you in a concentration camp. We poached anyway, but we never got caught, although once or twice we got away only by a cat's whisker. We bred rabbits but at times we put up snares in well-known hare runs, especially in turnip fields. Hares can grow to four times the weight of a rabbit and would feed a family for a week. Göring appointed *Reich Jägermeisters* (hunting managers), who were sort of supervisory game wardens for specific areas, and they in turn appointed *Forstmeisters* (forest manager) who walked all day (sometimes at night too) around their designated area, which was usually ten square kilometres, carrying a shotgun with permission to shoot at any poacher who did not stop when challenged. Before the war Göring, as Reichsminister for Forest and Wildlife (among his many other titles) had hunted in the Reichswald after the Rhineland occupation in 1936. Hunting was strictly reserved for special permit-holders and still is. Even a fishing license was not easy to come by during the war. Göring's laws against poaching, introduced in 1934–35 were severe. Sachsenhausen and Flossenbürg were full of violators. Concentration camp names like these were unknown to us then. We were told the *Konzentrationslagern* were places for re-education. There were none anywhere near us, not even within a hundred miles, as we discovered after the war.

Pheasants were a specialty for us to catch, and Brother Len invented an ingenious trap. I think some other poacher must have told him how to do it. We would drop a handful of corn in a specific area where these wild birds gathered. It would be called 'seeding the field' today. Once the birds grew accustomed to the free meal, they would show up every morning on schedule. The trap wasn't really a trap at all. We cut a foot square piece of brown packing paper and folded it diagonal and glued the diagonal sides together. That way we had a triangular paper bag. Then we opened the bag and put a small pebble inside so the wind wouldn't blow it away. We then smeared a bit of sticky kraut molasses around the inside of the bag and put a few bits of corn in front of the bag and more inside. Most of the corn was put right at the small tip of the bag. The bird came and picked up the first few kernels of corn in front, then proceeded to pick up the corn inside the bag. Once the head or neck feathers came in contact with the sticky molasses, the bag stuck to the bird's head. It would run in circles until we chased it down. They wouldn't fly away if they couldn't see where they were going.

Nobody had a shotgun as far as I know, except old Brögger Flönz. He treated anyone out in the fields with suspicion except the farmers. One day, early in the war, a big bomb dropped about a mile outside town in a field. No one was hurt and soon the huge crater filled up with ground water, so we went swimming in it – stark naked of course. Flönz caught us swimming once and came walking up, gun over his shoulder and asked us what we were doing. Brother Len, who always had answer for everything, said 'Fishing'.

'No fishing allowed here,' he yelled, 'you ought to know that. I'm going to report you to the school headmaster. Now get out and get dressed.'

It had not occurred to Flönz that the 'fish pond' was a bomb crater. People in positions like that were the real dummies of the system and of no use for anything. There were plenty of them around, right up to the end of hostilities.

I remember one Friday in the spring of 1944, I was told by Mum to go by tram to Krefeld and get some horsemeat. Rumours of unrationed food spread like wildfire and on that day I was armed with a shopping bag and eight Reichsmarks to get me to the city, buy the horsemeat (*Trab Trab* as we called it), and get home. Sounds simple, but nothing was simple in a country full of desperate people. The driver and conductor of the tram were not known to me, otherwise I could have gotten a free fifty-Pfennigs ride. I left home at 5:00 a.m. to be in the queue by 6:00 a.m. A lot of other people apparently had the same idea because the tram was full all the way to Krefeld. Since it was early morning, there was no danger from attacking fighter-bombers, and the RAF night shift was finished hours earlier. The end of the line was near the Krefeld water tower since the tracks had not been repaired from the last bombing and we had to walk the rest of the way.

There was already a line about a hundred feet long after our mile walk, but we all expected to get a share from the butcher. Some people said that six horses had been slaughtered the day before and a little arithmetic made me think that I had a good chance of getting some of the meat even if I was the hundredth person in line. It was still two hours before the shop would open and daylight was coming fast and with it, the chance of a fighter-bomber visit. By 7:30 a.m., there were several hundred hungry people in line. I feared the opening of the shop more than the fighter-bombers. I knew there would be a stampede to get into the place first. Hungry men and furious housewives can be more fearsome than a bullet-spitting Thunderbolt. Someone up there in Heaven must have been reading my thoughts; a flight of P-38s came to my rescue. Under normal circumstances a dreaded bunch of killers like this would have scattered everyone, but these were not normal circumstances, even for wartime. No alert had been sounded. Maybe no one had expected an early morning visit but nevertheless, here they came, stitching up the tarmac and cobblestone streets with their machine guns. The milling crowd forgot the horsemeat and scattered into alleyways and front yard ditches. I jumped to the front door of the shop, seeking shelter in the doorway. The P-38s came back around a few times but no one was hurt, even when a drop tank was released. It fell into a garden nearby. Before the people in the crowd recovered their wits, the shop door opened and I was the first one in. Then the stampede started but I got the meat, neatly wrapped in the daily Nazi newspaper, and left the place in a hurry.

When I got back to the tram station, I discovered that I had spent all the money on meat and the tram ride to Krefeld and had none left for the fare home. With no other transportation available, it looked like an eleven-mile walk home for me. I made three miles the first hour and got as far as the huge DEW Steel Works, a very dangerous place to hang around in a war. But rescue was at hand in the form of the tram. It had stopped at the DEW station and before it could get away, I jumped on the back bumper of the last car. Nobody on the tram, including the driver, could see me. People along the road could see me, but only after the tram had passed by. I hung on to the tram with one hand and the horsemeat with the other and made it home with my treasure.

*   *   *

Spring weeds were a welcome change of diet for us. We didn't call them weeds (*Unkraut*) of course; they were still vegetables (*Gemüse*) to us. One has to know which weeds are okay to eat and when someone discovered that a particular plant was edible, the news spread like wildfire from home to home. I wondered how that first person figured out that something like stinging nettles was edible. That person must have really been starving. The roots can reach a foot or longer and can be cooked like any vegetable and eaten. I don't think I've ever seen it for sale except as an herbal treatment for an enlarged prostate, but if you want to dig your own, this is how you can prepare it: Cut off all the green parts and the very bottom tip of the roots and discard. Wash the roots in warm water and make sure all dirt is removed. They can then be cooked whole like carrots or grated and put into soups. They can be cut into pieces after cooking and mixed with green lettuce, olive oil, sweet vinegar and a teaspoon of sugar to make a tasty cold salad. Some people add a finely-chopped onion to the salad but I never have been very fond of eating onions with sugar.

A few other weeds that we regularly ate were:

Yarrow (*Achillea*): The name was derived from the Greek hero Achilles who was supposed to have healed wounds he received in battle with this plant. This grows in almost any garden and the plants can be found in any garden centre. Normally it has white flower heads but variants are known in yellow and pink. We used the flowers for making tea, alone or with other wild plants. The plant itself is quite bitter.

Ground Ivy (*Glechoma*): This was used like yarrow but we ate the cooked leaves as well.

Masterwort (*Angelica*): This was picked when the plant was just putting on new leaves. The leaves were eaten as in a salad or cooked as a vegetable. Older plants are said to have medicinal uses as well. Flowers and seeds cannot be eaten.

Dandelion (*Taraxacum*): This is a good plant to eat cooked, like spinach or just raw, like lettuce. The flower stems are too bitter to eat but are not poisonous.

A winter food source for us that is mostly ignored today is Viper Grass, also known as Black Root or Scorzonera. We used this weed in salads by washing the roots first and then thinly slicing or grating them. Mixed with celery, pepper and salt, the combination is quite good. They can also be cooked but they will turn brown and not look like anything to eat. We found that if the roots are boiled first, then peeled, they are much better. We also mashed them and then fried them as a sort of pancake. Ginger roots were also used in salads but they were prized as the main ingredient in a home-brewed Schnapps called *Ratzeputz* which loosely translates to 'rat cleaner', 'rat plaster' or 'rat poison'. That was a good name. It burnt like rat poison. A spoonful of ground red pepper was often added to each bottle to make it even more potent. Our soldiers in Russia loved it during the cold winter of 1941/42. On the fronts a saying was created that went something like: 'My last word shall be "*Ratzeputz*"; after drinking it, I won't mind being kaput.'

After the terribly cold winter of 1941/42 was over, our schoolteachers told us that to keep our soldiers from freezing in the next winter, a clothes drive by the WHW was being started. I found this rather disturbing; we had been told in 1941 that the war was almost won, so now it was 1942 and we were looking forward to the next winter already? My brother Len naturally knew more about this and he convinced me to listen. He knew a lot more about lots of things, or so he thought. His view was that since our Wehrmacht had to occupy a large slice of Russia even after we finished beating the 'Ivans' (the Russians), the soldiers would need warm clothes for the winter occupation. My remark that I had not seen a naked Russian in pictures from the Eastern Front, and that they surely had cloth mills and tailors enough in Russia to dress their 128 million inhabitants fell on deaf ears. In any case, I was surely not going to give the WHW any of my warm winter sweaters – so Len had a better idea. It was early spring and the farmers in our area were already busy sowing wheat, rye, barley, and oats. To protect the fields from hungry birds, the farmers put up scarecrows everywhere, complete with hats on top. We sneaked out into the fields about midnight one night, and high up we heard a lone British snooper plane we nicknamed 'Iron Gustav' on his normal rounds, taking night photos of our area for future bombing raids. We knew he had no bombs, so we proceeded with Len's plan. We undressed a few of the scarecrows and stuffed the clothes in a hemp sack. Our teacher was delighted the next day and we were given time off from homework. We did that a few nights, but then a farmhand started patrolling the fields and that put a stop to our pilfering. Later in 1943, when fighter-bomber attacks increased, the scarecrows disappeared altogether. The pilots would fire at anything anywhere that looked remotely like a human being, even scarecrows.

To stop birds from invading the fields, we were told to take sparrow and starling nests out wherever we found them. They usually built under the eaves of houses. The reward was five Pfennigs (about two cents) for every dead baby bird we collected. That might sound terrible today, but in order to survive; we had to protect our food resources. A proclamation by the authorities said that each sparrow could consume two ounces of grain per day, and with millions of the creatures around, this amounted to several tons of wasted food that could be used to feed people. In 1946, we received no reward for killing sparrows; instead we plucked them like chickens and ate them ourselves. You soon come to realise that eating sparrows can keep you alive, that is, if you can kill enough of them, and without a gun of any kind, that's not an easy thing to do.

*   *   *

It was a dangerous life for schoolchildren late in the war. There were no school buses; you walked to school even if it was three or four miles. You kept a constant eye on the sky and listened for the sound of engines. One plane 20,000 feet up doesn't make much noise, but 500 bombers with four engines each can be heard for miles. Air-raid shelters in schools were not reinforced, and after D-day, when fighter-bombers swarmed over our area on any clear day, all schools were closed. The Party *Bonzen* had nothing better to say other than, after Germany's final victory, lessons would be resumed, new schools would be built, and life would be much better. This was declared in an official Party proclamation sent to each school child's family.

'The only thing missing is an Iron Cross for us,' I said to Brother Len after reading this worthless proclamation.

'Medals are for soldiers at the front,' he replied.

'Is that so? We are at the front too; remember Goebbels telling us that we here on the home front are also doing our bit for victory'?

'Yes,' Len answered, 'but the front is artillery, trenches, machine guns, and an enemy opposite you.'

'We've got that here Len. We have trenches all around us. We don't have any artillery yet, but 1,000-pound bombs surely do as much damage as 105mm shells and we get machine gun fire aplenty from the *Jabos*. Our front is not in front of us, it's above us. By the way, the 88 crew needs a new loader, so why don't you have a word with the captain and volunteer for the job, and while you're at it, tell him that we're not on the front and see what he has to say about it.'

'I'm not a flak man; I can't be stuck in a fixed position.'

'Neither am I, big brother, but I do my share at the quads, and I would gladly help out at the 88s if the shells weren't too heavy for me to lift.'

Our argument was eventually interrupted by sirens sounding an imminent air raid, but no planes showed up in our area. The quads stayed silent and the 88s didn't bother with fighter-bombers anyway. We didn't see any planes of any sort this time. Maybe it was a false alarm. By this time, there were no drills and we took every alarm to be the real thing. One day soon after that, the *Jabos* attacked an outlying farms and later Len was in the vicinity with a group of Hitler Youths building a plank bridge across an anti-tank ditch so the farmer could get his harvest into his barn. Several cows, grazing peacefully in the farmer's field, had been the victims of an eager P-47 pilot and the normal procedure was to inform the local veterinarian who then decided what to do with dead and injured animals. The vet came after an hour, and brought along a police constable who had the authority to shoot and kill any injured livestock. After their inspection, a truck was then ordered to the field to take the dead animals to the *Abdeckerei*, or 'Knackers Yard'. We had a better name for that establishment – the 'Soap Factory'. The truck did not come until after dark. Trucks in open fields were easy targets for fighter-bombers. One calf had a severed head and somehow, before the truck came, Len managed to bring the bloody head home. I for one was not very pleased to see this thing on our table but Mum was in high spirits and out came her box of recipes. I couldn't imagine the anatomy and cooking lesson we were all about to get.

It takes strong hands, an open mind and, above all, an empty stomach to extract the brain from a cow's head. The brain was placed in a basin with cold water to soak the blood out, and then the veins were removed with a sharp knife. After that job was done, it was put into a saucepan and covered in water. A teaspoon of salt and two tablespoons of vinegar were added along with several herbs and spices. It was boiled for twenty minutes on a low heat and served at dinner with tomato salad and butter. The leftovers were fried the next day and eaten with bread – sort of a calf-brain sandwich. No one ever mentioned anything about finding a calf in the field with no head. There was not much that was thrown away in those days. Lungs were cooked in the same way as brains and used in a ragout; hearts and even udders were also turned into palatable dishes.

*   *   *

May in Germany is the month when Yellow Broom (Scotch Broom) is in full flower and it was used for making many medicines. Ten- to fourteen-year-old kids picked them and dandelion flowers by the sackfull. Mum had learned from her mother and grandmother about cures for almost anything. Tea was made from potato peelings that treated the most persistent stomach or kidney problems. Bandages were washed and used over and over again, but later in the war, they were half paper and just dissolved if you tried to wash them. My brother Len got a bad infection from stepping on a rusty nail and the doctor gave us a bag of salt of some sort to treat it. He soaked the foot for a couple of hours in the hot salty water and the swelling went down. He was up and around in a couple of days but not quite healthy enough to help with the chores of course.

Most of the home remedies we had are not found in America or I have not seen them. Common names for plants are different here, but I can recognise some of the ones we used. For a common cold, we would get a pair of long socks and soak them in a half-and-half solution of apple vinegar and water; then put the wet socks on, wrap warm towels over the socks, and just lie down for a couple of hours – it worked wonders. We had long socks up to just below our knees back then. Another cold remedy that worked required ingredients we couldn't get easily later in the war: boil a mixture of water, milk and wine (3:3:1 ratio) add lemon juice and sugar and drink hot. A third cure was made of hot white schnapps (gin will do) mixed with a dash of pepper and black root or ginger powder.

One of the great remedies for coughs, colds and headaches was made from unpeeled boiled potatoes. Mash them up, wrap a few spoonfuls in a cloth and put it on your forehead or, for coughs, on your chest. I guarantee this recipe.

Potato peelings were also dried in the oven and used as a remedy for head and shoulder joint ache. The hot peelings were put in a pillow case and slept on. For diarrhoea we boiled oak bark, then mixed the water from it with an equal part of wine and boiled the combination again for a few minutes and drank it hot. General stomach pains were relieved by chewing a lemon peel – if we had one. Indigestion was common with the things we had to eat but there was a cure for that and it came straight from the office of Dr. Leonardo Conti, the *Reichsgesundheitsführer* (Health Minister). It was two tablespoons of apple vinegar, one teaspoon of sugar, and a teaspoon of 'Kaiser Natron', which was a brand of baking soda. This was mixed with enough water to dissolve everything and drunk. We discovered that another great remedy for things like swollen joints and muscle pain is cottage cheese: smear cottage cheese over the affected area and wrap with a cloth. Leave it on several hours. For an earache we used onions cut up in strips and stuck in the ear.

Chapter 9

Invasion, Pirates and the Shrinking Reich

On 7 June 1944, an important announcement came over the radio and the next day the news was carried in all the newspaper: '*Die Invasion hat begonnen*' (The Invasion has begun). Almost 200,000 Allied soldiers had landed on the beaches of Normandy the day before. Many more would come ashore in the months to come. By July, the Allied troops had captured the first German fighter bases in France and this brought us within easy range of the fighter-bombers. They descended like locusts and we soon learned how to recognise each one. Things got busy at the quads; the schools soon closed and did not re-open until after the war. We were busier than ever trying to keep the invading planes away from our towns and factories. Their targets were also our food supply.

Hitler, in desperation, called on the youth of Germany to help resist the Allied invasion and they volunteered in droves. Many still had innocent kindergarten faces, but each wanted to do his part. They dug ditches, cleared rubble, helped at anti-aircraft batteries or learned how to operate *Panzerfausts*. Others volunteered for sniper training and the American 84th Infantry had to deal with them in Aachen. Some were as young as ten years old. Himmler in an October 1944 speech said that, 'Our children will fight like Werewolves and defeat the Allies'. One involvement of ten- and twelve-year-old boys and girls that I know something about was in November 1944 during Operation Clipper (the British attack on Geilenkirchen). Near Leiffahrt, about six miles north-east of Geilenkirchen, the Germans were trying to slow the Allied advance. A US M3 halftrack with ten soldiers on the back had hit a road mine just outside Würm on the Leiffahrt road and two GIs were injured. The other soldiers and the driver scattered and took cover in a partially-destroyed barn. They watched four kids who were pulling a two-wheel cart loaded with anti-personnel mines. They were placing them on a footpath along the railway track. That they were kids was obvious. The boys wore short pants despite the late November cold, and the girls, with pigtails and skirts, were helping pull the cart. The GIs didn't see any firearms on them so they decided to rush the group and after all four had been captured, they asked the children their ages. '*Zehn, Zehn, Zwölf, Dreizehn*' (ten, ten, twelve, and thirteen), was the answer. I don't know what those ten GIs did with the kids. That detail was not recorded in the company record that I had a look at after the war. One of the girls, I actually knew. Her name was Liesel Keuper and I think she was killed after the war, in late 1945, when she stepped on a mine in a Geilenkirchen suburb. Another German boy died in the same explosion. He was buried by the blast and a wooden cross was stuck in the ground on the spot. A sign was quickly put up that read 'Achtung Minen'. During the clean-up of that minefield, his body was exhumed and buried. The devastation of Operation Clipper was complete and the scars on the countryside are still visible today.

Some people might think that all the children of Germany were so indoctrinated by the Nazi political system that they readily looked forward to the day they would be old enough to be sworn into the Hitler Youth and march through the towns with banners waving. I can tell you that this was not the case. Long before the outbreak of the war, there existed a youth movement that opposed the strict discipline of the Hitler Youth. They wanted freedom of choice, to go where they wanted, and to spend their free time the way they chose. They were of course a minority, but nevertheless they became a nuisance to the Nazis. They called themselves 'Edelweiss Pirates' and 'Navajos'. One group of Navajos operated in our area. They had their own flags, sang their own songs and despised the traditional Hitler Youth uniforms. The Edelweiss Pirates wore an edelweiss flower pin on their shirts or caps. On many occasions these groups attacked small Hitler Youth detachments, usually late at night. They carried no weapons, except perhaps a knife of some sort. They painted anti-Nazi slogans on walls, pulled down Nazi flags and were called vandals by local Party members. To say they were well organised and politically motivated by some nationwide anti-Nazi conspiracy would be an exaggeration, but they were a thorn in the side of the establishment. In Germany at the time, a child could leave school at the age of fourteen and work in a factory or become an apprentice for a trade, become a member of the Hitler Youth, and at age seventeen, be called into the RAD. Most were satisfied with this life because they knew nothing better; not much else to do anyway.

Some of the Edelweiss Pirates and Navajos were sons of Communists or Social Democrats, whose fathers had been locked up in concentration camps long ago or murdered by the Gestapo. Some were sons of criminals, and only a very few of them were truly politically motivated. They did not align themselves with any Allied-supported resistance groups. By 1944 the Edelweiss Pirates became such a nuisance that the Gestapo headquarters (in Düsseldorf) for our district and the *Sicherheitsdienst* (SD – the SS Security Police) office in Cologne decided to do away with them once and for all. Cologne in 1944 was a huge pile of rubble and the Navajos had successfully evaded the Gestapo by living in the cellars of bombed-out buildings. Some enemies of the Nazis such as criminals, escaped prisoners and even a few POWs and Jews were harboured by them. They were all awaiting the end of the war, which was on the horizon by mid-1944. Somehow, the Gestapo infiltrated this group and in the autumn of 1944, they raided a cell in a Cologne suburb. The 'enemies of the Reich' they were harbouring went back to the concentration camps and the young boys were imprisoned and tortured. In November 1944, a group of about a dozen was publicly hanged in Cologne.

Brother Len told me about the Edelweiss Pirates and said that they had to be caught. The activities of the Pirates were well known in the Rhineland long before 1944. A few investigators have suggested that the Edelweiss Pirates were somehow connected to the assassination attempt on Hitler of 20 July 1944. That is absolute nonsense; nor can it be said that this group took their ideas from the '*Rote Kapelle*' (Red Orchestra). This was a group of university students, mainly from southern Germany, and almost all had been arrested by 1944. The July 20th conspirators would never have trusted a misguided group of teenagers with their plans. After the occupation of the Rhineland in March 1945, the Pirates by no means folded; they denounced former Nazis to the Allies, who were only too eager to get their hands on anyone who had proudly worn the brown uniform. Then the Pirates started to attack German men and women who associated with the occupation powers. That attracted the attention of Allied military personnel assigned to keep the peace in the area. At least one Pirate, named Heinz Deventer, was sentenced to death by a British military tribunal in 1946 in Uelzen (Lower Saxony). I don't know if he was executed or what specific crime he was charged with.

*   *   *

Unlike the Nazis, who had strictly enforced a law that forbade us listening to enemy radio broadcasts, nobody cared what we listened to after our area was occupied by the Allies. Some writers, long after the end of the war, maintained that Allied forces confiscated all radios from German families. That simply is not true. No one confiscated ours and I don't know anyone in our town who claimed theirs was taken away. I remember well a squad of Dutch volunteers listening to a Berlin speech by Goebbels on our radio. This was on 5 or 6 March 1945, after our town was occupied. They had been fighting alongside the US 104th Division and were using our house for temporary quarters. Our electricity was working again after five days in the dark. The town had its own power plant and it had escaped the bombings that began in February. The Dutch soldiers understood German perfectly and had a heck of a good time poking fun at what our Propaganda Minister was saying. The speech by

Goebbels made it clear that he still believed in final victory and that we should as well. He said that if the war was lost, Germany would be better off living under the hammer and sickle than the British and Americans. He had detested the British for years, particularly Churchill, whom he described as the arch enemy, a gangster and the destroyer of Europe. By this time however, a separate agreement with Stalin was out of the question, but Goebbels had high hopes that the West would eventually fall out with the Communists over who would exercise control over Poland. Since the Yalta Conference in February, Stalin had broken every agreement he had signed with Roosevelt and Churchill. Goebbels wasn't so very wrong in his predictions. The 'Iron Curtain', a phrase he himself invented, came down across Germany soon after the end of the war.

The secret Werewolf organisation had been founded by Himmler in September 1944, but Goebbels mentioned it openly in his speech and called for Germany's youth to join it. They were a group of fanatical Hitler Youth volunteers who still believed that the war was far from lost for Germany even in 1945. Some were brave enough to get within forty yards of a Sherman tank with a *Panzerfaust*. Shooting one at this range was just about suicide. The Wehrwolves were assigned to operate behind American and British lines on the left bank of the Rhine River. The intent was to sabotage Allied installations, assassinate those who were responsible for surrendering cities without a fight, and generally create havoc in the occupied areas. No mention was made by Goebbels of the Eastern front. The Werewolves were supposed to strike fear in the Allies, but not much came of the organisation. The mayor of Aachen was assassinated and a seventeen-year-old girl who was supposedly a member of the Werewolves was said to be involved in the operation. A few attempts were made to destroy bridges, and a small convoy of Canadian trucks was attacked in the Reichswald, but that was all.

All this was far removed from our limited universe. Before we were occupied, our local Hitler Youth detachment was far too busy digging defence ditches or helping bring in the crops to be involved with such last-ditch attacks. Everyone knew 'no farms, no food'. By late 1944, Brother Len had also started working on the local farms, sometimes being gone for days, and with Dad far away and Granddad Willem dead, the task of supplementing our meagre rations at home fell to me. Even a twelve-year-old can become an expert gardener when starving is the only other choice. Watching the vegetables and rabbits grow made me proud of the work I was doing for our family. A fully grown cauliflower is a beautiful sight if you're hungry. Being hungry also improves your sense of smell I discovered. We could smell fresh-baked bread from a mile away and on *Pannas* day, the smell of meat fat cooking travelled even farther.

Because of the downturn of the war and the advancing Allies in the summer of 1944, there were no more Hitler Youth parades in town. It was ditch-digging time and the boys (and at times girls) had to bring their own food for the day. Len, who was their number-one digger, missed the pea soup they had been fed after their parades most of all. He had to live on black bread and turnip sandwiches from home. I was lucky, the quads' cook had to feed the crew, alert or no alert, and if they were having something good, I made sure I got my share. Food is not the only essential thing to keep one alive, however. You can freeze to death much quicker than you can starve to death. The government's WHW organisation was always begging for warm clothes for the front-line troops, but civilians feel the cold too and it was common for the temperature to fall to well below freezing. We made mittens from rabbit skins, untanned of course, so that after a few days on our hands, they stunk to high heaven. Old wool coats with holes in them were made into hats and chicken feathers were washed and dried and stuffed into pillow cases. Wool socks were darned and I darned more than my share of them. Even spinning wheels were dug out of attics and barns and once again put to use turning sheep wool into knitting yarn – when we could get the wool.

*   *   *

One night in May 1944, a raid was in progress on the cities of Moers and Rheinhausen (near Duisburg); with the Thyssen steel works the target. From the top of the hill where the quads were, we could see the chimney stacks of the Rheinhausen Steel and Copper mill. In clear weather, we could see the coal slag heaps of Essen Krupp. The eight huge chimneys of the DEW in Krefeld were only ten miles away. It was a commanding high point where the quads stood. To the north, only six miles away, the huge copper dome of the M-G water tower could be seen. Over the years, the copper had turned green by oxidation and was clearly visible from the air, standing smack in the middle of the city. Krefeld had one too and both were easy reference points for attackers. We were close enough to the attack to be a possible target as well so our air-raid sirens were screaming.

The streets were empty except for Mr Vink who was doing his rounds. Brother Len and I took the opportunity to sneak across a few fields to a nearby Wehrmacht bakery. The bakers were not to be seen. They were probably hiding in the deep cellars outside in the yard. Under a canvas canopy stood rows and rows of freshly-baked loaves cooling down. There were round ones, short ones and long ones, but in the dark, we just grabbed the longest ones, not knowing what kind it was. Running back home across the railway tracks, my still warm loaf broke in half. I picked up the two pieces and got home without encountering a soul. Len suggested another raid on the bread wonderland right then and I would have agreed with him, but alas, the RAF finished their destruction of Thyssen and headed for home. We liberated about fourteen pounds of black bread that night and we hoped to get more in the future. A few nights after that, the smell of fresh-baked bread wafted across the fields to us and we knew where that smell was coming from. We knew it was wrong, but we prayed for a full alert. We even prayed for the RAF, and both prayers were answered. We didn't know it, but this time the target was supposed to be Düsseldorf. For some unknown reason, the bombers dropped most of their load far off target and hit a few roof tile factories in our area. Our second bread raid was thwarted by two Wehrmacht guards and a bunch of POWs who were already loading the bread onto trucks. Nevertheless, fourteen pounds of black bread during the previous raid wasn't bad for one night's work, and for a considerable time after that, we lived on black bread and prune soup. This soup was Mum's own invention. We had plenty of prunes courtesy of a large plum tree in our garden. Mum would soak about two pounds of the bread for a night in water and the next day, put it in a pan with a handful of prunes and boil it for about two hours until it had the consistency of black mud. Then two tablespoons of vinegar were added and eight ounces of sugar or molasses, along with some cinnamon or ground cloves. We ate it hot or cold, but because of the coarse barley the bread was made from late in the war, it never seemed to get soft even when it was boiled with the prunes.

All this foraging for something to eat to supplement our rations and home-canned food was Brother Len's and my responsibility. Other people had kids too and they did the same thing, but there was never any rivalry. We were all in the same boat and we knew it. After years of war, we more or less treated pilfering as an adventure. We didn't think of it as a crime anymore. This was a war the whole nation was involved in one way or another and our simple lives were at stake almost every day. I'm not saying that we were explicitly targeted, but German children grew up to be German soldiers; we knew that and so did the Allies.

Up to the summer of 1944, we hadn't felt much of the war's destruction. We lived away from the big cities; Dusseldorf was thirty-five miles and Cologne forty. That doesn't sound far today, but even ten miles away from the exploding bombs seemed safe at the time. With fascination we watched the red skies above the burning cities, the burning distant Ruhr area every night, and the plying searchlight beams. We cheered when a bomber was hit and came crashing down in flames and were eager to read the news next day in the paper: 'Last night enemy bombers crossed into the north-western Reich area and bombs were dropped on several locations in the Rhineland. Cultural establishments, churches and hospitals were hit and the civilian population sustained some losses. Twenty-four of the attacking bombers were shot down by our defences. Night fighter patrols shot down another seven of the attackers.' We didn't believe everything we read, but there was no hiding from a shooting war after June 1944 when the Allies landed at the Normandy beaches. A few airfields the Allies captured in northern France a month later added to our misery and the area behind the German front line as far east as the Rhine became a hunting ground for fighter-bombers. From then on, digging potatoes, weeding or watering the garden or simply walking to the shop for half a loaf of bread became a dangerous business.

From their elevated seats, the pilots could see every movement and they shot at anything that moved. We jumped from one house's front-door lintel to the next as the noise of the engine receded into the distance and listened to hear if another plane was following. Night time was the best time to go out, but if there was an alert on, no one was allowed in the streets except the air-raid wardens. For October 1944, I remember that in our logbook at the quads was recorded 340 alerts for that month alone and that's about ten per day. These were just the daylight alerts, as our 20mm quads were only on standby at night in October 1944. Evening alerts were for our big brothers, the 88s. The air-raid warning system in Germany worked very well with a few exceptions. The *Drathfunk*, a radio transmitted warning system, would warn us of any approaching bomber force from the direction of the Friesian Islands. Terschelling was our main warning station; there were also stations on Helgoland and Norderney and we knew what the number of our area was on the alert grid map.

By October 1944, many town and villages west of the Rhine had evacuated children and old folks to Saxony, Mecklenburg or even Silesia, but many were reluctant to leave their homes. After all, it wasn't only the Western Allies advancing toward the German border; out in the East there was a far greater menace poised to storm into the Fatherland. In October, this enemy was still far away, even though a few Russian attacks had brought the Red Army into the south-eastern parts of East Prussia, capturing a few places like Goldap in Poland. According to reports, the Russians had raped every woman and child and had nailed Party officials to barn doors. We heard the Party leader of one village was tied between four horses and pulled apart. The vengeful Russian soldiers were showing no mercy; they hadn't been shown any by their conquerors in the past three years. When these tales of terror were heard by the people who had been evacuated from the west to the east, many chose to pack up and go back to their homes, fighter-bombers or no fighter-bombers. They'd rather be shot by a .50 calibre bullet or pulverised by a bomb than be nailed to a barn door.

Wehrmacht soldiers of lower ranks at the front had it even worse than us later in the war. My dad told me that in Russia they mostly lived off the land. Those soldiers who were stationed at home bases in Germany had their own company kitchens and were reasonably well fed. In September 1944, a tent city of Wehrmacht sprang up about five miles from our house and sometimes civilians would stand in the queue hoping to get a bowl of something from the cook. I don't know why the soldiers were there. Perhaps it was an assembly point for a division assigned to reinforce the expected Hürtgen Forest battle that would begin in October, or they might have been there awaiting the 'Go' for the Ardennes battle of December. The camp was well camouflaged in a pine forest. A few fighter-bombers flew right over the assembly and missed the comings and goings, but then on a sunny September day, the tent city was not so lucky. Several field kitchens were in use that day and the smoke from burning pine branches that the cooks used to heat their stoves gave them away. This was just too tempting a target. Probably it was a lone Mosquito that spotted the smoke and reported it to a fighter-bomber base in Belgium. By then there were almost a hundred Allied bases behind the lines.

Soon the first wave of *Jabos* arrived and circled around to get oriented. The kitchen fires were immediately doused with water but it was too late. Several civilians, including children, were at the campsite. Soldiers and civilians scattered in all directions looking for shelter. There were only a few slit trenches and one Westwall bunker that could hold at the most a hundred people. The rest just crouched down behind trees. About twenty P-47s raked the forest over from end to end. No bombs were dropped, but it was carnage of the first magnitude. Being about five miles from the attack, our quads were out of range most of the time, but we nevertheless let loose with all we had. The 88s were out of it; the *Jabos* were too low and they couldn't lower their barrels to that shallow an angle. The attack lasted about six minutes, and when it was over, 120 dead were counted, including fifteen children. I didn't see the camp after the attack, but Brother Len's Hitler Youth group went there to help out, and from what he told us later, it must have been an awful sight. Even the search for a mouthful of food was a dangerous undertaking in those days.

*   *   *

The Hürtgen Forest battle soon got in full swing; Operation Clipper was set to go off shortly just north of Aachen and far to the south, General Patton was hammering at the door of 'Fortress Metz'. Only the centre, from the Eifel Hills to the Ardennes, was quiet. The border area was, and still is, the nearest thing to a jungle in central Europe. There were deep gullies, majestic pine trees, raging creeks, forest trails and only a few rough roads, unsuitable for heavy armour even in good weather. But good weather in the autumn in this part of Europe is rare. The area is often shrouded in fog and it rains for days on end, and in the winter of 1944, it must have reminded the Wehrmacht soldier of deepest Russia, with strong blizzards and ice storms.

After the Western Allies reached the German border in September–October 1944, and Operation Market-Garden and Operation Clipper ended, the front lines south of the Hürtgen Forest went into hibernation, only to be rudely awakened on 16 December, the beginning of the Ardennes Offensive. In the interval, civilians travelled from west to east and east to west, often in plain view of half-asleep German guards in Westwall pillboxes or American GIs brewing coffee along the Lanzerath Highway. I can vouch for that as my mother and I crossed these lines in late October 1944 into Luxembourg on a trip to Wiltz, but we got delayed on our way home in mid-December by Germans preparing for the coming battle and Americans who had no idea it was coming. We didn't get out until the end of December. Farmers were still tending their fields when the battle began, harvesting beets, ploughing, and sowing while shells going both directions whistled overhead. In the late months of 1944 through early 1945, it was not uncommon to see civilians travelling across front lines, either to get away from the Allied bombing or to put some distance between themselves and both armies. The front-line soldiers, Allies or Wehrmacht, couldn't do much for the civilians. The days of orderly evacuation had long since passed, but Mum and I reached Wiltz without incident. Where were the P-47s then? Well, the weather in those border areas is usually lousy from October to January and Hitler knew it. The Allied pilots didn't fly and the Germans sat in their bunkers with GIs only a mile to the west of them. '*Leben und leben lassen*' (live and let live) seemed to be the order of the day for a brief period before the Battle of the Bulge began. Winters can be extremely cold in that part of the country, with temperatures of -25°C common and no soldier is going to move if he doesn't have to.

Our seven-week journey to Wiltz and back opened our eyes to the overwhelming force that Germany was up against. It was also the first time in my life I tasted coffee made from real coffee beans, corned beef, spam, chocolate raisin bars, and above all, chewing gum. The first time I was given a stick of gum by an American GI, I flatly refused to put it into my mouth. It made me think of chewing tobacco and I wanted none of it. Eventually, I got up the courage and tried it. I was surprised that it had nothing to do with tobacco. We made it home by New Year's Day 1945 and things there had really gone from bad to worse. Food was almost non-existent; Brother Len had lost a few pounds, Aunt Carol looked like a spider with a few legs missing, and the winter vegetables were buried under two feet of snow. Mum immediately set about making things right. She really could make a meal of nothing and that's about all that was left. We brought a few goodies from the Americans back with us which were shared with friends; like powdered instant coffee and real bread.

We had been told that the American GIs had even less to eat than our Wehrmacht troops, but Mum and I found out differently during our trip behind the Allied lines. We saw how the GIs lived for ourselves, which made us think that maybe the rest of the propaganda was lies too. Maybe General Patton wasn't a coward and maybe Eisenhower wasn't a Jew after all. We had the good fortune to come in contact with a mortar platoon of the US 28th Infantry Division that was billeted in our relatives' house where we were staying. Their rations and food supplies were out of this world. Our visit with them only lasted a few days, but it was a real education. That mortar platoon was detailed to guard a river bridge, but was subsequently driven off by overwhelming German forces. The wounded, and we knew their names by then, were treated by my relatives and me. The Germans held the western part of the town, so we made sure that the wounded GIs were sneaked out of Wiltz in an M3 halftrack and taken to Bastogne, some fifteen miles away. One of the wounded was a Texan named Oddis; at least that's what I understood from the other GIs who called him by that name. Whether they reached the safety of Bastogne, I didn't know until fifty-five years later. On a Battle of the Bulge website someone asked for information regarding a mortar platoon that had been in Wiltz on Tuesday 19 December 1944. I replied in an email and said that I knew of a mortar platoon that was there and a wounded guy named Oddis and told the whole story. Well, the soldier's name was actually Odis Wise, and it was his son who had posted the inquiry on the website. I wrote to him telling him the story of the bridge, his father's specific wounds and we both knew then that we were talking about the same person. Sadly, Odis died in 1998, long before I read the website post. Another GI named Dellora was the mortar platoon's machine gunner, and he was killed that 19 December. I visited a Second World War museum in Pigeon Forge, Tennessee in 2002 and went to the wall of remembrance, and there I found the machine gunner's name and the following statement: 'C. Dellora, Killed in Action December 19, 1944, ETO (European Theater of Operations).'

*   *   *

Our *Volkssturm* unit was officially formed in M-G in late September 1944 and called up for service the next year in early February. These were sixty-year-old and older granddads and young boys from the local Hitler Youth. A retired colonel who lived up the street from us was made their company commander. Now, during Hitler's reign there were very few retired officers. If a general lost a battle and was scolded by Hitler, the general's first words were, 'I resign my command'. Hitler always refused to accept the resignation, and rightly so.

'I am the one who decides who resigns', he would say. No soldier, and that included generals, could simply resign and go home because something didn't go well at the front. The colonel who commanded our *Volkssturm* retired long before Hitler came to power. As I remember, he was seventy-four in 1945; a bit too old to be fighting General Patton.

The weapons they had were a conglomeration of rifles from Denmark, France and Italy with hardly any ammunition. The villages in our area managed to mobilise nearly 200 men and boys in September and they were out almost every day in early February for training. Only about half of them even had a rifle. They only had five rounds of ammunition for practice and five more rounds to keep with the rifle. Each man was given a *Panzerfaust*, but no uniform or helmet. Some showed up for training wearing their Sunday hats and armbands with a swastika and '*Volkssturm*' stitched on it.

Mr Geisler, our town barber, was also a First World War veteran and well over sixty years old, so he was never drafted, but he was called up. He could cut a head of hair in five minutes with his hand-operated clippers. You never knew exactly what it was going to look like, but we boys knew it would be short, very short. Girls had pigtails that their mothers braided for them and most kept that style well into their twenties. I remember one Sunday afternoon seeing Mr Geisler marching with a group of other old men. He had a *Panzerfaust* over his shoulder and could hardly keep up. They certainly didn't look like our Wehrmacht we saw marching through town only a few years before. I didn't see how we could ever win a war with that kind of army.

On 26 February, this motley collection of 'Reich Defenders' assembled and I heard that only a few diehards showed up; twenty-seven of them to be exact and that no amount of propaganda could persuade the others to fall in. I was told they were ordered to assemble at a local farm the following day to be fed into a defensive line. What happened to the twenty-seven men and boys that did show up? I have no idea, but I think it's safe to say they did not take on the American 104th Infantry Division. Before they were dismissed by the colonel, the first American artillery shell to hit our village fell into the garden of a neighbour. Everyone heard the whistle of the incoming round and the explosion but it was a 105mm shell and no big deal to people who had lived through four years of 1,000lb and bigger bombs being dropped on them. But those who were there said that first shell scattered our *Volkssturm* and the roll call the next day brought only nine dedicated men to the assembly point. A local 63-year-old watchmaker and First World War veteran assumed command and sent them home. He then jumped on his bicycle and left, not to be seen again until April when the fighting was all over in our town. This was the end of our local *Volkssturm* defence. Their equipment and weapons turned up years later in garden sheds, ponds and septic tanks. The farmer who found such weapons would throw them into their sludge ponds or manure heaps rather than having to answer questions from the advancing Allies. Many a *Panzerfaust* and machine gun disappeared in that way under tons of horse and cow manure. Even tanks and anti-aircraft guns were pushed or pulled into slurry pits. Some were dug out sixty years later to be sold to reenactors who restored them to working condition and use them today in recreating long-forgotten battles. I remember a local farmer who found a *Nebelwerfer* (rocket launcher) when he drained his pond in 1983. A restoration team from Holland bought it and restored it for a Second World War museum.

Little Fred and I were cutting clover for our rabbits along a footpath near our house when that first shell landed. I knew it wasn't very far away. We jumped into a slit trench and then heard the downtown air-raid siren start to wail. The artillery fire continued for several minutes before all was quiet again. The quiet after an air raid was a very strange kind of quiet out away from the city. Everyone listened and tried not to breathe too loud, as if the bombers could hear and know you were still alive and come back. As soon as we could move, we raced home and I deposited little Fred with Aunt Carol and went up to the quads. The bombing was all over and the planes gone before they even got off a shot.

After February 1945, not much news reached us as to how the war was going, but we could easily guess. We heard second-hand that BBC broadcasts had mentioned a few towns captured by the Allies. Krefeld, Cologne, and Moers were taken at the beginning of March. During the time from 1 March to 8 May 1945, the news about how the war was going came from our radio. We could only pick up the *Deutschlandsender* station, which was in Berlin and still held by the government. German stations in the medium-wave band had either ceased transmitting or were severely jammed by the Allies. The *Deutschlandsender* was a special pet project of Goebbels and was so powerful that it couldn't be jammed very well, but the news we got from it was taken by all with a grain of salt. Most of the broadcast was propaganda anyway. We heard 'Hold out for final victory', over and over. We also heard things like: 'Yesterday over a 150 enemy bombers were shot down. Russian attacks near Stettin were repulsed with heavy losses to the enemy; seventy-two tanks were destroyed. On the Hungarian front, our SS troops re-took the city of Stuhlweissenburg, and south-west of the city, the Bolsheviks gained only two kilometres of ground. On the western front, all American attacks near Griesheim were contained and in Frankfurt, heavy street fighting is in progress.'

We could read maps, and it was easy to see who was advancing and it wasn't us. We did believe a few of the Berlin broadcasts however. Around the middle of April, the radio gave us the news that three looters who had participated in a bread riot in Rahsfeld had been beheaded on orders from Goebbels. The announcement went on to say that this should be a warning to others not to break the law. This was more frightening to us than the bombers overhead. It seemed our own government had turned against its citizens. Sure, catch a thief and put him in jail and we would all cheer, but to execute people for trying to steal bread, which all of us had done, was just terrifying.

Chapter 10

End of the War; Beginning of the Starving

During the winter nights of January and February 1945, we sat around the kitchen table and talked about what life would be like after the war and what would be in store for us. Of course, Brother Len still believed in final victory for Germany, but he was the only one. I maintained that it was time for all of us to start learning English or French. We argued for a while, and high up we heard the drone of RAF Lancasters and Halifaxes going east and our 88s banging away not far off. Our local quads were out of business at night, but our searchlights were scanning the sky trying to catch an intruder in their beams. Berlin Radio had a special message to the people that night from Goebbels himself. 'On our western front, the Allies have tried again unsuccessfully to penetrate our great Westwall near Straelen but were repulsed. American forces committed all their reserves to gain a foothold around Zülpich and south of München-Gladbach.'

'That's us Len,' I yelled, 'you heard it; south of München-Gladbach.'

'Yeah I heard it,' Len replied, 'but we're defending ourselves well and we're counter-attacking to reverse all enemy penetrations.'

'Len, you sound like Goebbels. Do you know that the *Amis* are already firing artillery into Baal, Linnich, and a few other places that are only twenty miles from us?'

'Shut up; let's hear what our Propaganda Minister has to say.'

Goebbels kept on ranting: 'Near Düren, in the area of the main Allied offensive, 200 American tanks were destroyed. West of the Ruhr, near Krefeld, heavy enemy fighter-bomber activity has been reported. Our light flak shot down twenty-seven P-38 and P-47 fighters.'

'We've shot down nothing in the last week,' I informed Len 'and as far as I know, neither has anyone else in our area. Krefeld is only twelve miles away and Giant would know about planes their quads shot down over there and he didn't say anything about it.'

'Well, the 88s might have got them.'

'I know two things, Brother Len; 88s don't waste ammunition on planes 200 feet up, and you only know how to dig holes in the ground.'

Goebbels went on: 'The enemy forces intending to reach the Rhine have been repulsed, but fighting is still going on in the Hürtgen Forest. On other fronts . . .'

'Turn that thing off,' Mum shouted from the kitchen, 'let's hear some music.'

Len turned the radio dial to Beromünster (Sursee/Lucerne) but the Swiss station was quiet. Kalundborg in Denmark was transmitting marching songs and Stockholm had news in Swedish. We couldn't understand what they were saying but we didn't turn the radio back to Goebbels' speech either.

*   *   *

The last days of February 1945 were the most dangerous times for civilians in the area along the western borders and the left bank of the Rhine River. Evacuations by that time had stopped altogether. There was nowhere to go, east or west. Germany was in a vice that would surely shut soon. Only a few diehards still believed in wonder weapons. The *Volkssturm* was useless and the Hitler Youth was eager but inexperienced. There were not many left who wanted to die for '*Führer, Volk und Vaterland*'. Once the US Ninth Army crossed the Roer River and the half-mile wide floodplain, there was not much the German Wehrmacht could do to stop them. Between the city of M-G and the Roer, the Wehrmacht could only muster a parachute regiment and a handful of Panther and Tiger tanks from the Panzer Lehr Division. Opposing them was the US 2nd Armoured Division, 'Hell on Wheels', equipped with some brand-new Pershing tanks. Those 46-ton monsters had a 90mm gun that could take on the Panthers and Tigers on equal terms. Supported by three infantry divisions and a huge armada of fighter-bombers, they advanced up to twenty miles a day and met only sporadic resistance. In some western suburbs, the Germans put up a resistance line and tried to stop the onslaught but to no avail. It was a different matter in some eastern suburbs. As the history of the US 2nd Armoured Division records; their Combat Command B bypassed the city of M-G, but in one suburb they met parts of the German 902nd Panzer Lehr Regiment supported by a Panzer Grenadier Battle Group. The Germans were ordered to attack late in the afternoon of 1 March, just as it started to snow. The Germans attacked, and in the ensuing firefight that lasted most of the night, they managed to push the Americans back to the outskirts of the city. The Americans lost about 110 dead and twenty-two tanks and halftracks. An unknown German tank gunner in a *Jagdpanther* destroyed five US tanks that night. The Germans lost four Panthers that they could ill afford to lose and then retreated toward the Rhine just before daylight came on 2 March. Ten civilians were killed and many others wounded that night because there was nowhere for them to go to get away from the fighting. The city fell late in the day on 2 March 1945.

A few days earlier, Brother Len had been ordered to report to the Hitler Youth headquarters to be deployed digging anti-tank ditches, his favourite pastime. We had no inkling of his whereabouts, but reports reached us that a whole battalion of Hitler Youth had tried to stop the 2nd Armoured Division just to the east of us, armed only with rifles and *Panzerfausts*. The entire unit was annihilated and we feared the worst. Alas, Len turned up a couple of days later. He had been captured by the 406th Regiment, 102nd US Infantry Division, before the fighting and sent home after interrogation. Brother Len was a bit put out by that; he had thought he was more important than to be sent home with a kick in the pants.

As early as the Hardt Woods battle (Battle of Jebsheim) that ended on February 2, there wasn't much point in the quads trying to defend the crumbling Reich any longer. The big guns were disabled when the Americans arrived, along with an assortment of 37mm guns and a Maultier *Nebelwerfer* that had found its way to our position. The crew dispersed and a few of the men managed to obtain civilian clothing and mingle with the local population in their shelters. Brother Len remarked afterward that it had been a lovely war, but it wasn't quite over.

After our school was closed indefinitely in August 1944, the local town administration took over the building. By 25 February 1945 there was nothing left to administrate, so those people who had supported the Nazis and feared the wrath of the Allies, left town, some on bicycles, the mayor in a car. They all fled across the Rhine. After the first air raid in February, some administrative departments were moved into the villages and into our school. It became the town council headquarters, still proudly displaying in huge Bakelite letters on the outside wall, 'Adolf Hitler Schule'. On 2 March 1945, the US 102nd Infantry Division used the letters for target practice. The local police force, which by February 1945 amounted to forty officers, was also in charge of the air-raid wardens, the Red Cross and some engineering units. They had made their headquarters in a bunker at the food-processing plant. High up on the roof was a covered concrete observation post. One could see the Rhine River to the east, and to the west, the view was all the way to Holland. On several occasions, this little bunker had been the target of fighter-bombers, but it survived the war without a scratch. The fire department and the police department left M-G on 28 February. When the US Army occupied the city on March 1, the police managed to get across the Rhine without incident. However, after the capture of the Remagen bridge by the US 9th Armoured Division and the crossing of the river by Montgomery's 21st Army Group, the police became part of the 300,000 Wehrmacht soldiers who were eventually surrounded in the Ruhr Cauldron. They all marched into captivity and were soon transported to Cherbourg as POWs.

When the shooting started late on 27 February 1945, the Nazi *Bonzen* loaded their belongings and some files on trucks and left the area around midnight, crossing the Rhine the following day. Only the Party chairman had the courage to stay behind. He and his wife committed suicide two days later. The *Bonzen* that fled returned weeks later as if nothing had happened. None of them had ever shouted '*Sieg Heil*' or '*Heil Hitler*', or so they said when they were interrogated, but the occupying forces were not convinced and locked up the whole bunch. The town by then had a US Colonel and a former Missouri police lieutenant as administrators. The police lieutenant spoke fluent German and had lived in Germany until he was twelve years old. His family had emigrated to the United States in 1920.

The GIs who 'liberated' our area – they were the enemy so we didn't exactly see it as liberation – were amazed by the destruction their Air Force had caused to the inner cities. Pictures of flattened Aachen, Cologne, and Düsseldorf with white surrender bed sheets hanging out of windows made headlines in Allied newspapers. The American media had a field day when their GIs took control of the city of Rheydt, a city not too far from our little village. A white bed sheet was fluttering from the top window of the house Dr. Goebbels was born in. Goebbels visited his hometown several times during the twelve years the Nazis were in power and Göring was also there a few times.

* * *

Older Americans can remember exactly where they were and what they were doing when they heard that President Kennedy had been assassinated. That was how it was for us when the war ended. It was a sunny day in early May and I was sitting in our garden watching the military traffic roll along. Across the road was a parking lot where field kitchens were preparing some sort of food. American GIs were sitting on doorsteps reading newspapers or playing some sort of card game. A huge black soldier was sitting on our neighbour's doorstep cleaning his fingernails with a bayonet. Suddenly there was shouting from the parking lot and a twin .50 calibre M2 machine gun started firing, with an unmistakable sound. Pistols and carbines were firing all around us. We just thought we were being attacked by the Wehrmacht or maybe the Luftwaffe but we didn't hear any planes. Since we were outside, we all ran for our vegetable bunker near the garden. The firing slowed and we could understand a few words the GIs were yelling, 'The war is over, Hitler's dead.' Hitler had committed suicide a few days earlier, but we didn't know it. The black soldier came running over, waving his bayonet and grinning from ear to ear and stood by the fence, 'Hitler's finished, Allies bang bang.' Yes, we had understood that finally the war was over. Celebrations by the *Amis* went on all night and they raided the wine cellar from the food-processing plant, but there were no incidents.

Generosity by the *Amis* was boundless beginning the very next day. It was like we had never been at war with them and they treated us like we had been allies. We smiled back when they smiled and we held our hands out for candy, coffee and cigarettes. Those were the 'three C's' for us and were among the first English words we learned. The coffee was for Mum and Aunt Carol. The candy was for me, and the cigarettes were for Giant or for trading. Brother Len wouldn't ask the GIs for anything. When Gunny left for Krefeld soon after the Americans arrived, we gave him the few cigarettes we had left and he traded them to the farmers in the area for butter or bacon. It was below the dignity of the farmers to ask for anything from the GIs, but they would certainly trade with us for American cigarettes. Because of the farmers' steaming compost heaps, usually placed right by the front door, most soldiers avoided their houses and left them alone.

With the arrival of the US Army came a new worry for us; how to obtain food with all the shops being closed. That problem was soon partially solved when people starting looting Nazi stockpiles. The Party men had already fled, most across the Rhine, but with a curfew in place, no one was allowed on the streets after sunset, so looting took place in broad daylight while the *Amis* watched. I discovered a cache of Wehrmacht bread in what had been a bowling alley and that hoard was ransacked by the locals. Even the GIs helped by making sure everyone got a fair share. We got more than most; after all, I had found it. Our kitchen window was only a short distance from the bowling alley, but bread doesn't keep indefinitely and a hundred loaves is a lot of bread to eat. Brother Len's suggestion that we can it in glass jars was rejected. We didn't have enough jars and Len hadn't been right about too many things lately. Our air-raid shelter was damp and the bread soon got mouldy. We brushed off the mould and ate it anyway. Next we tried the attic under the roof; it was much drier there. We put the bread in cotton sacks and hung them up between the rafters. A little axle grease smeared on the strings and nails stopped the mice. We were well stocked with bread, but other things were in short supply, so we swapped German medals, badges and WHW pins for GI rations containing butter, sausage, Spam, and other goodies. One GI gave us coffee in return for water from our still-running tap. The electricity was out again, however, and would stay out for a long time.

In the first few weeks after the end of the war, Nazi doctrine was still too fresh in people's minds. They thought we would all be put into labour camps or worse if we took anything from the occupiers. Among some of those who had been in power, there was enough guilt to go around and it spread to others; collective guilt they call it now. The personal experience of my family told me different and I was not much affected by the new local propaganda. Some people took to the Americans right away, some took a while, and a few never wanted anything to do with them at all. The GIs in our area didn't loot, but a sort of swapping ground was established early on; a fancy *Schneewittchen* (Snow White) alarm clock for a tin of Nescafe or an Iron Cross for a can of Spam or a K-ration. Soon young children were running around with blown up condoms, thinking they were GI party balloons. Within a few months, every home had something from the Americans in it. I suppose the children were the first to break the ice; maybe it was the 'Scheving Jum' as we pronounced it (chewing gum), the candy bars and the oranges that did the trick. The mothers and Frauleins (German men were rarely seen) were attracted to the smell of real coffee the GIs brewed on their tanks. Chelsea and Lucky Strike cigarettes, white bread, tinned butter and liver pate won over the rest temporarily and the huge sacks of biscuit flour after the Marshall Plan went into effect made it permanent. Hunger was the dominant factor that broke down the barriers and kept them down.

The American GIs couldn't feed everyone, and they only occupied part of Germany. We were in the same dire straits we had been in during 1918. There was peace, but no food. Germany was again a ghost country and famine became widespread. Children went to school hungry and left school at 1:00 p.m. even hungrier, despite the Allies' soup kitchens. Some schools created sleeping hours for younger children during school time. We had to put our heads on our desks and rest or sleep. This was supposed to make us forget about being hungry, but the classrooms were cold and no one slept or rested. There was no coal for heating the place, so we were cold and hungry. When we left school, we had to queue up outside one shop or another for a few ounces of meat and eight ounces of flour or coal. Children did not play anymore. Of course, some people still looked well fed, mainly ex-Nazis who had managed to slip through the de-nazification net or Frauleins who had an American GI or British soldier as a friend. The hungry folks looked at them with disdain. 'Good meals are a crime' was the slogan of the time. If you had enough to eat, you probably did not get it legally or morally. Long queues for the evening meal at convents and hospitals were already formed by 2:00 p.m. Scrawny children with billycans (cooking pots) in their hands waited patiently for whatever was left over.

Soon after, German housewives developed the most sophisticated meals using Spam and potatoes. For a while after the surrender, Spam could be had from any good GI. They didn't seem to care for it very much and were anxious to trade it for something. All that was needed was a German medal and a few words in English – especially Spam, and a deal would be made. Three small cans of Spam for an Iron Cross was the going rate. The bigger round five-pound cans could be had for three or four medals, or the affection of a German Fraulein. One enterprising local 23-year-old woman in our area was well known for her dealings with the GIs and eventually the American Military Police, who had gotten wind of her business, arrested her. She was caught in bed with an American Staff Sergeant from the quartermaster's store. The hoard of food they found at her house would have kept a platoon of GIs fed for two weeks. She was released after a few days with a warning. Reichsmark fines were worthless because Reichsmarks were worthless. She was back in business soon and I think eventually ended up in Brauweiler Prison for Women. Spam was not on ration cards after the war and it was not available in shops.

Officially, a curfew was ordered immediately after our area was occupied, and people were only allowed to move around outside from 9:00 a.m. to 11:00 a.m. to search for a shop that was open but there were none. The curfew was really because of the heavy American military traffic and the few diehard Nazis in our area that might cause trouble. Some of them believed a counter-attack was coming that would recapture the Rhineland. We had a first-hand look at the equipment the Americans brought along with them and knew there would be no such retaliation. We kids stood in the gardens, even during curfew hours, and watched the trucks and tanks go by. There were Shermans, M3s, M5s and M8s, Hellcats and occasionally a brand-new Pershing with its 90mm gun would roll past. These monsters were a match even for our Tigers and Panthers. We were not on the road and the GIs didn't seem to care if we watched. Brother Len pointed at the high-topped M5s that we called *Puckelpanzers* (Hunchback tanks) and commented, 'Ours are better.'

'Well, where were ours when we needed them'? I replied.

During the Allied invasion, the US infantry, always looking for a way to hitch a ride to advance even faster, confiscated a few German military and civilian trucks with empty petrol tanks that had been abandoned by the retreating Wehrmacht. After being refuelled, they made good transportation for the weary footsoldiers. It was a hilarious sight to see a squad of GIs, armed to the teeth, hanging for dear life on the back of 'Arndt Transport GMBH' trucks. The company still exists today and still transports vegetables all over Germany. Some GIs found a few three-wheeled pick-up trucks. These were popular before and during the war as substitute transport for small loads. They had two wheels on the back axle, but only one in front and were powered by a two-stroke engine. With the arrangement of their wheels, however, they couldn't cross the tread bridge across the Rhine, so the GIs burned them on the spot. Trams in Krefeld were commandeered, but without power, the things wouldn't move so they were bulldozed off the road.

The local city administration had completely broken down during these turbulent days even before 'liberation', so the occupying powers had to introduce some sort of local government to provide basic services. The ration card system and the postal service needed immediate attention. The Allies printed some postage stamps marked a.m. Post for 'Allied Military Post' that were used alongside German stamps with Hitler's profile on them partially covered with an ink spot. German ration cards were still printed for the time being with the issuing authority stamp inked over the Nazi eagle and swastika. The point system on the ration cards was the same as that used before the end of the war, but most of the items were not available in the shops that soon reopened their doors. The few items that were available were scattered all over the town and there was no coordinated distribution of anything. We had to walk miles randomly from one shop to another to get the few rationed items that we needed. Until June 1948, we still used the Reichsmark, even though it was practically worthless. I remember paying 500 Reichsmarks for a movie ticket in 1948. Before the war, this would have paid the rent on a nice house for a year. Ration cards were used up until 1949; we got them once a month for food. Later, they were different pastel colours for different items; then came the shoe cards, next the clothing cards, and permits were needed for everything else. The list was endless. Nothing had changed for us.

Our two local butchers opened their doors again after the surrender but with a very limited selection. The meat ration card might have shown points for 200 grams (eight ounces) of fat, which included bacon, but if the shop only had a few pounds for distribution, you were lucky to get two ounces. That was a couple of thin slices and it was supposed to last for a week. Fatback was not sliced and was issued in four- to five-ounce squares. Other meat, mainly pork, required several points, but if it was not available, you took what was. Bones, with the last molecule of meat stripped off, were sold one pound per card holder, but no ration points were needed. This system was the same for all groceries except fresh vegetables that could be bought at small farmer-operated vegetable shops. Beef was rarely seen even before the end of the war and it was just as rare after the war. Cattle grazing in pastures made easy targets for fighter-bombers and cows don't grow in a few weeks to slaughtering size. Pigs were kept under the cover of sheds at all times before the end of the war. *Bezugschein* (permits) for other essentials came from the local economic office, just like during the war, and they stated exactly the item to be issued. Each item required a separate permit and it was still an endless task filling in the required forms. The men in charge of distribution and permits had to make sure that things were issued to those who really needed them. I remember one man, a Herr Sonnenschein, at the local economic office being attacked by an irate housewife over a permit for a pair of slippers. I'm sure this was not an isolated incident.

Soon enough, the main roads were cleared of rubble and once the power was back on, electric trams were put back on their tracks and started running. A twenty-Pfennig ticket could get you to almost any town since all cities in the Ruhr were connected by tram. M-G had fourteen different lines at the time and some ran for sixteen miles from the point of departure with stops at every other street corner. Until the de-nazification programme started in earnest, these services were operated by the same people who had been in charge during the Third Reich; that is, if they weren't among those who disappeared before the *Amis* came. Goebbels told us that if we lost the war, Germany would be occupied for at least fifteen years. This information had leaked out of the Yalta conference and he used it in his propaganda in print and on the radio. If that was true, we thought, then why would they want to bomb the cities into rubble they would soon occupy? It made no sense.

Since our area was occupied in early March, gardens needed to be planted if there was to be any food for our family. Food storage facilities were empty and had been for some time, which just added to the misery of the have-nots who hoped they would get at least one meal a day after the war. Whether Germany could look forward to a good harvest in 1945 depended on the farmers that still had horses and ploughs. Former Wehrmacht soldiers cleared millions of mines from fields before they could be sown. Some of them were as small as matchboxes but they could still maim or kill. At times, farmers took the task of mine-clearing upon themselves. If they suspected there were mines in a field, they used one horse and an eighteen-foot wide harrow. They would walk fifty feet behind, holding the lines from the horse. This worked in some cases, but often the horse was killed and sometimes the farmer as well. Later, when tractors were available, the harrow was pulled about 100 feet behind. To this day, those hellish explosives are found in fields and they are still dangerous.

*   *   *

In mid-summer 1945, Dad came home from POW camp. He had been in Denmark when the war ended and since there had been no fighting there, the Wehrmacht just surrendered to the Danish Resistance and suffered no reprisals from the Danes. They in turn called in some officers of the British Army to make sure that no high-ranking Nazis were among them. The Danes were not interested in keeping POWs; they wanted to get on with their own lives. After a few weeks in holding camps, under shelter and given good meals, the majority of the POWs were released. They were given a Red Cross pass, a travel permit and twenty cigarettes, and told to go home. With no transportation available, it took Dad two weeks to get home. He went to see Mr Abel who still had his job as transport manager for the electric-tram company in town. He was overjoyed to see Dad, and glad to have a driver back. The tram lines had been repaired, rubble was soon cleared from the streets and the overhead cables reconnected, and by August, Dad was back in his old job. He stayed on this job until the trams were replaced by buses in the mid-1950s. He then worked his way through several construction jobs; the rebuilding of bomb-ravaged Germany was in full swing. Later he even worked as a janitor in a school for children of British military officers. He died in 1976 with the knowledge that most of his immediate family had survived the terrible war years. Aunt Carol eventually married again in 1946 and moved to a town near Frankfurt. I never saw her again after she moved and even Dad lost touch with her. I'll always remember her, however, because she was the link to reality for our family. She lost her husband and personally experienced the emotional pain that the war brought, while we only felt it second-hand. She was a strong woman who inspired the rest of us to be strong when things were really bad.

Mr Vink resumed his job as a furnace stoker for the food-processing plant in our town after the war. There were no more shouts of 'Lights Out' for him. He retired sometime in the 1950s. The children, and some adults, may have made fun of him, but he no doubt saved the lives of many of us. I realise now that his was a thankless job that he could have refused, but he, like so many other unsung heroes, did his part in trying to keep us safe. I can see today that he actually did his job well as opposed to so many other officials of the Nazi era who did not. He didn't personally benefit from the triumphs or tragedies. He was simply doing his job, trying to keep as many of us alive as possible.

By 1949 Brother Len had completed a metalworking apprenticeship and found a temporary job at a farm near the Hürtgen Forest area, milking cows and cutting *Binsen*, which was the coarse grass preferred by basket weavers. It grew wild all along the Rur River (not the Ruhr) and basket weaving was a big industry in that area at the time. In 1944, there had been a huge battle there and quite often a cow or an unsuspecting farmer became a casualty of the mines left in the forest. During the summer of 1949, I joined Len for two weeks. The farmer that he worked for allowed me to sleep in the straw barn with the mice, sparrows, and nesting owls. After the afternoon milking and feeding, he had free time and at that latitude and time of year, there was daylight until 11:00

p.m. We had plenty of opportunity to search the countryside for war relics and scrap metal. Anti-tank ditches had filled with water and in one, near the village of Siersdorf, we found a US M8 armoured car, which was no doubt left during Operation Clipper. There was no way for us to recover it and it might be still there. A local schoolboy took us to some hidden Westwall bunkers that even the farmers in the area didn't know about. In those days it wasn't safe to venture out in the Hürtgen Forest and most people were smart enough to stay out. Some bunkers still had shells and grenades stored in them and others had rusty bed frames arranged like the place had been an aid post during the battle. Helmets, both American and German were everywhere and they would bring about a dime as scrap. Today they are worth a few hundred dollars each. Recently, a friend who lives in the forest found a box with four 20mm barrels preserved in grease. Today there is not much of a market for those things but our Gunnery Sergeant would have given his right arm for them in early 1945.

The end of hostilities brought 'Beer Hall Strategists' from the First World War out of their holes like moles from the ground. Mostly they all had nothing better to say than, 'We told you so'. Brother Len, although not a veteran, despite his claim of being an 'Old Hand', maintained that the Westwall should never have been breached and that the Wehrmacht should have obeyed orders and done their duty. Len had dug anti-tank ditches in the vicinity of the wall, and he was disappointed that he had not been awarded a Westwall medal. This *Beton Orden* medal was for bunker workers only, like the RAD and OT Engineers, not for the Hitler Youth. This medal was jokingly called the 'Concrete Medal' by the recipients because of the millions of tons of concrete they used in constructing the wall's bunkers.

In July 1945, the Americans left and handed M-G over to the British. We were in the British zone of Germany after the country was divided up. The *Tommies* immediately occupied a few factories that had ceased production and established an 'Advanced Base Ordnance Depot', probably foreseeing clashes with the Russians who occupied the eastern half of Germany. For us youngsters who had swapped Nazi relics with the Americans for candy, cigarettes and other goodies, times became pretty hard. It wasn't that the British were less friendly; they just didn't have things to spare like the American GIs. On rare occasions, the soldiers threw us an orange or a half-eaten sandwich and watched in delight as we fought over every bite. We knew they had a rubbish dump near the back wall facing the railway tracks and at night we climbed the wall to search for whatever might be edible, like rotting fruit and mouldy cheese. Even beech nuts were collected and used in baking without any harmful effects. The depot, being set up as an advance base for weapons and ammunition, was closely guarded, first by RPs (Regimental Police), then later by Latvian auxiliaries with rifles, but no ammunition – as one good-natured Latvian informed us. The guards patrolled the perimeter in pairs and we had thirty minutes to get over the wall, search for useable items, and get back to safety before the guards came around again. They knew we were there but they hardly ever challenged us. It was like a cat-and-mouse game at times. They were cats without claws and we were mice who could outrun them. Mostly we went for rotting oranges. The peel was dried and then ground to powder in one of our coffee grinders. Brother Len wanted to use one of our grinders to turn his toenail clippings into bone meal for the garden but we drew the line at that.

At the start of the Allied occupation, children often successfully begged the soldiers for scraps of food, candy, coffee, or a leftover meal, but when most of the soldiers left, they had to start digging in their gardens again. There was never enough food to go around. The inner cities had no gardens and the women were pressed into clearing millions of tons of rubble. A new word came into being to describe them. The *Trümmerfrau* was the average woman whose husband was KIA, MIA or WIA (killed, missing or wounded in action). With a scarf to protect her head and a shovel in her hands, she went to work clearing the roads of rubble, or filling in bomb craters with the hope of finding something useful she could take home with her. With the NSV gone and no welfare organisation to feed the hungry, begging for food and prostitution were the only choices. The black market flourished but the prices were astronomical and only a few people could afford any of the things for sale; most didn't have anything of value to trade.

At the end of the war, politically-oriented youth organisations were banned in Germany except for the *Deutschen Katholischen Jugend* (DKJ – the German Catholic Youth Association). Brother Len despised that group, mostly because some of its members were former Edelweiss Pirates. Within a year things changed. The Social Democrat Party (SDP), which had been forbidden by the Nazis, was allowed to recruit new members. The Falcons was a youth group promoted by the SDP and this group, like the SDP, opposed the Communists and was hardly on speaking terms with the DKJ. The Falcons wore a red falcon lapel pin, had flags, and marched through towns singing old pre-Nazi songs. They held youth camps in the country and assembled in weekly meetings to tell their members how nice it was to live in a devastated Germany governed by military occupation, and how they should all look forward to the day when the country would become a social democracy. Had anything really changed since the end of the war? Brother Len joined as soon as the Falcons were established in our area, and with his Hitler Youth leadership skills, he became a group leader in no time. Brother Len, as I have stated earlier, was not very keen on housework and homework, and I think, when the war was over and Germany had lost, his world sort of collapsed around him until he joined the Falcons. There was no more '*Heil Hitler*'; this time the greeting was 'Friendship'. What did matter was that he was back in command, albeit 'without portfolio', which was a Nazi term meaning an honorary position without much authority. Throughout his life, he was always in command of something, whether it was the Falcons, a motorcycle club or a railway preservation society.

*   *   *

The local factories that had escaped major destruction tried to manufacture something to sell, no matter what it was. There had been a factory just outside town that built sweet-wrapping machines before the war. During the war it was converted into making parts for U-boats. That must have taken some doing to convert a sweet-wrapping machine into a U-boat component. After the war there was no demand for U-boat parts or sweet-wrapping machines so they started making two-wheel carts. Now that was something everyone could use. The wheels were U-boat steering wheels two feet in diameter. The cost of making these carts was minimal and a few thousand of them were made and mostly used by the *Trümmerfrau* to cart the city's rubble to a dump outside town. Day and night the clanking of iron wheels on cobblestone streets could be heard all over town.

Brother Len got a job in that factory as a toolmaker. Having a paying job away from home in those days was a drain on a family's food resources, as the pay didn't cover even what the worker ate and the job took him away from the garden. The pay was only forty-five Marks a month, about $8 at the time, and factory work in 1946 was hard, with nearly all of the work being done without machinery. The most they could muster was a few sets of acetylene welding units and a drill press. There was no canteen, no washing facilities and the work was forty-eight hours a week. Len's demand from Mum for his eight-hour workday was six double sandwiches with hard black bread and a pat of vile-smelling margarine. Sometimes he got a paper-thin slice of meat and a little jam. In the winter when things were bad, he would get a bowl of a green concoction called oxtail soup. Why it was named that, I don't know. It had nothing in common with the backside of a cow, except maybe the colour and the smell. I never knew what was in it. It was sold in shops out of a big bucket by the spoonful, which you mixed with water and boiled into a soup. It tasted similar to a bouillon cube that had been soaked in cod liver oil.

Chapter 11

After the End: Refugees from Trizonesia and God Bless George Marshall

Before March 1945, the NSV had seen to it that bombed-out citizens and those who were really starving were given a hot meal once a day. It might have been just cabbage soup and two slices of bread or barley porridge, but it was food. This organisation was banned, like anything else Nazi, immediately after the war. The Allies had no intention of allowing this organisation to continue feeding a population that had supported the Nazis and was still filled with Nazi sympathisers. With shops closed and the whole food supply in turmoil, people lived on handouts from those who still had a little more than those who had absolutely nothing. There was no local government, no town council, no school system and no institution to turn to for a loaf of bread. The transportation system was in ruins and things got worse once winter arrived. Farmers who still had a horse or two were, to some extent, able to till their fields, but they had to search their barns for scattered seeds to plant.

After the war, fledgling political groups such as the Social Democrat Party, the Christian Democrats and a few other minor ones set up welfare programmes that had the blessing of the Allied administration. They eventually began taking on some of the former duties of the NSV in 1946. With the promise by the Allies of a future general election, these would-be parties clamoured for support and they knew how to get it. Soup kitchens were set up again, with the NSV labels on the distribution pots having been removed. Not much had changed, except maybe the soup was even worse than before the end of the war. The Allies supplied the Germans with some basic food, but the German cooks, who couldn't read English, didn't know half the time what they were making or how to make it. For instance, soup kitchens were given sacks of biscuit flour. Now, in Germany a biscuit is something like a cookie and there was no yeast, sugar or fat to make cookies, so they invented biscuit-flour soup. That was bad enough, but the flour hadn't been stored well so it was often mouldy and came with a good supply of worms. We also got cornmeal, but we were suspicious of it because it was yellow. German cornmeal was always made from white corn. We soon figured out it was edible, with or without worms.

The Social Democrats used an air-raid shelter near the school as their soup kitchen. The Falcons collected old Wehrmacht mess kits, filled them with soup and added a crust of cornbread, then delivered them to people who could not come to the distribution centre. They never failed to tell the recipient that the food came from the Social Democrats, even though it had first come from the United States. Since the Christian Democrats had been mildly tolerated by the Nazis, former NSV workers were soon drawn to their kitchens. In 1947, the woman in charge of the soup kitchen was the former chairwoman of the NSV in our town. This didn't please the Social Democrats, but the woman did have previous experience. The job (and most of the food) was the same, only the uniform had changed – so much for de-nazification.

Anyone over the age of eighteen, or for that matter even younger, who had served in any service branch of the Reich, went through a de-nazification process that was instituted by the Allies as soon as possible after the surrender. Many thousands slipped through this net and became 'respectable' citizens under the new rulers. We lost half our teachers in town who had been Party members out of necessity. The other half were allowed to resume teaching by the autumn of 1945, but a lot of schools were still closed a year after that. Late in the summer of 1945, our school reopened but most of the teachers were new to us. Our teacher had been discharged from an Allied POW camp in June. He hadn't become a Party member and was relieved of his job early in the war. All teachers during the Third Reich had to be affiliated with the *Nationalsozialistische Lehrerbund* (the National Socialist Teachers Organisation). Most who joined were given a cushy job and those who didn't were put into a Wehrmacht uniform in short order. I guess it's no surprise that by 1944 some classrooms had sixty-plus children for one teacher. Our new teacher had been part of a Luftwaffe ground crew, refuelling fighter planes at an air base near Luneburg.

Many schools had bomb damage and when our school reopened, we were sent home when it rained because of all the holes in the roof. In the winter there was no heat and we were often sent home when the weather was really cold, although it was not much warmer at home. Writing pads were sold by two school supply merchants who demanded a permit signed by the school principal before you could purchase them. To us, that sounded like the way things had always been. Our principal was a refugee from the city of Breslau in Silesia and had not been a Party member. His son, however, had worn the uniform of the SS Totenkopf and soon enough the ever-present Allied agents looking for ex-Nazis were tipped off. A search of the house revealed the son's SS uniform hanging in a closet. Alf, as the son was called, was arrested and went into a POW stockade, then for good measure, they arrested our principal for failing to report his son to the authorities. They released him six weeks later. Alf came back home in 1947 after spending two years in a re-education camp in deepest, darkest Oklahoma. While we were literally scraping the bottom of the barrel to find something to eat, this SS guy was fed white bread, real coffee and Spam, and smoked Chesterfields in a camp near Tishomingo.

*   *   *

The European Recovery Plan (ERP), better known as the Marshall Plan, was not introduced until 1947 and we didn't get our first CARE (Cooperative for American Remittance to Europe) packages of food until the spring of 1948. The years 1945 to 1947 were the worst for us and without some outside assistance, mostly from the United States, a lot more German adults and children would have starved during that time. Help was offered to all European states that had participated in the war, regardless of which side they were on. Even Russia was offered help, but they refused. The Iron Curtain was already coming down between East and West. The ration cards and coupons introduced in September 1939 were still issued, though not in great quantity and without the swastika and eagle on the front. Fresh fruit was not rationed – after all, there were many orchards around and those people who had no fruit to pick and no garden could always jump a fence and pilfer. *Verboten?* Yes it was, but a lot was *verboten* then, even more than during the Third Reich. The civil servants who had made laws while wearing a brown shirt were still making laws. Some eventually died of old age at their posts; others were pensioned off after serving the occupation government for a few years.

When the ERP became operational, things improved slightly. The Caritas Catholic Organisation received CARE parcels and distributed them to the needy. The eastern refugees in the camps were the first in line. They needed assistance more than anyone else. They had no gardens, no work, and lived on handouts and food from former NSV soup kitchens. One day we also got one of these CARE parcels and in anticipation, we crowded around the table to inspect the goodies. Alas, the labels were all in English and to figure out what was in some of the packages required some guessing and tasting. A packet of powdered egg stumped us. We tried boiling it, brewing it and roasting it. We finally gave up and asked a British soldier who was standing guard at the depot across the road what the stuff was. The guard drew a chicken on a piece of paper and an egg under it. When Len came back and showed us the paper, we were none the wiser. Was it powdered chicken or powdered egg? Finally Mum mixed water with it and put the mixture in a frying pan for a few minutes, and there it was – a fried egg. Orange and lemon juice powder was also a challenge.

I had never tasted anything so sour. It took some experimenting before we finally mixed it with enough water and found it to be good to drink.

Black marketeering then became not just a pastime, but a way of life. It was still illegal, but at least they couldn't send you to a concentration camp if you got caught. The police would just confiscate your items in most cases and send you off with a warning. The black marketeers had meeting places, mostly in pubs, and these places were known under code names. The Alfa Hotel and Pub was known as 'The Elastic Corner'. The Black Horse Pub was 'The Dirty Spoon' and the old Brauhaus was 'The Bloody Rooster'. Scores of other seedy trading places were established. They were called 'Puffs' and usually a woman was in charge, called a 'Puff Mutter'. The main currency was Chesterfield, Camel and Lucky Strike American cigarettes, Nescafe instant coffee, or nylon stockings. The girls without a GI boyfriend had to make do with '1A Plus' leg paint, a sort of eyebrow pencil used to draw seams on their legs for the appearance of wearing stockings. When the American GIs left in July 1945 and the British moved in, nothing changed except the cigarettes. They were now Players, Navy Cut, Woodbines or Senior Service and there was more tea than coffee being traded. The British Military Policemen were also more eager to stop and search a suspected black marketeer than the Americans had been.

Most men and a few women smoked when I was a boy and they were issued ration cards for cigarettes, cigars, or loose tobacco with rolling papers. By 1942 the popular brand name was *Sondermischung* (Special Mixture) *R 6*, but what exactly was special about the mixture, nobody knew. When I was younger, nobody smoked in our family except Granddad, and he smoked a pipe. He grew the tobacco himself, dried it and cut the leaves with our bread slicer. Later, even until 1948, the tobacco stalks were also ground up and rolled into cigarettes. Someone always had a few tobacco seeds to swap for a pound of margarine or a linen towel. After March 1945, American brands of cigarettes like Camel, Lucky Strike or Chelsea were for Frauleins only. We had no Frauleins in our family and by that time Granddad Willem had died, so we had no need for tobacco except as trading material.

Some non-smokers rolled cigarettes after the war from the loose tobacco they could get on their ration cards and sold them for twenty Pfennigs each. If you wanted to buy more than twenty, money was not accepted. Payment was then a cabbage, a jar of pickles or even a pair of scissors. The have-nots took to the streets as they always had and picked up cigarette butts and re-rolled them when they had enough. Giant told me after the war that at Christmastime in 1944, he swapped a large jar of pickled onions for forty home-rolled cigarettes. Who knows where the tobacco had come from but he said he was glad to get them.

*   *   *

I remember one day in the winter of 1946 when Brother Len and I went by tram to Düsseldorf to visit an old aunt in Hilden, just east of the city. The area was in shambles due to the continuous bombing of 1943–4. Women were clearing rubble, sorting good bricks from bad, hammering, nailing and cutting half-burned beams for firewood. Their children stood in long queues at open-air kitchens hoping to get a ladle of watery soup and a slice of hard black bread. If they were unlucky, and many were, they went home empty handed and lived with another twenty-four hours of hunger. This aunt in Hilden had a large garden and was a bit of a miser and hoarder. Her husband had been killed in Norway and they had no children. She was nevertheless an energetic person and grew most of her vegetables herself. Brother Len and I did some repair work on her house over the three days we stayed with her and as a reward, she gave us about fifty pounds of potatoes. We had two sacks, one with about twenty pounds in it for me to carry and Len had the heavier one.

We decided to make our way home early on Sunday morning to avoid crowds of beggars and we managed to get from Hilden to the city centre to catch the #14 tram to M-G without a problem. About thirty people were also on the tram, suspiciously eyeing our sacks and no doubt they knew what was in them. We moved to the rear door with our treasures and some of the people edged nearer. Only the stern eye of the conductor kept them at a respectful distance. A woman seated near us whispered to Len, 'Potatoes huh? I'll give you twenty-five Marks for that bag'. Len declined of course, so the woman tried her offer on me. I looked for help to Len and he grabbed my sack and put it under his seat. We eventually disembarked the tram in München-Gladbach without further confrontation, but in order to catch the next one, we had to pass a *Ross Schlächterei* (a horse butcher) and a long line of folks waited by the door to get a pound or two of horsemeat. We quickly marched past with our sacks over our shoulders, but a little girl, about ten or eleven years old pulled at my coat. 'Please, do you have a potato for me?' she asked.

'How do you know I have potatoes in this sack?' I asked in reply.

'I can smell them,' was her answer. 'I'll pay you for some.'

'Pay me? How much?'

'Twenty Pfennigs is all I have, and I only want one potato. My mother is in the horsemeat queue but I don't think she will get any; we were last in the line.'

I dropped the sack. Her eyes, big as saucers in her skinny face, lit up. I took three potatoes out and handed them to the girl.

'And you can keep your twenty Pfennigs.'

Len was mumbling something like 'ungrateful brats', but we went on at a brisk pace and got the #9 tram just in time, before the crowd at the horsemeat shop was told that no more meat was available.

* * *

Brother Len eventually got a new job in a factory that made kitchen stoves. He operated a sheet metal press that made the necessary holes for the fire and ash boxes. With him knowing it all, he used his fingers to remove punched metal sheets when they got stuck in the press instead of using the tool made for the job. One day the press came down before he got his fingers out and both his index fingers were cut off. He was taken to the local hospital and we went to see him that night. Considering the pain it must have caused him, he was in good spirits, but I couldn't help remarking to him that his nose-picking days were over. This meant now that he was exempt from house and garden work for the foreseeable future. He got through six years of war, being shot at by fighter planes and bombed by bombers and never got so much as a scratch and then, a year after the end of the war, he lost two fingers. There were far worse accidents than losing fingers, however. The amount of unexploded German and American ordnance that was just lying around was unbelievable. There were grenades of all shapes and sizes, and artillery and tank cannon shells, but most dangerous of all were the mines and unexploded bombs. Mines were laid by the thousands by both sides during the war. Paths were cleared by engineers during the fighting, but after the war, if you strayed off the path they had cleared, you most certainly bought yourself a ticket to eternity. If you wanted to steal cabbage from a farmer's field in the night, you had to make sure you stayed on a beaten path.

The forests near us were full of mines. It has been estimated that there were 15,000 of them laid in the Hürtgen forest alone. To venture out into this area to collect firewood was strictly prohibited. Mother Nature eventually helped out. During a huge thunderstorm in 1946, lightning set the forest ablaze and most of the mines exploded from the heat. Others in fields and gardens are still being discovered to this day.

On one hot summer day after the war in 1945, Len and I cycled a few miles toward the forest where he had dug anti-tank ditches the year before. We went through the fields because there were cows in them so we figured there must not be any mines about. We rode through the 'Dragon's Teeth' (reinforced concrete tank-traps) and came to a part of the anti-tank ditch that had filled with water. There was no one around, so we decided to have a cool swim in our underwear. I was the first to dive in and a few feet below the surface, I knocked my head on something. I called Len over to have a look. It was a heavy box.

Len and I dragged it to the bank and opened it up. There were several German 'potato-masher' type hand grenades in it. They were a little rusty but we could clearly read the label that said: '*Zündung 7 Sekunden*' (seven-second fuse).

'Let's make a few bangs,' Brother Len suggested.

'You ever thrown one of those things?' I asked.

'No, but I've seen an instructor demonstrating how to do it in HJ camp.'

'Look Len,' I warned, 'we're not in an HJ camp now and there's no instructor, and if it says seven seconds fuse, I bet it will go off in three, so let me get out of the way first.'

I was glad Len took my advice just for once and we carefully slid the box back into the water. That ditch was later filled in with debris from the town and I daresay the box is still there.

The Westwall, or Siegfried Line that had been praised so much by Hitler during the war, and was breached by the Allies in short order, was another source of exploration for us, although it was *verboten*. In Germany everything was (and still is) *verboten*. I recently heard a saying that describes post-war Europe pretty well. 'In England, everything is allowed, except that which is forbidden. In Germany, everything is forbidden except that which is allowed. In Italy, everything is allowed, including that which is forbidden. In Russia, everything is forbidden, including that which is allowed.' One needs to be a lawyer to know what is allowed and what is *verboten* in Germany even today. Anyway, most of these bunkers had been blown to kingdom come by the Americans as soon as they captured the line. They pumped the bunkers full of water and used high explosives to crack the concrete so it could be broken up and hauled away. The Allies didn't find all of them however. I found one in 2004 near a village in the Saar province. It was completely overgrown and not even the owner of the land knew it was there. It was a small bunker, about eighteen by fourteen feet, but the machine-gun mount was still there and a rusty camp bed. Those bunkers that are still in good shape and situated on privately-owned land are used as toolsheds or hay barns, but those on government land are out of bounds – *verboten*. Some are excellent places for growing mushrooms. The railway tunnel that ran to the bridge at Remagen is now a mushroom farm and the bridge towers house a museum.

*   *   *

Just after the war, the first groups of refugees arrived from East Prussia and Silesia. Some had been walking west for a month. As a predominately Catholic region, we naturally looked upon these mostly Protestant transients with suspicion. They were looking for '*Brot und Arbeit*' (bread and work) like everyone else. This was a slogan the Nazis claimed to have invented, but it was the Communists in 1917 who first used it. Hitler, when he came into power, ordered Göring to get the economy going again after the Depression, producing weapons that would be needed in the war he saw coming. This put people to work on a scale that had never been seen in Germany. People bought bread and a lot more. During the war, however, this slogan soon fell flat. Yes, the work was there, but the bread was nowhere in sight. Some wise guy claimed he had overheard a speech by Göring once, saying that there was enough food for all Germans to last for a lifetime. Sure, there was enough I suppose, as long as you didn't eat it or died young. For those who did eat it and didn't die young, there was far from enough bread or anything else to eat for that matter. Another popular slogan of the time was, '*Jeder muß Kartoffel pflanzen*' (Everybody must plant Potatoes). We asked ourselves if that included those with no garden and not even a balcony. Did it include the aged and the infirm, the disabled war veterans, and the children? What about the nurses and doctors who were on call twenty-four hours a day during the worst air raids? You can't grow potatoes in a pot on a windowsill in the city.

'Wheels must turn for victory' was another hollow saying we heard all during the war. By early 1945, the only wheels turning were the wheels on carts and prams being pulled and pushed by the millions of refugees trying to escape the advancing Ivans. There were soup kitchens set up along the way for the refugees (and soldiers too), but there were so many of them, the kitchens couldn't keep up and anywhere civilians or soldiers congregated was a target for the fighter-bombers. Refugees died or were killed by the thousands and had to be left by the roadside. Even though she had a family to feed herself, my Mum joined in and helped the NSV feed as many as possible. We had a hundred-litre (about twenty-five gallon) galvanised steel tub we bathed in which was used to make potato soup for the refugees. They originated from places I had never heard of but I could find them on a map. One group was from the far away Masurian Lake district in eastern Prussia, near the Lithuanian border. We used to describe that area as the country where foxes and hares say 'Good night' to each other in *Kauderwelsch*, which was a mixture of German, Polish and Lithuanian, but they understood my mother's shout of '*Kartoffel Suppe, Kartoffel Suppe*', and lined up in an orderly manner. There was no pushing or queue-jumping; they were too tired after the 600-mile trek.

Mother made simple potato soup for them in our bathtub: ten pounds of potatoes, boiled with the skin on. Five stalks of leek were added along with a few strips of pigs' trotter, pepper, salt, a few handfuls of barley and finally a pound of flour was thrown in to bind the concoction together. The poor people fell on the soup like the French fell on the Saarland after the First World War. More refugees came a few weeks later from Pomerania and Upper Silesia, but eventually, the welcome by local people wore off. The area of Germany occupied by France, the US and the UK, which we called 'Trizonesia', became an overflow destination for people from Upper Silesia. This inspired some clever writer to create the saying, 'We are the occupants of Trizonesia, and you are the displaced mob from Upper Silesia'.

There was not enough housing for our own bombed-out people after the surrender, so some sort of temporary accommodation was needed for all the refugees. The community air-raid shelters were all that was available. They were equipped with metal bed frames and a table or two and the men subdivided the shelters with blankets hanging down from the ceilings. One such shelter near us housed 600 men, women and children. Living conditions were not much better than in a concentration camp. Cooking was done in shifts or food was supplied by local welfare organisations (the former NSV). There were four toilets and four baths for all of them. Many took advantage of the public baths in town rather than wait two weeks for a reservation in theirs. Washing was done using zinc tubs and cold water. There was not enough wood or coal to heat water just for washing clothes. There was nothing for these poor people to do; no radio, no entertainment for the children and no work for the men. Of course the women always had plenty to do. To Brother Len this was a good place to canvass for new Falcon members. Once he gave them the propaganda line about a future socialist government with equality for everyone, the youngsters from ten to sixteen came to the meetings in droves. Not all of them fit in well, claiming they had been a 'von' (higher Prussian society, estate owner) in East Prussia or Silesia. But a von or a Graf (count), or a Freiherr (baron), or a Freiin (baroness) was not treated with any more reverence than the fourteen-year-old boy with the Polish name of Frantek who had arrived without any relatives or parents and only knew his home city had been Elbing.

I took Frantek to the next Falcons meeting. We had somehow acquired a table tennis set from somewhere and a few musical instruments so there was some entertainment for youngsters. It turned out that Frantek was an excellent table tennis player and a year later he helped the Falcon team win the local trophy and get into the regional league. I asked him what had happened to his parents on the trek from Poland. At first he wouldn't answer, but a week or so later, when I took him to our home and we shared a meagre meal of fried potatoes and onions, he opened up. The story he told us made our hair stand on end. We knew that the Russians had taken terrible revenge on the German population once they crossed the border into the old Reich, but we never knew the details.

Frantek and his mother (his father had been missing in action since 1943) had left Elbing with a large group of other refugees on a cold and snowy January day in 1945 and took to a road that was supposed to take them to the Vistula River. The Soviet Army was twenty miles south of them at the time. The group was moving in a westerly direction and making about fifteen miles per day. Frantek estimated there were about 500 people in that trek, some pushing prams, some with hand carts and some with just a bundle slung over their shoulders. On their second day out, during a blinding snowstorm, they heard the sound of engines and the clanking of tracks to the south. Occasionally they could also hear cannon and machine gun fire. Then suddenly the dark shapes of Russian T-34 tanks appeared out of the blizzard, and seeing the trek, they opened up with all they had, raking the group from left to right with machine guns. The tanks just smashed into the humanity and rolled forward and back over prams with babies in them, over men, women and children and their carts. Those who could still run managed to reach a forest a mile or so to the north. The blinding snowstorm prevented the tanks from chasing them. They turned east and disappeared into the whiteness. Hundreds were killed. The badly injured froze to death.

Frantek never knew what happened to his mother. He just ran and never looked back. He finally met up with another trek going west and stayed with them all the way to Berlin. There he joined another group that eventually brought him to our area. Many other refugees had similar tales to tell and just how many died or were murdered on these frozen treks will never be known, but estimates run into the hundreds of thousands. Eventually over seven million refugees arrived in the four zones of Germany. By 1950, many thousands had emigrated to countries like Argentina, Brazil, the United States and Canada. All these people fleeing the Russians had to be fed somehow. It was impossible to give them a decent place to live, so a lot of them moved into two-room pre-fabricated huts, but at least they had a roof over their heads and a small cooking stove to prepare a meal and could keep reasonably warm in the cold winter months. The winter of 1946/47 was brutally cold. At times, the temperature in the mountains fell to -40°C. Welfare organisations worked overtime but with the limited amount of food they had, it was necessary to return to the substitutes that were used the year before. Dishes were invented that no one would touch today. I remember in that winter we had crow once. Even after cooking the thing for twenty-four hours, it was still as tough as old leather, but it was protein. With hardly any meat or fats, people ate what was available.

Chapter 12

1946 Road Trip

By mid-1946, most schools in Germany had reopened and the clearing-up of destroyed cities had begun. There was no rebuilding yet because of the lack of cement and skilled labour. Food was more important than cement, and besides, most of the cement-making facilities had been destroyed during the war or were being dismantled by the Russians for shipment east. At the Yalta Conference, Stalin demanded that Russia be compensated for the ruins the Germans had left behind during their stay and cement factories were high on his list. Churchill and Roosevelt agreed, so as soon as peace was declared, the dismantling of German factories began. Cars and trucks, those that were left, began to disappear until the only vehicles remaining were a few Holzvergasers no one wanted.

Brother Len used Dad's old bicycle to get around. Gunny borrowed it just after the war, but brought it back later that year after he started his black-market business in scrap copper. Dad got the bike from the local military occupation office and used it to get to work. He had to be at work as a tram driver by 6:00 a.m. and it was four miles to the depot. With the help of a school friend named Robert, who later emigrated to Canada, I was able to build a bicycle out of parts we collected. It was a bit rusty and the tyres were water hoses, but it got me around. Easter 1946 was around the third weekend in April and we got a sixteen-day vacation from school. Brother Len was out of work with his amputated fingers, so we decided to take a bicycle tour of the Fatherland, or at least part of it. So with our parent's blessing, we loaded our bikes with everything we thought we would need and took off in search of adventure. I can't imagine today why they let us do that, but we were growing up and had shown them that we were responsible kids. We took two ex-military tent halves, our old quilts and a sheet for a sleeping bag, two mess tins with cups, a very small *Spiritus* (alcohol) stove, and some black bread and marmalade. Len said that if worse came to worse and we couldn't find any food, we could always break into a turnip bunker. He didn't think it would come to that because April is a busy time for farmers and they were very short on labour. He thought that most of them would be glad to feed us in exchange for a day's work.

The weather was glorious when we set off and headed south. Our intention was to get to the Rhine and cross somewhere if we could find a rebuilt bridge. Neither of us had ever seen high mountains and Len suggested a route through the foothills of the Alps. The first day was pure torture. Having no real tyres on our bikes, every pothole rattled our teeth, and there were lots of potholes to be found in 1946. We did forty miles that day, made it to Cologne and set up camp right by the river. We found no bridge the next day so we pedalled on along the left bank until we came to Linz. There we found a ferry in operation that took us across. The ferry master warned us that we were entering the American zone of occupation and that they had checkpoints searching for war criminals.

'Do we look like war criminals?' Len asked.

'No,' he replied, 'but nevertheless, the *Amis* are very strict when it comes to people crossing from one zone into another.'

'Well, we'll take our chances, and we're only going to Bavaria to visit an old aunt,' Len lied.

'With those bikes you won't even get to Frankfurt,' a nosy passenger chimed in.

'We are cycling experts and we have plenty of spare parts,' Len continued to lie.

This bantering went on until the ferry reached the eastern bank. There were no checkpoints there, but nevertheless we decided to go off the main highway and take a secondary road. Our map was from an old school atlas with very few details, but at least it showed the major cities, highways and mountains, and we knew which way south was. Near Idstein we called at a farm and begged for a bite to eat. The farmer's wife took pity on us and gave us a sandwich. In those days, thousands of people were roaming the countryside; refugees, drifters, homeless people and ex-Eastern POWs who had no intention of going back to Soviet-occupied Latvia, Lithuania or Poland. Some of them even asked the police for help and often they got an empty cell, a straw mattress, a cup of some kind of coffee and a slice of bread for the night. We considered ourselves lucky, having two bicycles and a few Reichsmarks in our pockets and above all, a place to go home to if things didn't turn out well. Call it an adventure, but the whole war had been an adventure for us, and Len for one, was sorry to see it end – especially with us on the losing side. Sometimes, in hilly country, we had to dismount and push our bikes along the road. We met lots of refugees with bags and parcels strapped to their backs. I'll never forget one couple we met south-east of Frankfurt headed east. The man about thirty-five years old and his wife or girlfriend was about thirty. Both were covered in dust and their clothes were filthy, but they were quite cheerful. After greeting them with a '*Guten Morgen*', we inquired where they were headed.

'We're on our way to Arnstadt in Thuringia,' the man answered.

'But that's in the Russian zone,' Len said, 'who wants to live there'?

'We've been drifting since the autumn of 1945,' the man said. 'Nobody wants us. I haven't been able to find work and we have nowhere to stay. All I have is a relative in Arnstadt, so we're making our way east.'

'Where do you sleep and how do you eat?' I asked.

'We stay in hay barns and beg for food or look for soup kitchens,' the woman, named Grete, answered.

We travelled along with them toward Aschaffenburg and near dusk we spotted a haystack in a field. There was no farm to be seen, so all four of us headed toward the stack. The hay smelled musty and was wet, but the man, his name was Peter, pulled some hay from the bottom of the stack until he found the way to the rick (frame) underneath. There was room under it for all of us and we shared a couple of sandwiches with them. We had no coffee powder – besides, making a fire for hot water in a haystack would be asking for trouble. At 7:00 a.m., we crawled out from the stack and made our way back to the road. We said goodbye to Peter and Grete and wished them well with the Bolsheviks in Arnstadt.

We had been on the road for five days. The Alps, Len's destination, were still far to the south and we were heading south-east according to our map.

'What are we going to do if ever we get to the Alps?' I asked him.

'Just see the mountains and look around.'

'Look Len, we only have eleven days left before school starts again, we aren't even near Bavaria, and this bike riding is killing me. I need a good wash. I'm full of hay seed and I'm hungry.'

Len consulted the map and agreed with me, but he said we would do two more days going south and then turn back. I had something to add to that. 'We still have twenty Marks; why not go by train? Bike transport is free on trains and we can have a wash in a station washroom.'

'Okay, we'll try that,' Len agreed, to my surprise.

We asked some locals in a village if there was a train station nearby and luckily, there was one only a few miles north, near Hasloch, I think. We bought two tickets for Schweinfurt. Rail travel was cheap then and our bicycles travelled in the baggage car free. We had an hour and twenty minutes to wait, so we looked for the *Aborten* (public toilet). There was a cast-iron water trough with a tap so we had a good wash, with cold water of course, and dried ourselves with our spare shirts. Food was only available with ration cards and we didn't have any. Begging was out; railway police watched everyone that came into the canteen area.

'It's like the Gestapo all over again,' Len said, with a nod toward two men dressed in black with railway badges on their caps.

We pushed our bikes to the platform after purchasing our tickets to Schweinfurt. After an hour, the train puffed its way into the station. The baggage car was right behind the coal car and a porter loaded our bikes into it. There were only four cars behind the engine. They were all third class with wooden seats. The passengers were mostly city folk with their bags containing cabbage, greens or clothing. Some, despite the warm spring weather, were wrapped up to their ears in coats and jackets to avoid carrying them. It was hard to even see their faces. It took two and a half hours to get to Schweinfurt. The main railway station there had no roof. The destruction in the city was still visible three years after the heavy raids on the SKF ball-bearing factories. We left the station on our bikes about 3:30 p.m. heading for Bamberg. In a forest near a town called Oberaubach we made camp near a creek, put up our tent halves and ate two sandwiches we had scrounged from a soup kitchen along the road and washed them down with acorn coffee we made using water from the creek. It was an eerie night. We were far off the beaten track and nowhere could we see any lights. Len had a large pocketknife as our only weapon. We felt like the trappers of the American Old West we used to read about. Early the next morning we set off again and, according to our map, we were heading for Bayreuth.

'That's where that Wagner guy was from,' I said to Len.

'Yeah, but we won't get a handout from them,' he answered.

'Len,' I pleaded, 'if we are that badly off, why don't we just turn toward home now?'

'We have plenty of time, don't worry.'

'What worries me is my stomach, I'm starving and begging at soup kitchens won't get us much.'

'Trust me, I'll find us something,' he mumbled.

Well, I didn't have much choice, so I just kept pedalling. I didn't worry too much though; Len was an expert in finding food. On the road, we found a can of grease in a ditch that came in mighty handy for lubricating our wheels' bearings and chains. We passed by a lumber camp and a huge *Büssing* truck loaded with tree trunks was waiting to pull out onto the road. The driver bade us a good morning and asked us where we came from and our destination. We told him we were going to Bayreuth and that it would be nice if he would give us a lift if he was heading that way. He said he wasn't going to Bayreuth but was on his way to a sawmill near Ochsenkopf (Ox Head), which was a village in the Fichtel Mountains. Len told him that would be okay, as we were on a vacation trip to see an old relative and wouldn't mind the detour. Glad to have some company, he lifted our bikes and tied them on top of the treetrunks. We climbed into the cab and off we went leaving a cloud of diesel smoke behind us. He stopped at a butcher's shop in a small village on the way and came out with a pound of *Pannas* for us. He told us that during the war he drove a supply truck on the Eastern Front and had made his way west when the Oder front collapsed. His home was in Kronach. We got to the sawmill that afternoon and thanked him for the ride and food. As soon as we got on our bikes, it started to rain. It wasn't a hard rain so we kept going, but after a few miles, we were soaked.

'What now Len?'

'Well, I think we'll go south one more day and then turn for home by a different route.'

I looked at the map and realised, 'We're almost in Czechoslovakia, Len.'

'We'll turn back before we get there,' he reassured me.

'Okay, as long as we get home before the Easter holiday is over, and by the way Len, today is Good Friday and it'll be Easter in two days. What are we going to do for Sunday?'

'I'll find out if there's a Falcon Club somewhere near here. I'll ask at the next town we come to. The Falcons will help us,' Len said confidently. We went another dozen or so kilometres that day and finally rolled into a town called Wunsiedel. There wasn't much war damage to be seen. At the local police station, we told the officer on duty that we were on a vacation tour and Len showed him his ID card from the Falcon Club. He informed us that we were in the American Zone without a permit, but since we were youngsters, he would let us off. There was no Falcon Club in Wunsiedel, but he directed us to a large refugee camp in an old building where we might get a hot meal, a wash, and a mattress to sleep on.

We told the man in charge of the camp that we had been on the road all day and asked if we could stay the night. He said something under his breath about Rhinelander refugees that we didn't understand, but a woman came and told us it would be okay if we stayed for the night. There was even warm water and a plate of fried potatoes, bacon, a fried egg and hot cocoa. This was fine dining for a couple of waifs like us.

'So that's how they live here in Bavaria', Len said, 'I'd like to stay here.'

'And I want to go home the day after Easter. I need another shirt, my coat is full of grease, and we have pedalled for three days in the rain. I can't understand this funny Bavarian accent either, so I just want to head home.'

'All right, this is as far as we go. We'll just explore the countryside around here over Easter and then head west to Bayreuth.'

'With a little luck, we'll be able to catch another ride with a truck driver.'

'We can take a train, if things don't work out, okay?'

'A train ride home suits me just fine.'

We explored the town on that Saturday before Easter and pedalled up and down the old cobblestone roads. There was even a decorated Easter tree in the middle of town by the *Rathaus* (city hall). A cafe was open selling cakes on ration coupons and serving *ersatz* coffee. After the bath the night before in the refugee camp, we looked quite respectable among all the homeless folks. A soup kitchen was dishing out food for those without coupons – and the soup wasn't sauerkraut. The local Bavarians were quite friendly to us outsiders. The Americans had designated the town as a tourist attraction for their soldiers. One of the prominent citizens of the town was at the same time in the dock at Nürnberg, accused of crimes against humanity: Rudolf Hess. Some of the accused in Nuremberg were hanged without, what we thought at the time, evidence of guilt, but there were much more important things for the ordinary German to worry about. The news was in the papers every day but we were sure it was mostly written for foreign readers.

That night we stayed again at the camp but we were up at 7:00 a.m. the next day; after all, it was Easter Sunday and everyone who could walk was going to church and we joined them. About 10:00 a.m., after church, we decided to head south for a few hours. Going east was out of the question; the Russians were only twelve miles away in that direction. The area around the Fichtel Mountains was similar to the countryside near our Eifel Mountains back home; rolling hills and deep forests, with farms in every valley. Somehow, we managed to get ourselves a little lost while exploring some of the trails off the main road. When we heard dogs barking in the distance, we thought we had strayed too close to the Russians. We pushed our bikes through the undergrowth and changed course to the west. We came upon a patch of broken trees that we couldn't get through, so we had to try to go around the splintered forest. Len found a broken wheel of some sort and declared it to be part of an aircraft, but I wasn't so sure.

'There's no airfield around here, Len,' I told him, 'it must be from a lumber wagon or something.'

'Not with this sort of tyre; this is a plane wheel.'

We searched the area and soon found twisted pieces of corrugated metal that told us this was an aeroplane crash site, which also explained why all the trees were broken the way they were. It was a big Junkers 52 transport plane. We found more pieces in the underbrush, an engine, rudder parts and lots of parts we couldn't identify. The plane must have crashed without catching fire, as we didn't see any burned trees in the area. By this time a lot of bushes had grown up, covering the scattered aircraft parts. No one had found the plane because it was in a forest of several hundred square miles and things could easily go unnoticed. Among the fallen trees, we discovered some steel and wooden boxes, but not a single Reichsmark. Neither did we find any bodies or evidence that anyone had died in the crash. We did find lots of official-looking papers from the Wehrmacht however. We decided to liberate as many of these as we could roll up in our tent halves and travel with. We didn't know what we were going to do with them but they were free and looked important. Len came up with the brilliant idea of selling them to the foreigners who had come to Nürnberg for the war crimes trials. We were only a day from there, he thought, and the stuff might fetch a few Marks.

'We've not even had a close look at that stuff, Len, so how do we know for sure it's important?'

He could see my point, but he was nevertheless certain that we should keep the papers, and we did. We stayed overnight in that forest among the squirrels and other unknown creatures. The next day was Easter Monday. We finally found a trail that led us out of the forest and we made it back to Bayreuth again by sunset. It had been a very long and tiring thirty-mile trip.

Tuesday found us in Franconia, Switzerland. In a wide valley, we stopped at a farm and asked the farmer if he had any work for us. We were about out of money and would be hungry soon. We needed work for a day or two before continuing our journey. The farmer had work for us to do, loading turnips and straw from the field. It was hard work but we knew we would at least get a good meal or two and maybe a little money as well. The farmer had an old single-cylinder Bulldog Lanz tractor to pull the cart as we loaded it. We worked until Wednesday, got good meals, and slept in a room above the hay in the barn. He even paid us twenty Marks before we left. We thanked the farmer and pedalled off for Bamberg, which was about twelve miles away. From there we caught a train to Frankfurt and got a connection to Cologne. We arrived in Cologne on Friday morning and that put us only about thirty miles from home. I was glad to be home and everyone was glad to see Len and me. School was to start the following Monday and I really didn't mind going back. We still had the papers we took from the Junkers 52 and we stored them in boxes in the attic. I wish I could find my way back to that plane crash now. In later years, I discovered that these documents were from one of seven planes that left Berlin for Munich in April 1945. Six of the planes made it but the seventh did not and no one bothered looking for it after the war. It was just another plane crash and there were thousands of those all over Germany.

Looking back now, I think that vacation with Len in 1946 was the greatest adventure of my life that didn't involve being shot at. Even our bikes did a great job in getting us around. We finally burned those tent halves in late 1946 but if I had known then what they would be worth today, I would have collected all I could find.

Chapter 13

Epilogue

Germany was then, and still is, a socialist country with more useless bureaucracy and laws than any other, including the former Soviet Union. Most laws that existed before the Second World War made good sense to the German people, but after 1940 the Gauleiters wrote their own rules, submitted them to Göring and with Hitler's blessing and approval, they became law. These laws were no joke although no one could figure out where they came from. Houses were built by the thousands when Hitler became Chancellor and loans were made interest-free. Any bank that charged interest on a house loan was breaking the law and subject to being closed down. No one knew how banks stayed in business, but the Nazis made sure they did. It's hard to imagine why the installation of central heating was forbidden by law in 1938, but it was. Radiators and even furnaces themselves were soon banned, so most houses installed the old-fashioned ceramic tile stoves. The small stoves were most often in the hallway, surrounded by ceramic tiles built up from floor to ceiling with a door to get to the fireplace. It would heat the whole house and many houses in modern Germany still use them. Another law required that six-inch pipes for drainage had to be used. Cast-iron pipes disappeared into the smelters and ceramic piping was introduced as a replacement.

Germany has never been a country that could sustain itself in food production and times got hard during the war for people at home. In the beginning (1939–40), things weren't so bad. Rations were adequate, but with most able-bodied men in uniform, labour was scarce. Farmers' sons, who were at first exempt from service, were called up and in their places came POWs. They worked for their food, not for their freedom, and their work, for obvious reasons, was never satisfactory. As an example, I had a friend here in the States from Westford, Massachusetts who was captured at Salerno in 1943 and spent his POW years on a farm in Pomerania. He told me that the German farm overseer gave him the name '*Schweinhund*' because he wouldn't work any harder than he absolutely had to. Another friend of mine from London was captured on Crete in May 1941. He spent his POW years in the Alkette factory in Berlin, a place where half-tracks were built, and he said he was very well treated. The food was good and he had the same meals in the mess hall as the

German workers, but of course when his shift was over, he was escorted back to the POW camp. Bob, my friend from Westford, was in the group of former prisoners led by American Colonel Hurley Fuller that made its way to the west at the end to the war. Sadly, both Bob and Maurice, my friend from London, are gone now.

'Papers please' is heard a lot more today in Germany than it ever was during the Third Reich. Identification cards are mandatory and you will pay a fine if you don't produce yours when asked by an official. Every inhabitant, whether a year old or 101, has to be registered with their name, address, religion and occupation at their local government registration office. These records are kept and if you move twenty-five yards up the road or 250 miles away, you must go to the registrar's office and fill out several forms. The German government keeps an eye on its citizens. The people in the registration office are even called *Ordnungspolizei* (Order Police) which is the same title used during the Nazi period and they regulate everything from the size of a gravestone to the colour of your roof tiles. During the war, this type of regulation was taken for granted because the people realised there was a war on that had to be won, but the mindset never changed after the war was over; it was just in hibernation. Today some people in Germany are asking themselves if they still live in the democracy that was created with such fanfare in 1949. I wonder how an American farmer would react if some government official told him that his seed potatoes had to be at least three inches in diameter.

* * *

Queuing for hours to get a little food was dangerous business if it was good flying weather. Only long after the war did I realise clearly that civilians, as much as the soldiers, were in the front line. Bombing cities from the air was regarded as 'Terror Strikes' by the Party, meant only to kill innocent civilians. This was total war and – make no mistake – civilians might not have done the fighting but they made it possible for the soldier to do his job and civilians were targeted by both sides. Whether it was a thousand-bomber raid on Hamburg or a 150-bomber raid on Coventry, or even an atomic bomb on Hiroshima, it made no difference; civilians died. Ten-year-old kids from the Hitler Youth working at flak positions were the hunters one minute, helping shoot down enemy planes, and the next minute they were the hunted as they stood in line for food. Farmers in fields who grew food for the soldiers and women in factories that made ammunition were targets as well. In a few years, when the last Second World War veteran is gone, the revisionists will have a field day with their theories, but I lived through that time. I know what total war is like. The objective of the German total war effort was to involve every citizen of the Reich in killing the enemy and everyone who supported the enemy, and to destroy everything that supported the enemy until there was no more enemy. That's not the way wars are fought today and it might just be that more people are killed because of it, and the reason that few things are settled by it.

Since everyone in our village had a garden or rented a vegetable patch, we were spared the very worst of the famine that lasted for two years after the war. Everyone did have to be careful when digging in their gardens however, to avoid being blown up by an unexploded mine or bomb. Many gardeners and farmers were maimed or even killed by those hidden leftovers from the war. On one of my recent walks across our old battlefields in the Hürtgen Forest, I found two horses grazing peacefully next to a stack of 150mm rockets from a German *Nebelwerfer*. I saw a farmer's cart that was standing rusted in the fields and noticed that its two wheels were from a 37mm anti-tank gun. Just outside Wiltz, overgrown by thorn bushes, I found an American howitzer in a roadside ditch, totally rusted but complete. The house where we lived was demolished in the late 1960s to make room for a block of condos. I've often wondered if they found our earthen air-raid shelter during the excavation, and what happened to the ammunition, pieces of shrapnel and air rifles Len and I hid there.

The war did teach us children of the Reich one essential thing: never take it for granted that you will not go hungry someday. I still have a garden and I make it the same way my granddad taught me. The vegetables we grew then would today be called 'organically grown' because all our fertilizer came from the compost heap. Today, those words don't mean too much except maybe in the price paid. We grew healthy food then without chemical fertilizer, although we would have used it if it was available and if it would have made our plants produce more food. Commercial growers today really don't have a choice but to use chemical fertilizer. Hobby gardeners like myself do. There were no such gardeners when I was a boy and no one grew flowers. You can't live on tulips, but we did discover that Nasturtium (Tropaeolum) leaves do make a nice salad. I remember one GI after the war saying that you could take a German and drop him in the Sahara Desert and give him two buckets of water a day, a spade of camel manure and a handful of seeds and he will have a garden in a few months. That's not much of an exaggeration.

I still preserve and store enough food to last me for several months and my mother's recipes are still being used to prepare it for the table. The Americans I have talked with who lived through the Great Depression are not so very different from the Germans who lived through the Second World War and survived the peace that came afterward.

*   *   *

München–Gladbach, as it was called then (the name was changed in 1960 to Mönchengladbach), was the city nearest to us with a fighter base just to the east. Hugo Junkers, the aircraft designer was born there, and Goebbels was born in the M-G suburb of Rheydt. Several thousand Jews lived in the city in 1938, but they were all deported to the East within a few years. The city could also rightly claim that it was the first town to have an air raid not aimed at industrial targets but at the population itself. In May 1940, forty RAF Wellington bombers attacked the city and killed scores of people. The British excuse at the time was that the main railway station was in the centre of the city, with a huge flak tower next door, and that the railway station had been the real target. We didn't believe it and we wouldn't have believed it even without our propaganda that called it a terror raid.

The Burgomeister of M-G was Werner Keyßner and he was a high-ranking NSDAP member from the early years of the Party. The city was bombed several times toward the end of the war, but the most destructive raids were in the autumn of 1944 and on 1 February 1945. It must be said however, that Keyßner saved the city from total destruction in 1945. On Hitler's orders, cities in the front line were to be turned into fortified positions, but Keyßner refused to sacrifice the city in the face of overwhelming forces. He was imprisoned after the war until 1948 and later became a representative of the Free Democratic Party (FDP) in M-G. Aachen had declared itself a fortress in October 1944 and had paid the price. It was substantially destroyed by US artillery. M-G was forty miles north-east of Aachen, and fifteen miles from the Rhine, and much larger than 'Fortress Aachen'. Keyßner was no 'Nettelbeck', and the US Army occupied the city in March 1945 without much ado. Joachim Nettelbeck had successfully defended 'Fortress Kolberg' against Napoleon Bonaparte in 1807 and his name was often brought up by the Party toward the end of the war. Dr. Goebbels was not amused when he heard the news of his home town's capture without a fight and he supposedly ordered Werewolves to assassinate Keyßner, but nothing came of it. About 65 per cent of M-G was destroyed during the war, but it was rebuilt from the ashes and is today once again a prosperous metropolis. The city's cathedral still stands proudly on a high hill and there are two major railway stations, an American football team and a hundred-year-old championship soccer team, Borussia.

The area west of M-G could be a gold mine today for tourists in search of unexplored Second World War locations. The city itself only has the high bunker as a memento, but just outside the city are many wartime fortifications; the Westwall was only a few miles away. There are still numerous bunkers around and the line of 'Dragon's Teeth' can be followed for many miles. Deep in the forest the foxholes and trenches are still visible and a track from a

Sherman tank is still embedded in a footpath. Most bunkers have been closed, or are too dangerous to go in. One, just outside the village of Bergstein, has been explored by many visitors even though a sign is posted warning of the dangers involved. Another bunker, on top of Hill 400 is closed altogether. Any GI who fought in the area in 1944–5 remembers Hill 400, known as the 'eye' of the German artillery. It was eventually taken by a US Ranger outfit in February 1945 after five months of wrangling with the German defenders. Ernest Hemingway named it 'Dead Man's Hill' after that infamous French Hill '*Mort Homme*'. Not too far away is the large Second World War open-air museum at Overloon; a must-see for any historian. The ex-fighter base is still there and proudly displays one of the very few Junkers 52s still in operation.

*   *   *

When I left school in 1950, I wanted to be an electrician or a heating engineer. The cold winters of the past few years probably had something to do with that, but heating was still primarily done with fireplaces and there wasn't much of a future there. Electricity and plumbing technology, however, was always progressing. I got a job in Cologne with a starting salary of twenty-five Deutschmarks a month, about $15 at the time. On weekends, Brother Len and I scoured the countryside for scrap metal and there was plenty to be found. Good prices were paid by scrap-metal dealers who didn't have trucks to collect the stuff themselves. In one week, I could make more than my job paid in a month. Our 'truck' was one of the wooden carts made in our town with wheels that were to have been submarine steering wheels. First we pulled up the thick copper cables at our old flak positions, and then later we searched the forests for abandoned and destroyed weapons, always in fear of stepping on a mine. We left ammunition where we found it, but burned out Wehrmacht trucks, iron girders, and old lead batteries were salvaged. Our ex-Gunnery Sergeant had a wood-burning truck and would take our scrap to the smelter for a share of the profit.

The Monschau area, Losheimer Graben and Elsenborn, from which the Battle of the Bulge was launched, is only an hour away from where we lived. The whole path of the advance can be followed. The Elsenborn highway displays a sign which reads, 'Highway to Hell' in English. A Panther tank is proudly mounted on a concrete plinth in Houfalize, and a monstrous King Tiger tank in La Gleize, the village where Jochen Peiper's battlegroup met its end in December 1944. Then there are the cemeteries – American just over the borders of Belgium and Luxembourg, German along the Westwall. The one near Vossenack in the Hürtgen forest is the burial place of General Walter Model. American General George Patton is buried in Ham, just outside

Luxembourg City. Vossenack has a military museum that is well worth a visit and a short walk downhill leads to the Kall Trail, which is a narrow path that rang the death knell for many US Sherman tanks. The Mestrenger Mill house, known by many US wounded, was rebuilt and is now a restaurant, accessible only by a narrow trail.

A reunion of ex-Wehrmacht and GIs who had fought over the area was held in 2004 on the 60th anniversary of the battle and a memorial, dedicated to both sides, was unveiled and now stands on the parapet of the Kall Bridge. I attended the dedication service. Seventeen American and forty or so German veterans were there. After the service, we all proceeded to the Mill Restaurant and had a splendid time. Some of the men strolled around the area to find the foxhole they had dug during that wet and cold November in 1944. An 86-year-old US veteran, who was a young lieutenant commanding a tank platoon in 1944, told of the misery and complications involved in getting his platoon down that narrow path. In one spot, American engineers had to blow a rock from a sharp turn so his Sherman could get around. The exact spot is still a dangerous curve for cars. The Germans avoided sending tanks into the forest. They had six years to explore the area before the battle and kept their armour on the few available roads. They also had plenty of mobile anti-tank guns concealed in bunkers and minefields to make life hell for the Americans. It truly was 'Hell in the Hürtgen Forest' as the GIs described it.

The American soldiers who occupied our area from the 102nd Infantry, nicknamed the Ozarks, didn't know that in March they would soon come across one of the most horrendous Nazi crimes committed outside a concentration camp. Although this didn't happen in our area, it was discovered by the same 102nd that occupied M-G. The Ozarks had only arrived in Europe in December 1944 and had fought their way across the Rur River. They had seen their fair share of fighting and in mid-April the division approached the town of Gardelegen. Inside the city were over a thousand inmates from Dora-Mittelbau. They were in the process of being moved to Neuengamme. The guards, on hearing that the US Army was only a few miles away, drove the prisoners into a huge barn and set fire to it. Only a handful escaped the inferno. The 102nd found the charred bodies a few days later, and the American Regimental Colonel ordered all able-bodied civilians of the area to give the dead a decent burial. The town is probably the only one in Germany where an American military order is still in effect. The order is posted at the cemetery and reads:

Here lie the bodies of 1016 men who were murdered by their captors. They were buried by the citizens of Gardelegen, who are hereby charged with the responsibility of maintaining their graves. The memory of these unfortunates will be kept in the hearts of freedom loving men everywhere.

This order is given by the commander of the 102nd Infantry Division, United States Army. Vandalism will be punished with the maximum penalties allowed by the military government.

Frank A. Keating, Major General
USA, Commanding

So, what did we, the so-called 'Children of the Third Reich', learn from the war? I can only speak for myself and say that I learned a great deal, and I'm sure others did as well. Some apparently didn't learn much, however, and continued believing the Nazi propaganda they had heard for years. We learned how to survive in depressing and dangerous circumstances. The war itself, the early Wehrmacht victories, our armaments rolling to the fronts, and even the enemy bombers dropping their loads, were all part of a great adventure to us youngsters. We shouted 'Sieg Heil' and 'Hurrah' when an enemy plane came down in flames. When bombs missed their targets and exploded somewhere in a field, we danced and pointed fingers at the bombers. We stood to attention at funerals when one of our comrades died during a raid. Above all, we tried our very best to get on with life. I still hoard things that are essential for survival. We never run out of food. We grow our own and preserve it and we hole up when the weather is bad. We watch while others invade grocery shops and buy emergency food that will be thrown away in a few days.

The veterans of the Second World War on both sides are rapidly disappearing and it is left to those remaining to write down the things they can still remember. First-hand accounts may not be perfect but they can contribute to the full story when it's finally told. The war claimed lives long after the shooting stopped. Hospitals were understaffed or in ruins and doctors who had served in the Wehrmacht were either in POW camps or dead. It was a long time before the Allies sorted out who had been Party members or collaborators and they were not in much of a hurry. Our large local hospital in Krefeld had been bombed despite the huge red cross on the roof. The top two stories were demolished and open to the whims of the weather. The St. Theresa Children's Hospital was in ruins. It had taken a direct hit in mid–February 1945, killing seven nurses and eighteen children. It was never rebuilt and the site is now a parking lot which surely covers the remains of many innocent dead.

To end the story told here, I should say more about an important character who followed along with no concern for bombs or wars, but who became a victim nevertheless. Little Fred, being only three-and-a-half years old at the end of the war, knew nothing but bombs and hunger his entire life. He was even born during an air raid and grew accustomed to the alarms and the explosions. As young as he was, he walked around the village on his own at times and everyone knew him. It was a full-time job keeping him under control. He talked to everyone and everything he met, including horses and cows. We couldn't understand half of what he said, but I suppose the animals could; they looked at him, standing by the fence, with their big animal eyes. Bringing up babies in those years, it was a never-ending job searching for something to feed them.

Fred was brought up on watery milk and soaked oats, and by the time he was ready for normal food, he got the same as the rest of us, only mashed up and mixed with cod liver oil. Life did not get any better for babies until well after 1948 and many died as a result of undernourishment and other ailments that young children got during that time. Baby Fred was one of them; he died in 1947 after becoming so weak he simply quit eating altogether. He was only six years old. I didn't realise there was anything wrong with him. He looked and acted like anyone else his age, but Mum knew he was getting weaker by the day. My parents took him to the partially bombed-out St. Theresa Children's Hospital in Krefeld, but there was not much they could do for him; it was too late. There were hundreds of children in the same condition and the ones who survived were older and stronger than Fred. We older kids somehow scraped through all this with minor problems, although none of us were what you could call healthy. And whatever happened to Brother Len? He died in Germany in 1986, long after his anti-tank ditches were gone, filled in after the war with rubble from our destroyed town.

An entire generation of German children's growth was stunted and I bet that one could find records proving it. Fred was buried in the children's section of Krefeld's main cemetery. Under German law, all graves were (and still are) removed after thirty years unless someone pays for the ground and only rich people could afford it after the war. It was a simple funeral; that's the only kind of funeral anyone had at the time. There were many of them every day, so they were not marked as special events and it was rare for anyone but the immediate family to attend. I still think of him now and then and wonder what he would have become if he had survived. My mother, Agnes Zander Gehlen, was buried in the same cemetery after she was killed by a drunk driver in 1968. The cemetery doesn't exist today and I've not been back there for over thirty years. The only thing left in remembrance of any of my relatives is a memorial plot for victims of the air raids of February 1945.

Recent nightmares like the attack of 11 September 2001 have replaced the imagery from world wars, but those who fought in and lived through them will never forget what total war really is. The ghosts of the Second World War are still around, but you have to look for them. They are not in front of your eyes every day as they were for us when the war ended. The bunkers and the trenches are not all gone and remain as visible legacies of battles fought more than seventy years ago.

Finally, we have the cemeteries, Allied and German, and most are well cared for by those who have loved ones there and by those who will someday join their comrades in that hallowed ground. Graves of known and unknown soldiers are added every year as remains are found in battlefields across Europe.

A small plaque placed on one of the graves in the Hürtgen Forest says it all:

To my beloved son; since your eyes closed, mine have not ceased crying.

Your loving mother

Appendix

Recipes from the Reich

A lthough there are numerous recipes included here, I advise the reader not to recklessly indulge in eating some of the things we ate in those times. We survived without too many problems, but I doubt that a 21st-century person could live healthily on what we had to eat. If you do try some of my mother's recipes and feel unwell afterward, don't blame me; for some of them I wouldn't recommend myself, but we did live on such things and so did millions of other Germans. A few recipes you will recognise, but you might not know how they were prepared seventy-plus years ago with only basic and sometimes improvised ingredients.

*   *   *

The humble *Kartoffel*, or potato as you know it, should have a special place in any book on German cooking. There are over ninety recipes for cooking them that I know of, but our favourite was and still is the *Reibekuchen* or potato cakes. They are cheap and easy to make, but don't make too many at once as they are not as good cold as they are hot and crispy. At home we made them like this.

Potato Cakes

3 or 4 large potatoes
1 medium onion
1 egg
1 teaspoon of cornflour (Yes, we did have cornflour during the war; it was commonly called 'Maizena' after the brand name.)
Salt to taste

Peel the potatoes and the onion and grate them on the fine setting. We used a hand-held manual grater, but any type will do. Add the egg, cornflour and salt to taste, then mix well in a bowl. Drop fry over medium heat in vegetable oil. You can make the cakes thin if you want them extra crispy or thick if you just want them crispy around the edges. You can fry several at one time in a large cast-iron skillet. We had no vegetable oil so we used whatever we had, usually chicken fat or lard. We always had rabbits but you don't get much fat from a rabbit. After a few minutes check to see if the underside is golden brown, if so, turn the cakes over and do the same until nice and brown and that's it. It's hard to cook them fast enough to keep up with everyone eating them. Granddad Willem loved the things. He could gobble down a dozen at mealtime.

Fried Potatoes the German Way

Potatoes were not often simply fried because it required a lot more fat, but this is how it was done and it's still a good way to make them today. Use only new freshly-dug potatoes. Wash them and boil for a few minutes with peels on. Drain the water and let them cool so you can handle them for scraping the thin skin off. Let them cool completely; it is no good frying warm potatoes, they turn into mush.

While the potatoes are cooling, cut up an onion very fine, not the typical American way, or use a coarse grater. Dice a hard ripe tomato, then fry the onion and tomato in butter until the onion browns lightly. Cut up the potatoes as normal for frying and fry on medium heat for 15–20 minutes, stirring often, until brown and add salt and pepper to taste. Mix in the onions and tomatoes and serve hot.

If we had potatoes or other vegetables left over and had to do something with them, we made *Kartoffelbrot* (potato bread) or *Gemüsebrot* (vegetable bread) using a recipe like this.

Potato Bread

2lbs (900g) all-purpose flour
1lb (450g) leftover potatoes or other vegetables
2 teaspoons salt
8oz (200g) cottage cheese
1 packet dry yeast

Dissolve the yeast in a bit of warm water with the salt. Mash the vegetables cold and mix in the flour and the dissolved yeast in a glass bowl. Add the cottage cheese and then add water until the mixture is not sticky and doesn't cling to the bowl. Knead as you would any other bread. Cover with a towel and leave for about an hour at room temperature. The dough will double in size as it rises. Then put the dough in a bread baking pan and leave it standing for another thirty minutes. A pre-heated oven is best and our coal or wood fired oven was warm any time day or night. A hot temperature is required at first;

about 400°F (230°C) on modern ovens, then you can reduce the temperature to about 250°F (130°C) after fifteen minutes. Spray lightly with water several times during the baking. Baking time is about an hour. A shiny golden-brown colour will tell you it's done. It can be sliced when cold and fried or just used as sandwich bread, although it is not good with sweet preserves. I tried strawberry jam on Kartoffelbrot, but I wouldn't recommend it. However, I knew people when I was a boy who would spread sweet molasses on pickled herrings to make them edible.

Of apples and potatoes, we had plenty; so how do you put the two together when that's all you have? You can make apple and potato stew or *Himmel und Erde* as it is called in German. The name means 'Heaven and Earth' but I don't know why it was called that unless it's because potatoes are from the earth and apples are grown up in trees.

Apple and Potato Stew

3lbs (1.35kg) potatoes
1lb (450g) apples
1 onion, chopped
4oz (100g) cured bacon, diced
Salt and vinegar to taste

Cut up the potatoes and boil in a quart of salted water. Peel the apples and cut them into slices and add them to the boiling potatoes. When done, add a teaspoon of sugar if you used sour apples. If you used sweet apples, add a tablespoon of wine vinegar. Fry the cut-up bacon with the onion and when golden-brown, pour over the boiled potatoes and apples. This recipe works well with pears too.

Another unusual dish was called *Blindes Huhn* (blind chicken), which has absolutely nothing to do with chickens, but it does require bacon, so maybe it should have been called *Blindes Schwein*.

Blind Chicken

½lb (225g) lean bacon, not sliced
1lb (450g) fresh green beans cut into 1-inch lengths
½lb (225g) fresh carrots, diced
2 apples, diced
1lb (450g) potatoes, diced
Salt, pepper, and chopped parsley

Boil the bacon in a quart (about 1 litre) of water for about an hour. Add the carrots, potatoes and green beans and boil until all are soft. Add the diced apples last because they don't take long to cook. After the apples are soft (about forty-five minutes), take the bacon out and cut it into small pieces and put back into the pot. Add salt, pepper and parsley to taste. Continue boiling at low heat but don't cook until everything goes to pieces. We also used chopped thistle roots instead of carrots and dried beans when fresh beans weren't available.

I've tried the following simple recipes with local tomatoes and they worked perfectly.

Roasted Tomatoes

Slice and roast a large onion in a frying pan with a minimum amount of oil. We used bacon fat if we had it or whatever was available, but you can use vegetable oil as well. Turn the onion slices over when brown, then add sliced tomatoes, salt, pepper and sprinkle with dried parsley. Simmer for about five minutes and serve. Granddad Willem spiced his with liquid Maggie seasoning, which has a flavour similar to soy sauce, to give it a tangy taste. Liquid Maggie was obtainable at times during the war and we grew parsley ourselves. In the autumn, we cut the parsley and bunched it and dried it by hanging it upside down in a dry sunny spot or we cut it up with scissors and dried it in the sun, then just put it in a glass jar with a lid.

Steamed Tomatoes

1 or 2lbs (225 or 450g) of tomatoes
2oz (50g) butter or margarine
1 onion
1 tablespoon chopped parsley
Salt, lovage, and pepper to taste

Don't use oversized tomatoes for this recipe; small or medium ones are best. Wash them first and cut them as if you intend to quarter the tomato but only cut half way through. Then put the butter into a baking dish and let the butter melt in the oven for a minute. Place the tomatoes in the dish and fill the cross cuts with finely chopped onion and the spices. Put in a hot oven for ten minutes and when done, sprinkle parsley over them and serve. This recipe works with mushrooms too.

Tomato Salad

Cut four medium-size ripe tomatoes into small pieces, do the same with a medium-size onion and add chopped greens of any variety to the mixture. Stir in a few drops of vegetable oil and a spoon of mayonnaise. Stir everything well and add salt and pepper to taste. Put in a cool place for an hour before serving. You can also add bits of cooked meat just before serving if you want.

Now this may sound like a salad you could get in any restaurant in America, but the difference is all in the preparation. Few cooks spend any time cutting up anything. A salad today looks like you just walked through the greengrocer's and put things on your plate. That is not a proper salad and salad bars have nothing to do with a real salad. Things have to be cut up finely if you want the flavours of all the ingredients to mix. That's the reason for the mixing and the one hour wait before eating. It really is a different taste and is not like the so-called salads you're used to. Now if you use a lot of carrots in the salad, you should add a tablespoon of vinegar to counteract the sweetness of the carrots. If you like really sweet salads, add a teaspoon of Demerara sugar while you are mixing things together. That kind of sugar was available to us at times during the war. After the invasion of Holland, there was lots of it that the Dutch had accumulated from their colonies of Surinam and Curacao. It's a brown coarse cane sugar and you can still buy it. It's still called Demerara sugar and today it's imported from Guyana.

One of our favourite ways of eating potatoes was in potato salad, but there was no mayonnaise – so we made our own. There are many ways of doing this but this is my mother's recipe. A recipe for potato salad follows.

Mayonnaise

1 cup of vegetable oil
1 egg yolk
Salt to taste
1 teaspoon of vinegar or lemon juice

Make sure before you start that all the ingredients are at the same temperature. You can warm the oil under hot water if needed. Beat the egg yolk with the salt until it thickens. You can use an electric mixer but it's almost as fast to do it by hand unless you're making a quart of the stuff. We never made that much because it would go bad before we could use all of it. The next step is the most critical. Add the mixed oil and vinegar in small amounts, even one drop at a time at first while continuing to beat the mixture. After the first two dozen drops, you can increase the amount added. Continue adding the oil and vinegar mix until the mayonnaise is creamy. Sometimes, depending on the temperature of the kitchen, the mayonnaise will become lumpy. You can recover from this by adding cold water a few drops at a time as you continue to beat the mixture. You can also add things like cream of mustard, celery salt, and pepper if you want. It may take a few tries to get this right, but once you figure out what works in your kitchen, you'll never buy mayonnaise again.

This is the German way of making potato salad. There are several variations and other ingredients can be added to please yourself. This is the way my mother made it for a family of four.

Potato Salad

1½lb (675g) potatoes
2 or 3 rashers of bacon
1 large onion
1 tablespoon cooking oil
2 tablespoons salad dressing or mayonnaise
A sprig each of parsley and celery, chopped
1 rollmop (herring fillet wrapped around a pickle) or 1 pickled herring
¼ cup white vinegar or the juice from the rollmops or herrings
Salt and pepper to taste

Boil the potatoes until they're just done through but not too soft. Remove them from the heat but do not drain. You want the potatoes to stay warm. Chop the onion and the herring into small pieces and put in a bowl with the vinegar or pickle juice. Add the cooking oil, chopped parsley, celery and salad dressing or mayonnaise and mix the ingredients well. Cut bacon into small pieces and fry until dark brown. Peel the still-warm potatoes, cut them into small (about half-inch) pieces, and put them into the herring mixture and stir continuously for a minute. The idea of doing this while the potatoes are still warm is that they will absorb the flavours of the mixture better. It does make a difference. Pour the hot bacon and the bacon fat over the potatoes and mix everything well. Add salt and pepper in the amount you want and mix again. Place in refrigerator to cool. Potato salad is great served with frankfurters or boiled eggs. Russian potato salad is similar, but they add a lightly-beaten raw egg and a sliced or chopped boiled egg to the mixture. This is an excellent dish for hot days. We never worried about it going bad in the heat of summer since it was always eaten by a hungry family soon after it was made.

The same basic recipe was used with any other vegetables we had. There were a few combinations of vegetables that were especially good: asparagus and tomatoes, cauliflower and tomatoes, beans and tomatoes, beans and cucumbers, celery and tomatoes, red cabbage and radishes, potatoes and cucumbers, and even apples and cucumbers (with ground nuts added if we had any). Our aim in those days was to stretch the available food as far as we could. Not much was thrown away and even potato peelings were washed and used. If they were too spotty, they went into the rabbit or chicken feed.

Another of our favourites was beet, instead of potato, salad.

Beet Salad

3lbs (1.35kg) raw beets
1 onion
2 whole dill pickles
1 apple, cored (and peeled if you want)
½ teaspoon sugar
2 tablespoons white or red vinegar
1 sprig parsley, chopped
Salt and pepper to taste

Boil beets until soft, peel and cube into ½-inch pieces. Cut up and mix everything but the beets. Add the sugar, parsley and salt and mix again. Now add the cut up beets, and then let the salad sit overnight in a refrigerator. If the beet cubes stick together, add a little cooking oil and mix again. This salad can also be made with boiled eggs, pickled herring, or leftover boiled meat of any sort.

In all these salads, you can add cut up hard-boiled eggs if you have them and again, the smaller the pieces the better.

To make a bean salad instead, you need fresh picked green beans; canned beans will do but the results won't be as good. Cut the beans into inch-long pieces and boil them with salt added, but don't boil them until they are soft. They have to be crispy to make a good salad. When cooked, drain the water and let them cool. Dice a small onion into very small pieces and add to the drained beans, add a tablespoon of vinegar and a spoon full of vegetable oil, some pepper or nutmeg, mix and let it really cool, stirring at times. Bean salad is served today as a starter, but we ate no starters, we ate what was on the table. The same salad was made with beet root. We also made herring salad from marinated herrings cut to pieces with a spoonful of our homemade mayonnaise added. Schnitzels are best served with this salad, but they were hard to come by.

Another pork recipe, that didn't get made very often even before the war, had the odd name of *Schneeschaufel*, which means snow shovel. I guess the sour cream is supposed to represent the snow and this is how it is made.

Schneeschaufel (Serves 4–6)

3lbs (1.35kg) of pork, preferably shoulder with the skin on
1 teaspoon of Caraway seed
1 tablespoon shortening
1 large onion
1 large carrot
½ cup of sweet beer (regular beer with ½ teaspoon of sugar added will do)
3 (or more) tablespoons of sour cream

First make multiple incisions into the skin of the pork diagonally with a sharp knife. Sprinkle salt and pepper over it and rub into the incisions. Melt the shortening in a roasting pan and put the pork in the pan. Cut up the carrot and onion and cover the meat with it. Add a cup of water, the caraway, and more salt if needed and roast for 1–1½ hours on medium heat in your oven. Baste the meat with the beer often during the baking. You can lower the heat and cook for a longer time if you want. This makes the pork skin soft as butter. When it's finally done, put it in cool place for an hour and then pour the sour cream over it. Your show shovel is now ready to serve. You can also use potatoes instead of carrots, or use both.

Contrary to modern cookbooks that list recipes for beef, lamb, or even chicken or turkey schnitzel, true German schnitzels (*Kotletts*) are made only from pork. In Austria, a schnitzel is nowadays made from veal. Schnitzel is an Austrian word anyway, so I guess they can make it the way they want. There is even a law there (no surprise) that says anything called a schnitzel must be made from veal. A schnitzel first has to be tenderized and this is done using a wooden mallet. An old saying in Germany goes that if you order a schnitzel in a restaurant and you cannot hear hammering from the kitchen, you won't get a good schnitzel. The pork cutlet has to be dipped in a beaten egg twice, salted and spiced, then dipped again in breadcrumbs and fried in a covered cast iron frying pan on low to medium heat, and turned often until golden brown on both sides. That's a simple schnitzel. Other ingredients make different schnitzels and may include mushrooms (with mushroom sauce), celery, cloves and onions. The names vary from *Jäger Schnitzel* to *Zigeuner Schnitzel*.

This soup starter mixture keeps quite well at room temperature because of the salt content and it can be stored in the refrigerator for a very long time.

Soup Starter

2 carrots
2 celery sticks or a handful of the greens from the tops of celery
2 garlic cloves
A handful of parsley
A handful of lovage or a half teaspoon of powdered lovage (ground lovage root or Ligusticum) or 'Liebstöckel', called Maggie Kraut by the Germans because of its slightly Maggie-seasoning taste
3 tablespoons salt
Black pepper to taste
Vegetable oil

Cut up the carrots, celery and garlic very fine. Put into a blender and add a small amount of the vegetable oil. Blend on slow speed and add oil until you make a thick paste. Add the rest of the ingredients and blend again on medium speed. Add oil as needed to keep the mixture from becoming too thick. Pour into jars and add a lid. Refrigerated, this keeps for months. Add to any soup or stew to improve the flavour. A little goes a long way though, so use sparingly. A little Maggie seasoning can also be added during the blending if desired.

Vegetable Cakes

½lb (225g) dried beans (lentils or peas)
1 medium onion
1 stale bread roll
2 eggs
Parsley
Salt to taste
2oz (50g) breadcrumbs

Boil the beans until almost soft enough to eat. Cut the onion into large pieces and boil for about a minute. Put both through the grinder along with the stale bread roll. To this mixture add the eggs, salt, some parsley and the breadcrumbs. We made our own breadcrumbs but you can use the ready-made ones just as well. Mix everything together and form into round balls and deep-fat fry until brown. It's sort of a vegetable hushpuppy without the cornbread. This is a simple and cheap meal. We also added mushrooms when we had them, but added a bit of marjoram to weaken the earthy taste. You can use oregano if you don't have marjoram. There is also an old southern United States recipe that's similar. You use black eye peas cooked done and mashed up. This is mixed with a little plain flour, an egg and red pepper, sage and even grated onions if you want. When fried in small patties until brown, it was used as a substitute for breakfast sausage during the Depression. With the sage and red pepper (and no onion), it does taste a little like pork sausage. Add some biscuits and milk gravy and you'll have a good breakfast for any true Southerner.

We also grew Savoy or Curly cabbage when we could get the seeds and it was a welcomed change. There are many ways to prepare it, but one of our favourites was a stew because it combined other things we might have already and it would feed the entire family. Beef is listed in the ingredients below, but rabbit was what we had most of the time.

Curly Cabbage Stew

2lbs (900g) Savoy cabbage
3 or 4 medium potatoes, peeled and sliced
1lb (450g) fatty beef, cubed
2oz (50g) vegetable oil
1 large onion, peeled and sliced
1 beef bouillon cube

Fry onion with the meat in your pot or pan with a little oil, then add the bouillon cube that has been crushed and dissolved in a cup (or more) of water, add the Savoy cabbage that you have cut into small pieces and the sliced potatoes. For spices you can use nutmeg, salt and parsley, and then simmer on low heat for 40 minutes and it's done.

Boiled sauerkraut (the German way) made from Savoy cabbage takes a while, so be patient. Canned sauerkraut is available anywhere if you haven't learned how to make your own yet. When you boil the sauerkraut, add salt and half a teaspoon of ground peppercorns and a piece of pork fatback. We used pigs' trotters mostly because they have a lot of fat for flavour and we weren't about to waste that. This has to boil for at least an hour on medium heat until the meat is tender. Don't drain off the water, that's where most of the nutrients are. When the sauerkraut is done, add some previously-cooked drained lima beans or white navy beans and mix with the kraut. Boiled kraut is good served with mashed potatoes. Of course, late in the war, even finding pigs' trotters was impossible, so it was sauerkraut soup and the horrible taste still lingers in my mouth. I haven't cooked it since the war.

Chicken Ragout (serves 4–6)

1 chicken (5–6lbs [2.2–2.7kg])
3oz (75g) butter
3oz (75g) all-purpose flour
4oz (100g) sour cream
1 or 2 bay leaves
Pinch of lovage (or Maggikraut), pepper, parsley and salt
1 onion
1 egg yolk

Boil the chicken for least for an hour until the meat comes off the bones easily, then mix the cooled liquid from the boiled chicken with the flour, butter, spices, and salt. Make sure not to mix the flour in very hot liquid or it will become lumpy. Then you can add the egg yolk and boil all this for a few minutes. Add the chicken meat and the sour cream last. We had no sour cream so we used a tablespoon of vinegar. Ragout was usually served with mashed potatoes and cauliflower but Kohlrabi will do as well.

Rabbit ragout is made in the same fashion but the rabbit needs longer to boil. In fact ragout can be made with any other scraps of meat; pork as well as beef. Even wild pigeons were trapped (illegally) and used during the war when we thought we could get away with it. Poaching could get you into serious trouble, especially repeated poaching.

Beer Soup

1 quart (1 litre) of beer
4oz (100g) sugar
Half a lemon
Cinnamon or ginger
2 egg yolks lightly beaten
1 cup milk
1 teaspoon cornflour

First you add the sugar to half the beer and put in a cinnamon or ginger stick. Heat this in a saucepan almost to boiling. If you have spices such as arrack or aniseed, you can add them at any point in the cooking for a little added flavour.

In a separate bowl, mix the egg yolks with the cold beer and stir until it foams. Add the cornflour, milk, and lemon and continue stirring. When this is mixed thoroughly, add to the hot beer and boil for one minute and it's done. You could drink it warm or cold and even turn it into a pudding by adding more cornflour and sugar during boiling.

If you have ever tried what the Germans call *Glühwein* or hot wine, usually drunk at Christmas parties, then why not try wine soup? Red or white, Moselle, Zinfandel or your average home brew will all do just fine for making this tasty soup.

Wine Soup

½ pint (275ml) of water
Cinnamon and cloves
2oz (50g) of rice or tapioca
½ pint (275ml) of wine
3oz (75g) of sugar

Boil the water with the cinnamon and two cloves and after it begins to boil, add the rice or tapioca. When the rice or tapioca is done, add the wine and heat up again until almost boiling; then add the sugar and it's done. You can also add a few cut up pieces of toast to the soup if you want, or even crackers. It takes about 20–30 minutes to make this soup and it can be eaten hot or cold.

Although Halloween wasn't celebrated until relatively recently in Germany, we grew lots of pumpkins during the war and after. In the autumn, when there were plenty of them, creative ways of preparing pumpkin for the table were found including a soup that is quite tasty.

Pumpkin Soup

1–1½lbs (450–675g) of cut-up pumpkin
2 pints (1 litre) water
Cinnamon
Lemon peel and apple peel
Teaspoon of cornflour
½ cup of white wine
Lemon juice
3oz (75g) sugar

Bring the cut-up pumpkin and water to a moderate boil. Add the cinnamon, lemon peel and apple peel. Mix the cornflour thoroughly in a bit of cold water and add to boiling pumpkin. When the mixture has returned to a boil, add the wine, lemon juice and sugar. Continue boiling for a few minutes and it's done.

There aren't too many meat recipes I can include because we didn't have much meat at the time, but I do want to give my mother's recipe for *Sauerbraten* since it is a traditional German dish, and we did have it occasionally until about 1941. Since I moved to the United States, I've often been asked how to make this dish because there are many ways to make it wrong and there's no fast way to make it at all. *Sauerbraten* marinade can be purchased in good shops but this is how it was done in my time by my mother. To make a good *Sauerbraten* you first need a cast iron pan with a lid. This *Sauerbraten* recipe takes time and if you want it for Sunday dinner, you'd better start on Thursday.

Sauerbraten on Sunday

3lbs (1.3kg) of bottom round beef roast without bone
2 large onions
3 bay leaves
1 pint (575ml) mixture of half wine vinegar and half water

Start on Thursday by putting the meat in a ceramic bowl with the wine vinegar and water mixture. Don't use a metal bowl because the acidity of the vinegar reacts with the metal and the result will have a metallic taste. Slice the onions and put under and over the beef. Add the bay leaves and a little salt, but you don't have to add the salt now if you prefer to add it after cooking. This goes in the refrigerator. Turn the beef over at least once a day. On Sunday, start early on the beef. Take it out of the bowl and dry it with a paper towel. Heat your cast-iron skillet with a small amount of oil. Slice the onion and layer the bottom of the pan with it, then lay the beef on top of it. Cover it with any remaining onion slices. Now you can add salt and pepper to taste if you didn't add the salt earlier. You can also add other herbs and spices that go well with beef at this time. Cover the pan with the lid and cook on a very low heat. You have to be patient because it has to cook very slowly and when the pan gets too dry, add a bit of water. The onions of course turn black from the roasting before the meat is ready. Check the progress and turn the beef every half hour. It might take two hours for the meat to cook, depending on the size of the portion. It is ready when you can insert a sharp kitchen knife easily. Take the meat out and use the juice for making gravy by adding more water mixed with a teaspoon of cornflour. Put the meat back into the pan with the gravy and let it cook for another 30 minutes. If you want it more sour, add a teaspoon of wine vinegar before the last 30 minutes of cooking. *Sauerbraten* is best served with boiled red cabbage and boiled potatoes.

One of the essential meals during the war was vegetable *Auflauf* (casserole), especially if you had a garden and very little meat to go around. The following vegetable recipes are well worth trying out. Meat can be added to any of them but it should be boiled separately, not fried or roasted.

Vegetable Casserole (*Auflauf*)

2 pints (1 litre)water
Salt to taste
2lbs (900g) of any vegetable
1lb (450g) potatoes
½ cup self-raising flour
1 onion

Grate or cut your vegetables (except the onions and potatoes) into small pieces and put into boiling salted water. Add the potatoes that have been sliced thin and continue boiling until all the vegetables are soft but not overcooked. Drain most of the water from the pan and transfer vegetables to a casserole pan. If you are including boiled meat in the recipe, add it now to the vegetables in the casserole pan and mix. Brown the flour with the onion in a skillet with a bit of oil and then add small amounts of water while continuing to stir, making a thickened gravy. Pour over the vegetables and put in the oven on medium heat for another 10 minutes. We made *Auflaufs* with carrots, kohlrabi, green beans, Savoy cabbage, turnips, sauerkraut, kale and white cabbage. For some reason though, it doesn't work well with red cabbage. We tried several times and it just never turned out right. If we didn't have any other vegetables, we made it anyway with just the potatoes.

Here are a few cottage cheese recipes we used; some are sweet, some are spicy. We ate it either way. Try some of them, but please, use cottage cheese from the shop. The smell of a gallon of milk that has been standing on the porch in 85-degree weather for a few days might change your mind about making your own, but if you're determined, this first recipe is for you.

Cottage Cheese

8oz (200g) milk curd, drain off any excess whey
Salt to your taste

2 tablespoons of fresh cut-up chives
1 teaspoon of fresh parsley and any other spices you like

Mix this and let it settle in the refrigerator for a few hours. Do not use dried chives or parsley unless you steep it in hot water for 30 minutes. This cottage cheese would most often be eaten on black bread. You can also add two tablespoons of freshly-grated carrot and a pinch of paprika instead of the chives, or the flesh of two large tomatoes and a grated onion. At times we added fried bacon pieces, but bacon was hard to come by, so we used fried 'garden bacon' (onions).

There are many other ways to prepare cottage cheese, but the way we liked it best was spread on bread with sliced tomato and cucumber or radishes. Chopped ham can also be added and when American GIs came in 1945 and introduced us to Spam, we naturally used it. 'Spam' was one of the first English words we learned and Spam and cottage cheese sandwiches were great eating for us. We discovered dozens of ways to prepare the stuff and would trade for it whenever we could.

Cottage Cheese Butter

5oz (125g) cottage cheese
3 tablespoons milk
5oz (125g) softened margarine or butter
1 small onion, finely chopped or grated
1 teaspoon fresh chives
Salt and pepper to taste

Mix the cottage cheese thoroughly with the milk and margarine. Add the onion, chives, salt and pepper and mix again. That's all there is to it and on freshly-baked bread, it is really good. We even tried to fry cottage cheese and after a few failures, my mother got it right and the end result was a rather nice dish.

Fried Cottage Cheese

2oz (50g) softened margarine or butter
2 eggs
1lb (450g) boiled potatoes, mashed
½lb (225g) cottage cheese
2oz (50g) flour

1 teaspoon each of salt and nutmeg or to taste
Pepper and chopped chives if available

Mix eggs and margarine thoroughly, and then add the mashed potatoes, cottage
cheese, flour and other ingredients. Form small patties from a tablespoon of
the mixture and fry in a pan until brown on both sides.

There were also many ways of preparing sweet cottage cheese using fruit or
berries. We had canned fruit in the winter that we had put up ourselves earlier
in the season and we used it with cottage cheese to make cheese cakes. All this
depended on the availability of sour milk. Cottage cheese was normally not
available at the market. The small amount of milk we got went mostly to baby
Fred or we used it to make soups to which we would add prunes or raisins.

Cottage Cheese Dumplings

4oz (100g) softened butter
3 eggs, lightly beaten
4oz (100g) cornflour
2oz (50g) sugar
1 teaspoon salt
1lb (450g) cottage cheese
½lb (225g) self-raising flour
Sugar and cinnamon

Beat the butter first until soft and foamy and then add the other ingredients
up through the cottage cheese. Add the ½lb of flour at little at a time until the
mixture gets thick and can kneaded but don't knead it very much, then roll out
the dough ¼-inch thick. Cut into 2-inch square dumplings. Once that is done,
immerse them in boiling water for ten minutes. Take the dumplings out and
brush with melted butter, then sprinkle a mixture of cinnamon and sugar over
them. Dumplings are easy to make and can be kneaded but a few rules have to
be remembered to avoid having them fall apart in the boiling water. Mix all the
ingredients well. Stiff dough works best, and boil one dumpling first to test the
water temperature and your dough. A rolling boil will sometimes disintegrate
the dumpling. To test the dumplings after boiling, cut one in half. It should be
dry and firm inside. You are using self-raising flour so expect the dumplings
to about double in thickness. When done, take them out of the boiling water,
drain the water off, and serve. The same basic recipe can be used to make
cottage cheese noodles. Use all-purpose flour instead of self-raising and only
one egg. You can let these noodles dry out and use them later in any recipe that

calls for them. Some of these recipes have butter as an ingredient but for us, real butter was a commodity that had vanished by late 1943. Our butter ration cards got us margarine that came in bricks that weighed about a pound. It was so hard you could not spread it and it smelled like gun oil and if you tried to fry anything in it, the result smelled like gun oil as well. Actually, I think the oil we used on the quads smelled better.

Modern *Pannas* (Scrapple)

2–3lbs (900–1,250g) of beef bones
A few ounces of sausage of any variety, if available, or chopped raw vegetables of your choice
1lb (450g) grits
2oz (50g) cornflour
Parsley and celery
1 small onion, finely chopped
Salt, pepper, and most important, you need the spice lovage
1 egg

Put the bones in a saucepan big enough to hold them and add salted water (about one teaspoon of salt per pint of water) to just cover the bones. Boil them for at least an hour and then take the bones out. Mix the grits, parsley, sausage (or chopped vegetables) and onion into the saucepan and boil until the grits are done. In a separate bowl, mix the cornflour with enough water to make a thick paste and add to the mixture. Add the lovage and the egg and boil for a few more minutes then pour into a bread tin and let cool. When cool, put the loaf in a refrigerator overnight. You can slice it and fry it until brown or just serve as it is. You cannot keep it for long even in a refrigerator. In cold winters, we froze it outside. Sometimes the temperature in January went down to -40°C. The *Pannas* we got during the war and shortly after had ground barley, stale bread and God knows what else in it, maybe roof rabbit, but nobody complained. I've not been able to find a grocery that sells lovage root but Liebstöckel is available and will work just fine as a substitute.

Turnips in Bread

A 2lb (900kg) loaf of black bread
4 turnips (rutabagas)
2 strips of bacon or 6oz (150g) ground beef
1 egg, lightly beaten

1 small sprig of parsley, chopped
1 onion
1 potato
1 tablespoon self-raising flour
Salt and pepper to taste

The black bread crust was hard as a brick during the war. If you wanted a piece you had to saw a slice off or use a special mechanical bread cutter that was also used to cut tobacco. To make this recipe, we sawed the loaf in half longways and scooped out the (somewhat) softer inner portion for making bread soup later.

Peel the potato, turnips and onion and dice into small pieces. Boil in salted water until soft. Pour off the water and add the egg, parsley, pepper and other spices if you have them. Nutmeg is also good in this recipe. Mash the ingredients together until it is all mixed well and then add the flour if the mixture is too thin; otherwise, leave it out. Stuff the mixture into both halves of black bread and put back together. You can use a skewer to hold the halves together, or if you originally cut the loaf longways, just put the top half back on. Put the bacon strips or ground beef into the bottom of a bread baking pan the size of your loaf and the turnip bread on top. Bake for 20–30 minutes on medium heat. The moisture of the ingredients will soften the crust of the black bread somewhat. When done, slice and serve hot or fry in cooking oil the next day. A loaf of today's rye bread works well for this recipe. Our turnip bread was delicious, worms or not.

Another very simple way of preparing turnips was to mash them after cooking and add a handful of raisins and a spoonful of sugar. This was most often spread on slices of bread and eaten as a sandwich. Turnips can also be fried after being mashed, like potatoes. We used turnips in most recipes that called for potatoes if we didn't have any. Mashed potatoes with raisins and sugar would be good to try today.

Now here is the recipe for cabbit stew we made for thirty-one people, and if you don't like rabbit, pork will do, or even chicken.

Rabbit and Carrot Stew

20lbs (9kg) washed and grated carrots
1 large skinned and gutted rabbit, cut up into small pieces
1lb (450g) fat, butter or margarine
5lbs (2.25kg) cooked rice; if no rice is available, tapioca will do
5 eggs lightly beaten or 1lb (450g) of powdered egg
5lbs (2.25kg) potatoes

½lb (225g) sugar
Salt, pepper and parsley in proportion to the ingredients

Grate carrots and put into a large casserole pan with the fat (butter or margarine) and sauté for five minutes on medium heat. Add the cooked rice or tapioca and continue cooking for another five minutes.

Meanwhile, enough water has to be boiling to make stew for thirty-one men. About four gallons (15 litres) should be sufficient. Into the boiling water, add the cut up potatoes, the rabbit and the spices. This has to boil for at least 90 minutes. After that time, add the contents of the casserole pan and simmer for another 30 minutes. Just before serving, add the eggs slowly and boil for another few minutes until they are cooked. Other spices can be added at this time if desired.

Tomato Soup

16oz (400g) tomato puree
1 onion, chopped
1 stick of leek, chopped
8oz (200g) of quick rice, elbow macaroni or tapioca
1 bouillon cube
1 tablespoon chopped parsley

Bring a quart (1 litre) of water to boil and add the chopped onion, the cut-up leek, the bouillon cube and the parsley. Allow this to come back to boil and add the rice or macaroni, and boil until soft. Do not drain the water after boiling, but add the tomato puree and stir well into the mixture. If the soup is too watery, a teaspoon of cornflour mixed with a bit of cold water and added to the boiling mixture will thicken it. Add pepper and salt and any other mixed spices to your taste. If you want the full effect of the war, serve outside with your lawn mower running full blast under the dining table.

Red Cabbage

Red cabbage is served today in many restaurants as a side dish and it's mostly cooked to bits and without taste, but for us, it was often the main course so it was important how it was cooked. With red cabbage dishes, one has to know the right ingredients, otherwise it is pretty bland. Red cabbage must be shredded before you boil it. It should be boiled on a low heat with a diced apple and a tablespoon of vinegar, a teaspoon of sugar, a bay leaf or two and salt to taste.

All this has to boil for at least an hour, so it's not for the fast food lover, but it is well worth the wait. This is for about 2lbs (900g) of red cabbage. After it has cooked and the cabbage is soft, drain off the water. In a separate bowl, mix a teaspoon of cornflour with a cup of water and pour over the cabbage. Let the cabbage come to a boil once again and it's done. If you want to make the cabbage a bit tastier, you can cut up a slice of bacon into small pieces, fry it until brown and then add chopped onion and let it cook together for a few minutes, then pour the bacon, onions, and the grease over the cabbage and mix together. It can be served with mashed or boiled potatoes, Schnitzel or pork chops, or just eaten by itself.

Pease Pudding

1lb (450g) dried peas
2oz (50g) butter or margarine
1 onion
Parsley or celery
Salt and pepper to taste

The dried peas have to be soaked in water for twenty-four hours then boiled on low heat until soft. This takes a couple of hours or more. Place the boiled peas in a sieve and mash them through with a large wooden spoon to separate the outer tough skin from the soft inner portion and drain any water away. Melt the butter and chop the onion into small pieces and add it to the butter in a frying pan. Stir until the onions are soft, not fried, and then add the strained peas. Heat until warm and it's done. Pease pudding is best served with sauerkraut or mashed potatoes. The same recipe will work with almost any beans.

In late summer, we had plenty of fruit and could make our own preserves, but without adequate sugar, the jam did not set nor could you keep it for long. So we had apple butter sandwiches, apple soup, apple roast, and the surviving rabbits had their fill of apples. As an example, here is a recipe for apple soup as we made it. We never peeled the apples, but we did cut the core out.

Apple Soup, á la 1946

2 large cooking apples, cored and cubed
½lb (225g) of hard black, rye or pumpernickel bread
4oz (100g) sugar
Pinch of cinnamon
2oz (50g) raisins or sultanas

Soak the bread in water for 30 minutes. Then bring a quart of water to boil, add the cubed apples and the raisins. Boil for about 10 minutes and then add the sugar. Lastly squeeze the water out of the bread, add it to the boiling stew and stir for a few minutes. We ate it hot or like pudding when it got cold and set to a paste.

Gemüse (Vegetable) Soup

1oz (25g) of margarine
1 small piece of celery root (celeriac, knob celery)
1 kohlrabi
1 carrot
1 parsley root (Hamburg parsley, Heimischer, similar to parsnip)
1 sprig of green parsley
1 onion
1 stick of leek
The inside white flesh of a cabbage or cauliflower
Salt and pepper to taste

Chop all the ingredients into small pieces and stir fry in the margarine for 8–10 minutes on low heat. Pour into another pan containing a quart of water at boil. Add spices. A bouillon cube can be added if available. Boil for an hour on low heat. Strain through a sieve and pour into a jar. Refrigerate until consumed as a drink. The strained residue can be used in stews or added to bread dough before baking.

Weed Soup

2oz (50g) margarine or butter
2 tablespoons olive oil
2oz (50g) all-purpose flour or quick rice
1 egg, lightly beaten
2 tablespoons sour cream
1 onion, chopped
3 tablespoons of Ground Ivy, Masterwort, Dandelion, or any of the other edible weeds mentioned earlier, chopped very fine. We used a pair of scissors to cut them up.

Put the chopped weeds into a frying pan, add the olive oil and the margarine (or butter) and cook for 5–7 minutes on medium heat until brown. Pour into saucepan, add 2–3 cups of water and bring to a boil. If you are using flour, mix it in a cup with cold water, and then add to the boiling water. If you are using rice, just add it to the boiling water. Boil for 15–20 minutes. Add spices such as lovage, salt, and pepper to taste. Add egg and stir into mixture until cooked. Stir in the sour cream and remove from the heat. For vegetarians, this is surely a change from the usual fare.

Another dish we made was *Sauerampfer* (*Rumex acetosa*, Sorrel, Spinach Dock) stew. It's a weed that grows abundantly in roadside ditches or meadows but do not use the flowers or the stems as they are very bitter. We only used the leaves. It can be eaten raw, and it has a somewhat sour taste that we liked. My mother had several recipes using this flavourful weed. Two good handfuls of *Sauerampfer* are enough for four people.

Sauerampfer

This *Sauerampfer* dish was made often and it is very simple. Wash the *Sauerampfer* and put it into a frying pan with a heaped teaspoon of butter or margarine and stir fry until the leaves are soft but not mushy. Transfer to a saucepan and cover the *Sauerampfer* with water that has had a bouillon cube dissolved in it. Add three diced potatoes and boil for 30 minutes. Crack an egg and beat it in a cup with a tablespoon of the hot *Sauerampfer* mix. When the potatoes are done, stir the egg mixture into the saucepan and let simmer for five minutes. Add salt, pepper, and some ground cloves and a pinch of sage and it's ready to eat. Carrots can also be added with the potatoes along with any dried vegetables for a little extra flavour.

Sauerampfersalat can be prepared like ordinary lettuce salad, but because of the slightly sour taste, we made a salad dressing of melted butter, margarine, or olive oil mixed with a teaspoon of sugar. The dressing also keeps the leaves from sticking together in a clump.

Sauerampfer Omelette

1 handful of *Sauerampfer*, washed and cut into small pieces
4 eggs
Grated cheese of your choice
Curry powder, Estragon (tarragon), salt, and pepper

This omelette is best made in a cast iron frying pan. Prepare the omelette as any other but beforehand, fry the *Sauerampfer* in a small amount of oil or butter and then add the beaten egg. Mix in the curry powder and estragon before cooking and add the grated cheese when the omelette is almost done.

Sauerampfer Pancakes

1 handful of washed *Sauerampfer* leaves
4oz (100g) butter, margarine or olive oil
4oz (100g) mushrooms
3 tablespoons white wine
2 teaspoons cornflour
3 eggs
½ cup fat-free milk (our milk was mostly fat-free anyway)
Salt and pepper to taste

Cut the *Sauerampfer* with scissors into thin strips and fry a few minutes in butter and put aside for later use. Slice the mushrooms and fry in a bit of butter or oil until they are light brown, then add the white wine and simmer on low heat. Mix a teaspoon of cornflour with a bit of water and add to the simmering mushrooms and boil the mixture for two minutes. Beat the three eggs with the milk and the rest of the cornflour and add salt, pepper, and a pinch of nutmeg and pour into a cast-iron frying pan. Lay the *Sauerampfer* on top and slowly fry until the cake is firm but not hard. Cover the cake with your prepared mushrooms and continue frying for a few minutes and it's ready to eat.

We also cooked Blutwurst with *Sauerampfer*, but this sausage is hard to find here in the United States. There are several German sources for it and most will ship anywhere. For those who want to try making it themselves, I have a good recipe but it is not for the squeamish. One first needs to know a butcher who can get the main ingredient for you, blood from a freshly-slaughtered pig. The sausage has to be made immediately with the fresh blood before it begins to decompose. There's no great effort required, but preparations made beforehand will pay off in the end, so collect all the ingredients before you go to the butcher.

Blutwurst

To make 2–3lbs (900–1,350g) of Blutwurst, you need, in addition to the pig blood, a half-pound of fresh bacon (not smoked), a cup of grits, rye flour or ground oats, and spices. Cut the bacon into very small pieces and put in a pan on medium heat. Add the grits and mix with water into a thin paste. Put a quart of the blood in a saucepan and bring to a rolling boil. Add the bacon and grits mixture and spices (salt, pepper and garlic powder). Boil for another 10 minutes or until the mixture thickens. Turn off the heat and pour this mixture into small glass jars with sealable lids. Put the jars into a boiling water bath for five minutes and then seal the jars with the lids. Let stand until cool and then refrigerate. That's all there is to it. A can of Blutwurst costs about $4 for 6oz (150g), plus shipping, but you can make your own for about a dollar a can. There is also the advantage of having the Blutwurst preserved in jars; it will keep for years. Fry a few slices with a beaten egg and garnish with *Sauerampfer* and you have a delicious meal. If you don't want to preserve the Blutwurst, just pour the mixture into a stone crock and refrigerate, but it must be eaten within a week or so. Liver sausage can be made the same way by running the liver through a meat grinder and adding water mixed with a bouillon cube. Homemade liver sausage is coarser than the pudding-style *Braunschweiger* from the supermarket and tastes much better.

Although I have scores of *Sauerampfer* recipes, this Second World War hors d'oeuvres recipe is especially good.

Sauerampfer hors d'oeuvres

½lb (225g) of butter or margarine, salted or unsalted
½lb (225g) cottage cheese
1 teaspoon chopped fresh garlic
1 bunch of parsley
Sprig of dill
1 tablespoon chopped chives
A few *Sauerampfer* leaves
A sprig of Pimpinelle (Sanguisorba minor, Rosaceae). If your shop doesn't have Pimpinelle, use a few cut-up slices of peeled cucumber.

Make sure the butter is at room temperature for better mixing and cut all herbs into small pieces; I use scissors. Mix everything into the cottage cheese and add salt and pepper to taste. Roll into inch-diameter balls. Serve on crackers or on pieces of toast. You can also add a half teaspoon of tomato puree to the mixture before rolling into balls for a little different taste.

Rum Fordsche Soup

8oz (200g) whole grain barley
1 stick of leek, chopped
3 potatoes, cubed

2 bread rolls, the older and harder the better
6 cups water
Salt and pepper to taste

Boil the barley for at least 1½ hours and add more water to keep the level about the same. After the boiling time, add the cut-up leek and potato cubes, salt, and pepper and boil until the potatoes are soft. Finally add the two bread rolls. They will soften and mix with the rest of the ingredients. That's all there is to it. This dish was also a staple for most POWs.

Frühling (spring) soup is made from a variety of spring vegetables, including spinach, asparagus, and early beans, cooked together for an hour. A handful of weeds of some variety was often added when there weren't enough vegetables. When done, tomato slices can be added to the hot soup before serving.

Spinach Soup

2oz (50g) butter or margarine
1 onion
2 tablespoons dried herbs (parsley, celery, chives)
8oz (200g) fresh spinach
2oz (50g) breadcrumbs
1 bread roll or 2 slices white bread
2 hard-boiled eggs
4 cups water

Cut up spinach and onion and put into frying pan with butter or margarine and let it wilt for a few minutes, add half of the water, the breadcrumbs and herbs, boil for 20 minutes, add more of the water if the soup thickens too fast. Slice the bread roll or use the two slices of white bread, and toast in the oven to golden brown, then cut into inch squares. Add the toasted bread to the soup mixture. Peel the two hard-boiled eggs and slice them; add them to the soup and it's done. Add salt, pepper, and a pinch of paprika if you want. This soup can also be made using leftover vegetables (cabbage, kale, cauliflower) and with frozen vegetables.

Noodle Dough

½lb (225g) all-purpose flour
2 eggs

¼ teaspoon salt
2 tablespoons water

Break the two eggs into a cup, add the salt and water and beat lightly. Add this to the flour slowly and knead into a dough that can be rolled out. It has to be rolled very thin. Cut into ½-inch strips 4 inches long. Place on trays or paper and put outside in the sun. They should be dried until hard. They can then be put into bags and stored.

One of our favourite pasta dishes was called *Maultaschen* (mouth pockets or mouth bags). The dough is prepared the same as for noodles, rolled out thin and then cut into 4 x 4 inch squares. Then a teaspoon of minced leftover vegetables or whatever's available is placed in the square. One edge of the square is then folded over to make a triangular pocket. The folded edges are then pressed together to form a seal. The pockets are then dried in the sun for a few hours only. To cook the *Maultaschen*, the pockets should be boiled in water containing a little salt and pepper for about 10 minutes. Any leftovers can be served cold in a salad or mixed with tomato puree or mayonnaise. Our homemade noodles were used in a variety of ways and since we always had apples in late summer, my mother came up with a recipe for apple noodles.

Apple Noodles

1lb (450g) cooking apples (firm apples)
½lb (225g) noodles
4oz (100g) sugar
1 lemon peel, diced
1oz (25g) unsalted butter
1 teaspoon cinnamon

Boil the noodles until soft and drain off the water. Peel and cut apples into small pieces and place in a pan with the butter and lemon peel. Add a cup of water and cook on medium heat for 8–10 minutes or until the apples are beginning to soften. Add the noodles, cinnamon, and sugar and mix well. We used plums at times too, but cherries didn't work well. Noodle salad can be made like potato salad and an added cut-up tomato or tomato puree gives it a nice flavour. Sometimes, when we had a can of corned beef from the GIs, we cooked the noodles, drained the water and added the corned beef, some chopped parsley and tomato puree. It was sort of spaghetti with meat sauce I guess.

We tried many drinks, even milk lemonade with a spoonful of schnapps, but I wouldn't recommend it. However, one cheap summer drink we made that I can recommend was elderflower champagne. I still make it today.

Elderflower Champagne

2–3 heads of elderflower in full bloom
2lbs (900kg) sugar
2 tablespoon white vinegar
1 gallon (4.5 litres) of cold water
1 lemon

Pick the flower heads when they are in full bloom and put into a ceramic or plastic bowl and add the lemon juice. Scrape the outside of the lemon (the zest) and add that to the bowl as well. Add the sugar and the vinegar and mix thoroughly. Add the cold water and let the mixture stand for twenty-four hours. Strain the mixture and fill your bottles. The screw-top water bottles work well. Only fill the bottles three-quarters full and collapse them before adding the screw top. This allows gasses to expand the bottle during fermentation. Lay the bottles on their sides and store in a cool place. The elderflower champagne is ready to drink in two weeks. If you bottle this in glass bottles, you need a valve, similar to those used in winemaking to allow the gasses to escape.

Making sweets and cookies had to be planned well in advance. Some of the ingredients weren't easy to come by, but Mum always managed to have something for us, especially at Christmastime.

Printen Cookies

¼lb (112g) butter or margarine
½lb (225g) *Rübenkraut* or Honey
½lb (225g) sugar
1 tablespoon of the mixed spices given above
1 teaspoon cocoa
1lb (450g) self-raising flour, or plain with a teaspoon of baking powder
1 egg
1 dash of salt

Mix the butter, honey (or *Rübenkraut*), sugar, spices, and cocoa in a bowl then transfer to a pan and heat slowly while continuing to stir. When everything has melted together, remove from heat and allow to cool for several minutes.

In a separate bowl, mix the flour, egg, and salt, then knead in the warm melted ingredients from the pan. It will be sticky, but just keep kneading until everything is mixed well. Cover the dough with a towel and set aside for a day. Do not refrigerate. Roll out the dough on a floured countertop to a thickness of about a quarter inch and cut into strips about two inches wide and four inches long. Place on a cookie sheet and bake on medium/high heat until golden brown. When done, the Printen can be iced with whatever you like. We used a sugar/water paste. Let the Printen cool in open air and try not to eat them for a day or two. They have to mature or they will be soft and soggy.

Spekulatius Cookies

1lb (450g) self-raising flour
½lb (225g) of sugar
1 teaspoon vanilla sugar or a couple of drops of vanilla essence
1 teaspoon ground cinnamon
1 egg, beaten lightly
6oz (150g) of softened unsalted butter
A small amount of ground cloves (maybe ¼ teaspoon)
3 tablespoons of whole milk

Put the flour into a large bowl and then add the rest of the ingredients except the butter and the egg and mix well. Add butter in small amounts and mix. This will make a stiff dough that should then be kneaded thoroughly. Roll out a fist sized ball of dough at a time on a floured tabletop to a thickness of about ⅛ inch and use your favourite Christmas cookie cutters to cut out the cookies. Place on a greased cookie sheet and brush each cookie with the beaten egg, then bake on medium heat for 15–20 minutes or until they are brown. You can leave them in the oven a little longer if you like hard crunchy cookies. Check on the progress often. We didn't have much in the way of temperature regulation in our wood-fired oven. The cookies burned easily, but we ate them anyway. You can add whatever kind of sugar decoration you want but don't go overboard. It is the taste of the cookie you want, not just the sugar. Let the cookies cool before eating if you can wait that long. We used two baking trays so we could put a new one in the oven as soon as one batch was done. Cookies were made whenever the oven was not being used for something else in the two weeks leading up to Christmas. Of course we didn't have self-raising flour and had to add our own baking powder, but today's self-raising flour works just as well or better.

Another favourite was Christmas *Pfefferkuchen* Cookies. If that sounds like pepper cookies to you, I can assure you there is no pepper in these cookies. I have no idea how they got the name, but they are great Christmas cookies and this is the modern way to make them. Instead of the instant pudding mix, we used Dutch cocoa, cornflour, sugar, milk, and a little salt.

Pfefferkuchen Cookies

½lb (225g) self-raising flour
1 packet of powdered instant chocolate pudding mix
½lb (225g) sugar
4oz (100g) of honey or sweet molasses
1 egg
4–5 tablespoons whole milk
¼ teaspoon ground cinnamon and cloves
3oz (75g) softened unsalted butter
3oz (75g) ground almonds or other nuts

Mix the instant pudding with the flour and the ground almonds or nuts, and then add sugar and mix again. Yes, we had instant pudding during the war, but you had to mix it with milk and sugar and cook it – if you had milk and sugar. Mostly Mum found other things to do with it. I don't know what was in it, but it seems to be about the same as the instant pudding mix you can buy today. Warm the honey or molasses and add the cinnamon, cloves, butter milk and egg to it and mix thoroughly. Add this to the flour, nuts and sugar mixture slowly and mix. Knead thoroughly and if the dough is a little soft, let it stand for 15 minutes and try again; then proceed as with the *Spekulatius* cookies for baking. You can decorate with sugar and additional ground nuts if you want, but they are good just as they are.

No German Christmas is completed without a *Christstollen* and in some specialty bakeries you can buy them ready-made well before Christmas, even here in America. There is a Polish version called *Potica* that is similar and it can also be found here occasionally. A proper *stollen* has to mature, like a good wine, and we used to make ours at the end of November through the beginning of December. To make your own is more adventurous and it surely tastes better too. There are several varieties, even a rum *stollen* using real rum, but you won't get drunk from eating it. The alcohol evaporates during baking, but you will have a nice rum-flavoured *stollen*. Here I will describe the simple *stollen* and if you want to make rum *stollen*, use less milk and add a dash of rum.

Christstollen (Fruitcake)

4oz (100g) of shortening
4oz (100g) softened unsalted butter
6oz (150g) sugar
1 egg, lightly beaten
1lb (450g) self-raising flour
¾ cup of milk
5oz (125g) raisins
2oz (50g) sultanas
2oz (50g) ground almonds or other nuts
½ teaspoon lemon extract

Melt the shortening and butter together on low heat. Add the egg, sugar, and lemon extract and mix this well. Then add half the flour with a bit of the milk; more flour and milk as you continue mixing. Lastly, add the ground nuts, raisins, and sultanas. Knead the dough thoroughly until stiff and roll into a loaf. You can get creative here and make a long loaf and coil it up if you want. Baking time with medium heat is 1 to 1½ hours. When the *stollen* is golden brown, remove it from the oven and brush it with butter and cover with icing sugar. You should store the *stollen* in a cool dry place. At Christmas you can decorate the result with green holly and candles.

Since I came to the US, my wife, who was born and raised in the mountains of Tennessee, has learned German cooking and baking from my mother's recipes. She can now make anything from a *Christstollen* to *Sauerbraten* as good as my mother used to. She has become an expert in cooking red cabbage and her *Apfeltaschen* (apple pockets) are better than the ones you buy today in bakeries in Germany. These are easy to make and I bet your first try will be a success. We had them whenever we had all the ingredients, but a few apples were always saved so we could make them at Christmastime.

Apfeltaschen (Apple Pockets)

8oz (200g) self-raising flour
8oz (200g) cottage cheese
3oz (75g) sugar
6oz (150g) softened salted butter
1 egg, lightly beaten
A few drops of vanilla essence

1lb (450g) cooking apples but you can use apple butter or cooked dried apples. If you use fresh apples, peel and boil them, add some sugar to taste and mash the cooked apples. If you use dried apples, cook them with a little water and sugar until soft and sweet.

The above ingredients (except the apples) are mixed into a dough and kneaded thoroughly. The dough is then rolled out on a floured surface to a thickness of about a quarter of an inch. With a saucer and knife, cut the dough into circles. Put a tablespoon of the apples in the centre. You can even add raisins at this point if you want. Then fold over and seal by pressing the edges together to form a half moon shaped pocket. Brush the tops with the beaten egg.

Bake for 20 minutes on a medium to high heat. After baking you can cover the Apfeltaschen with icing sugar if you want. We use any apples; it doesn't matter whether the apples are the expensive ones from the grocery shop or those that fell from your neighbour's tree. This recipe can also be used for coffee cakes but you cut the dough into small squares and fill with strawberry or peach preserves or even cooked pumpkin. Sugar was always rationed during the war so we usually used less than the recipe called for. At times we used syrup from sugar beets but the baked result is rather dark brown. Since coming to the Southern United States from Germany, I've also seen another version of the *Apfeltaschen*, but the dough is rolled out much thinner and they are fried in oil. They're commonly called fried apple pies and they are also very good. Finding enough oil to fry anything was a problem during the war, so things were mostly baked or boiled.

A German tradition was, and still is, *Kaffeetrinken am Sonntag* (Sunday afternoon tea, or coffee). Tea in itself was never a favourite drink in Germany. They left that to the British, who knew more about tea than anyone else. This took place on Sunday afternoons around 4:00 p.m., but with acorn or barley roast, it was hardly enjoyable. Usually a sort of cake or flan was served and even during the worst food shortages, there was always some sort of cake that could be made. Making a *Torte*, as it was called, was the cheapest way for the housewife to present some sort of sweet dish on the Sunday table. It's still made today and sold in any cake shop in Germany, but you can make it yourself, and the ingredients are better now than they were seventy years ago.

German *Torte* (Cake)

6oz (150g) self-raising flour

4oz (100g) sugar

4oz (100g) unsalted margarine or butter

1 egg
1 teaspoon vanilla sugar or ½ teaspoon vanilla extract added to the sugar

Simply mix all the ingredients and knead the dough for several minutes. We used to do it by hand, but there are electric kitchen utensils now that can do it for you. Roll the dough to a thickness of about ½-inch and put into a greased pie pan. We had a special *Torte* dish, but you can use any suitable pie pan. Bake for 20–30 minutes on medium heat. When done, tip the *Torte* out upside down and top with whatever fruit you like, from fresh to canned. When sugar was rationed, we sometimes used two or three saccharin tablets diluted in a bit of hot water in place of the sugar. The *Torte* was sort of bitter-sweet but still it was better than no cake at all. If you want to be imaginative, add a handful of raisins to the flour before mixing. We never had a raisin shortage during the war; there were plenty of grapes growing all over southern Germany.

Not all *ersatz* food was bad. We had an *ersatz* recipe for cookies when none were to be found that was really very good. It was called *Falsches Alpenbrot* or fake Alpinebread. It was a replacement for the well-known Bavarian cookie of the same name. I haven't made any since right after the war, but it's worth a try. We used unsliced black bread in those days, but I think modern white bread would produce better results.

Falsches Alpenbrot (Fake Applebread)

6 slices of thick white bread
1 heaping tablespoon of cocoa
8oz (200g) sugar
4oz (100g) softened salted butter
A pinch each of cinnamon and ground cloves

Dice the bread slices into 1-inch squares. Put them on a baking tray and very slowly let them bake. Turn them often until they are deep brown. Remove from oven and let them dry out for a day. After that, usually the next day, melt the butter over low heat and stir in the sugar and cocoa. Mix well or it will become lumpy. Add the spices and keep stirring. Take the pan off the heat and pour your bread squares into the pan. Let them soak for about 30 minutes then take them out one by one and put on a tray. Let them sit for a day or two and they are ready to serve. They are really good as a dessert covered with vanilla pudding or wrapped in gold or silver foil and hung on the tree at Christmastime.

Some of Mother's recipes mention vanilla sugar. This does not grow in nature of course and it's hard to find in shops but you can make your own easily. All you need is sugar and a few vanilla pods, which are available in good groceries. Put two or three vanilla pods in a glass jar then pour a pound of sugar over it. You can also use icing sugar. Put a lid on the jar and store in your cupboard. Shake the jar once a week. The longer it stands, the better the vanilla sugar. One teaspoonful for recipes that call for a pound of flour is sufficient. My mother did the same with cinnamon; two teaspoons of ground cinnamon to a pound of sugar. It was great sprinkled over rice pudding.

Index